" NOT SO BLACK AND WHITE "

An Invitation to Honest Conversations
about Race and Faith

REGGIE DABBS & JOHN DRIVER

ZONDERVAN
BOOKS

ZONDERVAN BOOKS

Not So Black and White
Copyright © 2021 by Reggie Dabbs and John Driver

Requests for information should be addressed to:
Zondervan, *3900 Sparks Dr. SE, Grand Rapids, Michigan 49546*

Zondervan titles may be purchased in bulk for educational, business, fundraising, or sales promotional use. For information, please email SpecialMarkets@Zondervan.com.

ISBN 978-0-310-36340-8 (softcover)
ISBN 978-0-310-36343-9 (audio)
ISBN 978-0-310-36342-2 (ebook)

Published in association with the literary agency of Wolgemuth & Associates, Inc.

Cover design: Jeff Miller / Faceout Studio
Cover illustration: Eky Studio / artjazz / Here / Ensuper / Shutterstock
Interior design: Sara Colley

Printed in the United States of America

21 22 23 24 25 26 27 28 29 30   /LSC/   12 11 10 9 8 7 6 5 4 3 2 1

This book is an answer to prayer. So much of what has made this conversation difficult is that it hasn't been much of a conversation. It has lacked nuance, carefulness, compassion, and humility. Reggie and John embody each of these things so well and help to lead us in an actual conversation about difficult matters. I love the fact that they don't pull any punches. However, it's clear on every page that their aim isn't to be harmful but to be helpful. They walk the tightrope between honesty and hope as well as I've seen in this conversation. I'm eager to see more prayers answered as people get this book into their hands and hearts.

—JOHN ONWUCHEKWA, pastor, Cornerstone Church, Atlanta; codirector, The Crete Collective; cofounder, Portrait Coffee

We need this book right now. While the world debates and open, honest conversations about race remain rare, Reggie Dabbs and John Driver model what real dialogue can look like, pointing the way to a biblical, historical approach to difficult discussions marked by a commitment to mercy and justice at the same time—with an attitude of humility being the mark that every Christian brings to the discussion.

—BILL HASLAM, former governor of Tennessee; author, *Faithful Presence: The Promise and the Peril of Faith in the Public Square*

If you want to be a part of the right conversations and actions surrounding our nation's complex history of slavery and racism, as well as the bonfire of racial issues and other "isms" ablaze around us today, stop everything you're doing and read this book. Reggie and John represent such a balanced and healthy perspective that will help every single reader.

—ISRAEL HOUGHTON, Grammy Award–winning recording artist

In a time when racism and social justice are such sensitive topics, and many people want to shy away from them out of fear of saying the wrong thing or being judged, Reggie and John address them head on with an authoritative yet graceful voice. They pose thought-provoking and convicting questions. Reading this book stopped me in my tracks and made me evaluate where I stand, as well as the mistakes I've made and the moments I have not been open to hearing other perspectives and experiences. It was fascinating to see both Black and white leaders be able to come together to discuss their individual experiences under the light of the gospel. Their humility, vulnerability, honesty, and no-nonsense approach are refreshing. No matter who you are and what sphere of life you are in, this book will challenge you to do better, because we all need to do better.

—DREW CASTILLO, youth pastor (to Bishop TD
Jakes), The Potter's House of Dallas

Yes, our world needs dreamers, but what it more desperately needs is doers. Reggie Dabbs and John Driver's fantastically creative new book breaks through the racial rhetoric and provides a powerful new map for doing. This great book is for all of us. It rises above the rest.

—SCOTT HAGAN, PhD, president, North Central University,
Minneapolis (location of George Floyd's funeral)

This book beautifully unlocks revolutionary insights hidden in plain sight of the gospel, history, and honest relationships to help us neither lose our minds in senseless political debates nor bury our heads in the sands of opposition-based thinking and self-righteous obstinance.

—BETH AND JEFF MCCORD, authors of the bestselling
Becoming Us: Using the Enneagram to Create a Thriving Gospel-Centered Marriage; founders, Your Enneagram Coach

For our dads—
and for anyone courageous enough to listen
and to change the way they think

CONTENTS

An Invitation to Honest Conversations about Race and Faith

May 25, 2020

The world watched as Derek Chauvin, a white officer in the Minneapolis Police Department, knelt on the neck of George Floyd, a Black man lying on his face in handcuffs in the middle of a downtown neighborhood. Chauvin kept his knee and the weight of his body on Floyd's neck for more than nine minutes. George begged for mercy. He said he couldn't breathe. He cried out for his mother. A crowd of onlookers also pleaded with Chauvin to let him breathe. Other police officers standing nearby did not intervene as George Floyd gasped for air and eventually stopped breathing. He lay unconscious on the pavement for nearly three minutes, with Chauvin's knee still on his neck. Floyd had no pulse when paramedics arrived and was later pronounced dead at the hospital.

As protests erupted around the nation and the world, a tired yet somehow disturbingly invigorated conversation was reignited in the church and on social media. Everyone seemed certain that they were right and everyone else was wrong. Humility, empathy, or any acknowledgment of the need to listen or possibly change one's thinking seemed to be exotic concepts.

Everything was cast as black and white, even though it was not.

May 26, 2020

The world wasn't watching the next day as a conservative white Christian nervously picked up his phone and called his longtime friend Reggie, who is Black. During their short conversation, they talked about uncomfortable things they had never discussed before.

"I'm sick to my stomach, man," John said as he paced across his living-room rug. His emotions were raw, and for some reason he felt insecure talking with his Black friend about George Floyd, as if he was just catching up on something he should already have known. "I mean, the cop pushed his face into the concrete . . . and Floyd screamed for his mama. I've been so mad and I've been crying. This ain't right."

"No, it ain't." Reggie wasn't trying to be short with John, but he was already exhausted from what he had been reading online after the murder. He wasn't sure where this conversation was going. A long pause ensued.

"I just can't believe what so many Christians are saying on social media," John huffed. "It's like they don't think George Floyd was a real person. How did we get here, Reggie?" No answer. John took a breath, then said, "Bro, are you okay?"

"I'm hanging in there." Reggie could tell he didn't sound very convincing. "This is tough, man, but I think something is changing. It has to."

"I know how *I* feel right now, but I can't imagine how *you* must feel." John took yet another deep breath. "I realize you're dealing with a lot right now, but could I ask you a few questions without offending you?"

"We've been friends for years. What do you want to know?"

John understood that once he asked, there was no going back. But it was time. "Have I missed it all these years? Is all of this 'systemic racism' that everyone is fighting about something you've experienced? What's it really like to be a Black man in America?"

John expected a delayed response, but Reggie jumped right in. "When I was teaching my son how to drive, the first thing I told him was to always lay his wallet on the seat next to him so he could get it without reaching into his back pocket if the police pulled him over."

"You're kidding me."

"No, I wish I was. But that's a snapshot of what it's like to be a Black man—and to have a Black son—in America. If Dominic ever gets pulled over, he knows to roll down all four windows, turn on the dome light so the officer can see him, and keep his hands at ten and two. I taught him *that* before I taught him to put on his seat belt."

"Man, we've been friends for more than a decade. How could I not know this? I guess I never asked." John's tone was apologetic, but even that felt weird.

"That's okay. It's something I don't really talk about, but I've had some crazy experiences. I can't tell you how many times white people have heard my presentations at different events and said afterward, 'You speak really well . . . for a Black man.' They think it's a compliment."

"That can't be true. Can some people really be that dense?"

"It's actually happened a lot. They also ask me if my parents are white. When I tell them, 'No, they're Black,' they seem surprised. Professors at my predominantly white Christian college told me I needed to speak better than the white students to make sure I never gave white people a reason to say, 'I couldn't understand him because he's Black.' I know white privilege is a touchy subject, but I've felt it when white people put me into a category that says, 'He shouldn't be able to speak like that. He shouldn't be able to reach me.'"

This was the first time Reggie had talked about racism with John. "Why haven't you spoken out about this stuff?"

"Because I've never wanted everything in my life to be about my race—and because I guess I didn't think it would change anything. But now I'm having conversations that help me think otherwise. The other day, one of my college roommates dismissed the issue of racism because he said we were all fine back in college—*me*, the Black guy; and *them*, everyone else at school. I reminded him of the night all my roommates burst into my dorm room wearing white sheets and ignited lighter fluid on my wall in the shape of a cross."

"No way that really happened! In the 1980s at a Christian college?"

"Oh, it happened. It was a joke. I knew they loved me and meant no harm. I laughed along with them at the time, which I probably shouldn't have done. They didn't realize how much that kind of stuff affected me. I never told them. But the worst wasn't their jokes. Most of my friends didn't know that Minneapolis police repeatedly stopped me when I walked home from work at night. I had to show my school ID and wait for them to verify my identity simply because I was a young Black man walking around at night. When I shared this with my roommate, the one who thought everything had been fine all those years ago, he was speechless. 'Why didn't you say anything?' he asked. I was, like, 'Bro, what could you have done?'"

John honestly didn't know. He struggled to find the right words, then admitted, "I hate to say it, Reggie, but I think a lot of white people feel that way—like we don't know what to do. We have assumed a lot about the lives of Black people in America. Some say that we've let our systems sin for us—all we have to do is look the other way and keep living our lives, hoping that better laws and less racist talk mean things are okay. We were taught to be colorblind—not to notice or talk about racial issues—so we wouldn't make our Black friends uncomfortable."

"I get it. Right or wrong, we've all had our reasons for not talking about racism in the past, but I think we've come to a place where it's something we have to talk about." It felt liberating to speak so boldly on the topic.

"I appreciate your willingness to talk about it now," John replied. "It's not your job to educate all the white people of the world about racism. It has to be exhausting. I know that you don't want everything in your life to be about race—and it shouldn't have to be. At times, I've been on the wrong side of this issue, as have many other people just like me. It's time for white people—especially Christians—to step up, listen up, and stand next to our Black friends who are leading us on these issues, so you don't have to carry the weight alone anymore." John paused in thought before adding, "I haven't been a very good friend to you on this one."

"Hey," Reggie replied in his distinctively gracious way, "you're showing up now. That's where we'll start."

• • •

This was the first of many conversations between two longtime friends—a Black man and a white man, both in full-time ministry. Throughout our friendship, we had spoken at many of the same events, shared countless dinners, talked on the phone thousands of times, and even written two books together. Yet somehow we had never talked honestly and directly about race.

That all changed in the aftermath of the protests and escalating violence that followed the brutal killings of Ahmaud Arbery, Breonna Taylor, George Floyd, and many others.[1] Sadly, there has always been racial injustice, and we hadn't been ignoring it, but these events made it impossible for us and many others to remain passive in any way. But what was the right way to engage on this issue? We decided to search for it together. That initial conversation we had about George Floyd led to many other honest conversations about race, faith, history, and what needs to change in our nation.

As we shared our own stories and talked about the church we both love and serve, we really listened to each other and dove into the ongoing legacy of slavery and racism in America. From these conversations, we concluded that contrary to those who claim that systemic racism is little more than the rantings of liberals, whiners, and troublemakers, it is still a gaping wound in the church and in our nation that won't be quickly or easily healed. Even so, there is hope.

The Uncomfortable Path to Healing

Racism in the United States is a wound first inflicted hundreds of years ago that continues to fester. At various times, we have been told to leave it in the past and just move on, but how can we move on from a wound that is full of countless shards of broken glass and is still bleeding? We can't merely wrap it in the gauze of rhetorical forgiveness—even if we quote Scripture—and hope that healing will magically occur.

Tending to the wound of racism isn't as black and white as many people want it to be, regardless of which polarized political or religious group we gravitate toward. The only path to healing is through individual and collective debridement—the painful but life-giving removal of the shards that inflicted the wound. That is, in part, what both of us intended for our initial conversations: to enter the hard but healing process required to address racism in all its forms.

In the chapters that follow, we invite you into some of our honest conversations, as well as the historical and theological explorations that followed. The good news is these conversations aren't happening on Twitter, Instagram, Facebook, around your dinner table, or at work, so we hope you can enter them with an open mind and heart, even if what you read makes you uncomfortable—and we hope it will.

Having uncomfortable conversations can feel like the worst thing. But reading a book about race that makes you uncomfortable can be the best thing for you—if you have the courage to keep reading. That's why we encourage you to pay attention to your reactions as you read, especially if you feel angry, defensive, or misunderstood. We refer to these reactions as insults. An insult can be a revelation that leads to growth and understanding. The key is to examine not just the topics that make you uncomfortable but also how you process and respond to them. Any insult you experience while reading is an invitation to be curious about why you feel this way. Ask yourself,

"Why am I so angry?"
"Why do I feel defensive?"
"Why do I feel threatened?"

How do you know when you're experiencing an insult? Here are some of the comments we've heard from white conservative Christians that reflect insults:

- "I'm so tired of being called a racist."
- "Everyone just needs a heart change. It's a sin problem, not a skin problem."
- "Systemic racism is a hoax. Show me the racist individuals and let's stop them!"
- "Whether it's about racism or anything else, both sides lie, and I can't believe anything at all."
- "All these social justice warriors are just watering down the gospel."
- "I can't speak up. What if I say the wrong thing? I'll wait for more facts."
- "I can't say, 'Black lives matter.' I'm not a liberal Marxist who hates America!"
- "What about abortion or Black-on-Black crime? Where are the riots for these issues?"
- "If you support any part of the antiracist movement, you must hate police and support anarchy."

You may have heard people say things like these or had similar thoughts yourself. When it comes to race, our thoughts can be incendiary and easily detonated. Why are we so quickly inflamed, so readily offended, so easily triggered? *That* is what we aim to address in this book: why the topic of racism tends to insult everyone who engages it—and why it doesn't have to be this way.

Jumping In

Neither of us has ever skydived, but we've seen it in movies. Imagine the big back door of an airplane opening, and you're standing there in your skydiving gear just waiting for the green light to step off the edge of the ramp. This moment of waiting probably produces the most anxiety and hesitation. When you're skydiving, you can't see your landing spot from twelve thousand feet in the air, so you have to trust that what feels like a blind leap into the ether is actually the first step to safely reaching solid ground.

Jumping into the unknown is also the hardest part of conversations.

There was an awkward moment in our first real talk about racism when we had to just jump in and say something. It wasn't pretty or proper. It never will be. Unlike sounding off on social media, there is no comfortable way to engage with real people on this issue. But no matter how uncomfortable it is, we really need to listen to real people and learn from them, not only in person but from reliable sources they produce. That is what we aim to help you do, which is why understanding the structure of this book is important.

The chapters in part 1, "Evaluating Our Own Ways of Thinking," are intended to help us become aware of how we've been conditioned to view issues of race. We all have various lenses or windows through which we view the world, and we need to be aware of what those are. When we evaluate our own ways of thinking, we have a chance to remove the bugs from our windshields so we can stop looking *at* the glass and start looking through it instead.

Fair warning: these early chapters might prompt an insulted feeling or two, mainly because we use terms and reference ideas you may have been conditioned to interpret a certain way or not even entertain. We want to explore not just the terms but also the conditioning. Problems must be named before they can be addressed, so we hope you will absorb any offense, if only temporarily. The way we define terms like *grace*, *justice*, and *gospel* may also feel insulting.

It might help to pretend you've never heard the words or the definitions before.

Our goal is to provide you with tools to mine deeply into Scripture, as well as into your beliefs about racism—beliefs you may not even be aware you have. This includes examining what the gospel teaches about changing the way we think and about changing the systems around us. If you are courageous enough to enter this process, you will see racism differently.

In part 2, "Taking Historical and Theological Inventories," we engage in a nonexhaustive but robust inventory of racial history, policy, and theology. Though we will define it in much greater detail later, by "inventory" we mean an honest, fearless look at the whole of an individual's or organization's experiences in the world, perspectives from which they view the world, and patterns of addressing the world—some of which we are aware of, but a number of which we are not.

Many in our nation and in the church are already taking inventories on race, while many others are fiercely resisting doing so out of fear of being labeled or perhaps being found wanting in some way. Instead of resisting the process of exploring the truth about our theology and history, the healthier action is to engage in doing so together, knowing that honesty and vulnerability are not threats to the gospel but its pillars.

To take an honest inventory, we first need to understand the history and legacies we've inherited from slavery, our nation's founders and founding documents, the Civil War, postwar Reconstruction, Jim Crow laws, the civil rights movement, and the origin of the religious right and its eventual convergence with the white evangelical church. As advocate and author Latasha Morrison says, "When we lack historical understanding, we lose part of our identity. We don't know where we came from and don't know what there is to celebrate or lament. Likewise, without knowing our history, it can be difficult to know what needs repairing, what needs reconciling."[2]

Each chapter opens with a portion of a real conversation between the two of us, sharing stories from our own experiences and the experiences of people we know or have met. These are not intended as scripts for you to use in conversations about race, because that rarely works. Instead, we hope that sharing a few of our conversations might help you see points of entry into similar conversations in your own context and give you courage to engage in them. While many conversations about race—the good kind—are not as plentiful as we'd like to see, many others—the destructive kind—seem to be happening all around us. Perhaps reading our conversations will help you discover solid footholds for climbing upward, while avoiding hazardous footholds that will send you crashing to the ground.

Throughout the book, our focus is primarily on what tends to insult white people, particularly white conservative Christians. However, this is not meant to be one-sided, reverse racism. We are not suggesting that all white people are racist or that there is any reason to feel guilt or shame over being born white. At the same time, we have to reckon with the fact that there is great insult when white people—especially white people within the church—refuse to even acknowledge the existence, much less the injustices, of systemic racism.

This book predominantly deals with issues of racism as they relate to white and Black Americans, but we acknowledge that this is not the only cultural relationship with a complex history, present, and future that needs addressing and change. These principles and conversations will also be helpful in fighting the sin of racism that affects Latinos, Asians, and the many nations of indigenous peoples in the Americas—or individuals and communities of any other ethnicity. Not addressing each of these in this book does not mean that they are not equally important. It means only that our time and context constrains us to this primary topic.

You will also notice that we capitalize the term *Black*, but not the term *white*. We are not elevating one race over another. Later in the book, we will deal with the social concept of race, including the concept of whiteness as distinct from cultural origins like Scottish, German, or Norwegian. From biblical and historical perspectives, we will explore whether whiteness even exists. But our reason for capitalizing *Black* comes from the shared cultural experiences of Black people in America who have been oppressed by the majority culture, which uses the concept of whiteness to create fear and suppress minorities.

Blackness emerged from African victims being unjustly forced into slavery. Over time, their shared experiences, in both religious and community contexts, developed into a sense of Blackness that fostered safe places in a system of oppression. As we have learned to be sensitive to the inventories of others whose experiences differ from our own, we want to show appropriate honor and sensitivity to our Black brothers and sisters, many of whom bear the surnames not of beloved patriarchs but of brutal slave masters. This is why we have capitalized *Black*. We know there are other ways to handle this. But we researched both the writings of our Black brothers and sisters and current journalistic standards and made this decision out of respect for the sensitivity of this topic. Our goal is to listen and respond in the present with respect and empathy, even if perspectives on the terms we use continue to morph over time.

As this preview of just one issue demonstrates, conversations on race are nuanced and complex. We hope that as you read, you will be challenged to embrace not only new ways of thinking but also new ways of acting. We hope that by the time you finish this book, you will be open to thinking differently as a gospel practice, and that the knowledge you gain about racism will equip you for whatever you choose to do in response.

We know the odds are pretty slim that those who think systemic racism and social unrest are little more than conspiracy theories or left-wing ploys will read this book. However, if this describes you, we are grateful that you are willing to be a part of these conversations.

Even if this doesn't describe you, chances are that it describes a person you know. Whether you are someone's child, parent, coworker, pastor, or friend, we encourage you to take this journey yourself before handing the book to that person and saying, "Here! Look how wrong you are!" Let us save you the time and heartache: that won't work. But if you are willing to take your own journey first, perhaps afterward you'll be able to humbly hand that person the book and say, "I'm learning and growing in this area, and I still have a long way to go. Can we grab a coffee and talk?"

We realize that what we've written might cost us some friends and gain us some foes. Many think we should just leave well enough alone. But we choose to talk about these topics because the gospel does—it addresses both racism and the disposition of those who encountered and affected it. Beyond that, it affects all of us. It affects you, whether or not you realize it. It takes humility to see this.

We are doing our best to share from a posture of humility. As you will discover, we are just two regular guys who have worked extensively with adults and kids in public schools and churches. We have varied experiences as a Black man and a white man, along with diverse insights into history, theology, and community. We want to humbly share from where we are.

There are many other authors, leaders, and theologians—Black and white—you should be reading and following. They have spent their careers studying and addressing racism in America. Their books, research, and posts have inspired and informed us, and we hope the resources we share will inspire and inform you as well. We would love nothing more than for you to read what they've written and follow them, because their ongoing work has paved the way for others like us.

Following the deaths of George Floyd and others, an estimated 15 to 26 million people in the United States participated in demonstrations. In terms of the number of participants, this may well be the largest civil rights movement in American history.[3] No matter how we feel about the messy middle of such demonstrations, we can't deny that something significant is happening.

We are also engaging racism as fathers. When our kids look back on this turbulent time, we want them to know that even though racism was a volatile issue, their parents chose to listen and engage with grace and truth. We have taken seriously the admonition of scholar and advocate Jemar Tisby to "create something. Write a blog post. Write a book. Write a sermon. Do a Sunday school class. Host a forum. Write a song or poem. Create something that speaks to social justice. As you do it, remember that it always helps to get feedback from a person from a different racial or ethnic background who is willing to help."[4] We can't necessarily change the world, but we can do something. We can refuse to remain unengaged.

We stand at the edge of the ramp with you, waiting to jump out of the plane, just as we stood at the edge of an uncomfortable conversation with each other. If you feel mired in confusion or anger because racial problems seem like black-and-white issues, yet you wonder whether there may be more shades (even some grays) to be explored, we invite you to step off the ramp and keep courageously reading all the way to the end. You won't be jumping alone. You won't free-fall the whole way. You have a parachute, and there's a landing zone. The safety of solid ground awaits us—of better ways to think, more accurate information and history to consider, and better conversations about race to have—but only if we jump together in honesty.

"

PART 1

EVALUATING OUR OWN WAYS OF THINKING

"

CHAPTER 1

LOOKING WHERE
WE'VE SLIPPED

I forgot that you went to college in Minneapolis, where George Floyd was killed. I can't imagine what seeing his murder was like for you."

"I used to work in the same neighborhood where he was killed." Reggie's words hit John like a ton of bricks. An event on the news that seemed to be from another world suddenly felt close and real.

"When I saw that policeman with his knee on George's neck, I didn't just see George Floyd—I saw myself." Reggie took a slow breath, then continued. "I saw Dominic, my son, a young Black man just going to work every day. I saw my nephew, Donovan, and my niece, Monique. They both live in Minneapolis. Bro, it could have happened to any of us."

John wasn't sure how to respond. "Man, I've honestly never imagined myself pinned under a cop's knee. I've always been told that these are just rare incidents that happen to criminals by cops who are 'bad apples.' You're telling me that you worry about this kind of thing for real?"

"I do. I really do. I guess I've learned to live with it."

"Live with it? Reggie, you shouldn't have to live with it. What could we do so you don't have to?" John was eager to fix the problem.

Reggie laughed. "Man, we can't just make this go away. It's going to take time. Like many Black people, I'm not asking for special treatment, just equal treatment. If I do wrong, take me to jail. If I rob or beat someone, or if I commit murder, put the handcuffs on me and take me to jail. But don't arrest me on the street, try me on the street, convict me on the street, and sentence me to death on the street. Let me have my chance. Black people just want the same respect everybody else gets."

"I guess I thought you already had it. I thought everyone in America had the chance to have it. I used to be a history teacher, and I railed against racism in theory, as if racism is only about the actions of immoral individuals. Ahmaud Arbery began to change things for me—not just that some crazy rednecks could do something so horrible, but that the system seemed to prevent justice for Ahmaud for months until the video emerged. And then when I saw the video of George Floyd, I cried—hearing a grown man crying for his mama just broke me. I told Laura, 'I'm tired of sitting here talking about this. We need to show up for something for a change!'"

"That's what we really need," Reggie quickly replied. "We don't need white Christians and leaders standing on the sidelines cheering us on. We need you guys on the front lines with us."

"I'm trying. But I have to be honest. When I first heard 'Black lives matter' back in 2014, my reaction was, 'Wait, don't all lives matter?' I didn't think of myself as racist, so it offended me because it felt like someone was insinuating that I was. I didn't cause slavery and I certainly didn't condone all this horrible violence, so I didn't know how to handle taking responsibility for possibly contributing to it in some way." There it was. John knew that he was stepping into honesty in a way that could offend his friend.

"What changed your mind?" Reggie asked.

"Well, it's still changing, but it began with my wife loving me well enough to tell me the truth. I was making a lot of logically sound points, but I wasn't doing the one thing our Black friends were asking me to do: listen."

Reggie was silent for a moment. Then he said, "Bro, she nailed it."

John chuckled. "She always does. It helped me start thinking differently. I stopped being more offended at the idea of being called a racist than I was over racism itself—at the way racism actually affects people whose lives are different from mine. People like you. At first, I was offended because I hadn't done anything wrong. Now I'm seeing that, well, I hadn't done anything at all."

$$\bullet \ \bullet \ \bullet$$

Systemic racism. Reverse racism. White supremacy. White privilege. White guilt. Virtue signaling. Black Lives Matter. Blue Lives Matter. All Lives Matter. The Lost Cause. Jim Crow. Civil rights. Unconscious bias. Affirmative action. Black-on-Black crime. Police brutality. Law and order. Mass incarceration. Segregated churches. Mass repentance. History. Heritage. Hate. Reparations. Revenge. Reconciliation.

These are hot-button terms that can ignite heated and even fiery discussions. Just reading them may have evoked an emotional reaction for you. That's because all of us have deeply held, intensely emotional opinions related to our way of seeing the world—even if we don't realize it.

In recent years in the United States, our deeply held opinions have coalesced around polarized mindsets, one conservative and one liberal. Clashing ideologies have split our nation, trapping us in cycles of mindless and heartless debates that play out in the news and on social media. In his book, *Faithful Presence*, former two-term Republican Tennessee governor Bill Haslam addresses the way various sources affect our perceptions: "Today, many news entities have an economic incentive to outrage. Stoking the fires of disagreement can be very profitable. Networks like CNN, Fox, and MSNBC have all learned that there is money to be made from emphasizing only one side of an argument. The madder I get at one side, the more I watch whoever is telling me how horrible that side is."[1] All this madness shapes the loud statements political and religious leaders make or omit (after all, saying nothing is a big statement). And yes, this also results in awkward conversations around many family dinner tables.

We are eyewitnesses to the death of meaningful dialogue. Conversation has devolved from a mutual exchange of ideas into something fruitless and harmful. In the media, it's all endless opponent bashing, feckless name-calling, or reckless grandstanding. Sadly, Christians aren't faring much better than anyone else in this dumpster-dive into insult that we now call public discourse. The new and accepted norm is to portray complete certainty about what's right and who's wrong in all matters, even when we know little about them. We have become too smart to listen, and thus too smart to learn.

Never have we been so entrenched in zealous yet unfruitful ways of thinking.

We are certain about everything, Christians especially. White

Christians have too often expressed their certainties in ways that sound much more like political beliefs than gospel ones. The conservative Christians among us have railed against "woke" Christians—anyone who is concerned about social issues—viewing them as misguided fools who have been hoodwinked into white guilt or a radical definition of *Black power* (a term most white people don't have any real context for). After all, we have a Black friend or coworker who agrees that all this social upheaval is just bad political theater. As a result, we feel no tension when attacking others in conversations or on social media because we believe we're defending Christianity or America, which to us go hand in hand.

While some of us rage against the woke machine, others of us retreat. We feel lost, with no idea how to rightly engage, so we either remain silent or settle for posting memes that are a watered-down scriptural version of "Can't we all just get along?" Even then, someone attacks us, leaving us to question whether there really is a race problem or if it's all just woke bluster. We feel immense pressure either to retreat or to join the name-calling game everyone else is playing.

When the only options are attack or retreat, there is no room for conversation, much less for the real or lasting change. But what if we told you that the gospel has so much more to offer than just a passive "Can't we all just get along?" It invites us into a whole new way of thinking, speaking, and being that truly is good news for those of us who feel trapped between dueling monologues. The gospel offers a path to healing, but we must believe it rightly to walk it. When what sounds like good news for us sounds more like bad news for those outside of our political tribes, the problem isn't with the gospel but with the way we're viewing or applying it. Not everyone will accept the gospel, but it should be good news for all.

If we are courageous enough to look at the way we think and talk (and do not think and talk) about race, we will discover that while we definitely have a racism problem, we have an even bigger gospel problem.

This is where you might be tempted to think, *Well, since I believe the gospel already, this doesn't apply to me.* Or worse, you might feel insulted that we've insinuated there is a problem with the way you think. This is a small glimpse into the bigger problem we are addressing—the binary, reactionary extremism that teaches us that we're either all right or all wrong, with nothing in between. This is the harmful kind of black-and-white thinking, and as we will see, it leads away from the belief in absolute truth we think we so strongly hold. This is why it is common these days for conservative Christians to respond to hard-to-dismiss challenges to their logic or viewpoints with "Well, you can't believe anything you hear these days, so who can know what's really true?"

Somehow, the loudest advocates of absolute truth can quickly deny it without creating tension within themselves. Why? Because they subconsciously believe that facts can be errant, but their thinking cannot. They would rather dismiss the facts than evaluate their way of thinking, believing, and being. This is not the way of the gospel.

Scripture reveals that only a fool (even a Christian fool) refuses to examine the way he or she looks at things. Take it from two Christian fools, this is actually good news.

What Foolish Thinking Really Is

Picture this scene. A fourteen-year-old Black girl who is pregnant for the second time comes home from school one day to an empty house. Inside, nothing remains but her first little baby screaming for his mama. Infuriated that she is pregnant again, her parents have abandoned her. She will never see them again. Soon, she will be living in an abandoned chicken coop with her *three* little babies because, although she doesn't yet know it, she is pregnant with twins.

When you imagine this young girl, what do you see? What conclusions do you draw about her? Is she an immoral person getting what she deserves? A casualty of her impoverished upbringing? A drain on the welfare system? Someone who should pull herself up by her bootstraps?

The things we see that aren't necessarily visually evident make up our assumptions, our biases, and our ways of thinking. Before we can see real people on the other side of our black-and-white lenses, we must first recognize what distorts those lenses. It's important to become aware of distorted viewpoints because they become the viewfinders through which we look at the world and other people in it. Our goal is to be wise, not foolish, in the way we view the world, especially something as significant as racism.

If we think our way of seeing the world is already crystal clear, we are modeling the biblical definition of foolishness. "The way of fools seems right to them, but the wise listen to advice" (Prov. 12:15 NIV). The English Standard Version says, "The way of a fool is right in his [or her] own eyes." Foolishness is not about errant facts; it's about the way we hold tightly to what seems right to us.

If it offends you to even consider that you might be foolish, this could be the start of really good news for you. Not because you aren't in fact foolish but because the Bible is an equal-opportunity offender—we all walk in foolishness at times. If you trust Scripture, then it's worth paying attention to anything in it that makes you feel insulted. This feeling reveals something important that we should take note of.

It's also important to understand that Scripture, especially the book of Proverbs, uses the term *fool* in multiple ways. When a proverb characterizes a person as foolish, it is not necessarily declaring that the person is foolish at all times and in all ways. Instead, many proverbs comment on the foolishness of specific situations, behaviors, and choices. Which means a person might be foolish in some situations and ways of thinking, yet not in others. For example, we may be wise in the way we handle finances but foolish in the way we speak to our families; or we may be wise in the way we work hard but foolish in refusing to accept instruction or advice. Both can be true.

As a first step in evaluating your thinking about race, we ask you to be open to the idea that you may not be wise in every thought and action. That idea should not be insulting; it's just a fact of the human condition. We need to grow in wisdom, just as Jesus did (Luke 2:52). Walking in God's ways (a phrase we will explore later) begins by being humble enough to examine—and to keep examining—not just your actions but also your thinking.

The consequences of failing to do so are evident in our society today. We do not listen because we no longer know how. We're so busy yelling and posting and shaming that there's no room for listening. We pick up the talking points of our favorite pundits or preachers and amplify them. We feel so insulted at even the prospect of entertaining differing viewpoints that we defend our own at all costs.

Proverbs again has something to offer: "*Fools* find no pleasure in understanding but delight in airing *their own* opinions" (18:2 NIV, emphasis added). Could a passage be more apropos for today? When was the last time we took pleasure in understanding someone else's opinion? Expertly broadcasting one's own opinion has become the highest, most hallowed accomplishment, a pathway to numerous followers, monetized ads, and even public office.

How might things be different if we took more pleasure in understanding issues and the people they affect than in sounding off? What if we paid more attention to whether our personal or organizational sentiments about racism sound more like Scripture than our favorite pundit's one-liners? What if we endeavored to respond with informed humility, sincere empathy, and a growing historical, theological, and relational understanding of racial matters? What if we desired to make a difference with both passion and gentleness?

This might sound too high minded for practical application, especially when civil unrest erupts and the internet burns hotter still. And yet these are not just sentimental musings but biblical principles and critical elements of the gospel. If we ignore them, we will descend into new depths of foolishness.

Think again of the fourteen-year-old girl. If we apply biblical wisdom, we attempt to examine not just her situation but the way we see her. Wisdom examines both what our eyes see and the eyes with which we see it. In the next chapter, you'll meet this girl in a way that might help you engage in this practice.

We don't have to be insulted by the truth that we might be foolish in some areas of life, that we might need to examine our ways and learn to think and act differently. Doing so positions us to receive the best news. This kind of thinking leads us away from sweeping statements of dismissive and sometimes cruel certainty into compassion, empathy, and wisdom—the kind of wisdom that doesn't just acknowledge how far everyone in our society has fallen but also sees where we've slipped.

Where We've Slipped

Misunderstanding or foolishness is not necessarily a failure, but it is a consequence of the human condition. Remember Peter's response when Jesus wrapped a towel around his waist and began to wash the disciples' feet? Peter was offended and initially refused: "You shall never wash my feet" (John 13:8). He didn't hesitate to rebuke Jesus, the Son of God, for challenging his self-defined standard of righteousness. Peter was convinced he was in alignment with God, even as he opposed him. He misunderstood what Jesus was both offering him and asking of him.

We are just as susceptible to misunderstanding. Resisting God's ways comes from being fallen human beings, a consequence of living in a broken-but-being-redeemed state. Peter failed initially, but not ultimately. He listened when Jesus said, "If I do not wash you, you have no share with me" (v. 8). Peter's response was immediate and wholehearted: "Lord, not my feet only but also my hands and my head!" (v. 9).

Again, misunderstanding is not necessarily failure; it is simply human. The failure is in refusing to listen or in denying the misunderstanding. Imagine Peter telling Jesus, "No way, Jesus. I have to stand my ground because you're wrong on this one." We fail when we defy biblical teaching with our own standards of righteousness, when we keep doing the same foolish things while expecting different results, when we pride ourselves on an unwavering commitment to our points of view.

Peter thought he was too humble for the humble Christ to serve him, too right for the Righteous One to wash him. He thought Jesus was wrong, but he really needed to address his own deep wrongness: the conviction that his way of thinking couldn't be wrong.

Many in Christian circles speak of racism as a sin problem—*someone else's sin problem*. We say things like "Racism has always been an issue and will always be until the end of the world." We act as if racism is immutable, a reality that exists without our consent, and therefore we have little or no obligation to address it. But this view contradicts Jesus' teaching, as we will see.

In writing this book, our primary objective is not to end racism in the world (though that would be incredible) but rather to do our part to end racism in the church—to root it out of church people and church systems so that Christians, Black and white together, can rightly influence our cultural systems instead of harm them. This is a goal all Christians should not only support but also wholeheartedly believe is possible and expected of those who follow Christ. Jesus' goal is a united family of devoted disciples who are devoid of racism, so it shouldn't seem too lofty an endeavor. According to the apostle Peter, "[God's] divine power has granted to us *all things* that pertain to life and godliness, through the knowledge of him who called us to his own glory and excellence" (2 Peter 1:3, emphasis added). We simply need to access the divine resources we already have. As pastor Thabiti Anyabwile says, "It's time to end the partisan and racist foolishness that blemishes the church."[2]

Then let's just do it, right? Well, it's not as simple—not as black and white—as we might think.

The United States prides itself on being a nation of courage and action. But it often takes more courage to listen than to take action. Doing rightly begins with believing rightly, which leads to speaking rightly. Right doing naturally follows right believing and right speaking. So the order is right thinking, right speaking, right doing. No other sequence can work, which is why Scripture is replete with examples. Moses had to adjust his self-condemned thinking when God called him. Bold words to Pharaoh eventually followed, as did a lot of action—from both Moses and God (Exodus 3; 6–12). Zacchaeus thought differently about his thieving lifestyle as a tax collector and spoke words of repentance, which were followed by the action of repaying with extreme interest those he had cheated (Luke 19:1–10). Rinse. Repeat.

We bypass this sequence when we rush headlong into "Just tell me what you want me to do about it." The danger is that we end up exercising a form of alternative political correctness (though we rail against political correctness) when we say or do things for the sake of social boundaries or appearances (such as believing that systemic racism is a hoax or ranting about being called racists), rather than out of changed hearts, minds, or systems. At worst, it is a cursory nod to civility while civilization burns to the ground.

Our nation has already tried this approach without success. Now we fight over the terms we use more than we fight against racism itself. Instead of cycling through right believing, speaking, and doing, ours is an endless cycle of attacks—attacks on social media, attacks from church pulpits, attacks on news outlets, attacks between political parties, and attacks when civil unrest erupts. It's time to stop chalking racial issues up to semantics or the actions of the evil right or evil left. As followers of Christ who affirm that all people are created in God's image, we do not have the option of treating others as subhuman or holding anyone in contempt. There is no place for the kind of thinking that says, "Either get on board with *our* way of thinking or get out of *our* country—or *our* churches."

Too many of us have spent our lives believing that positive legal changes and a general decrease in racial slurs or racist jokes means that racism is largely dead and buried. But there are aspects of racism we've not been burying so much as planting. Racism has continued to grow in unseen places for some of us, and in more visible places for many others.

An old African proverb says, "Look not where you fell but where you slipped." We can't address a wound or problem without examining its causes and ongoing contributing factors. Yelling about where we've fallen is easy, but looking where we've slipped takes humility, courage, and patience. It's time to look where we've slipped in the past and where we are still slipping today. We need to deal with the ideological and historical root systems of injustice, bitterness, ignorance, and stubbornness over which we continue to trip. We must seek to understand before we seek to be understood. And we must do so with humility so we can see our role in the bigger story of racism in the United States without being insulted by the idea that we have a role in it.

We cannot receive from Jesus what we do not think we need. It's time to examine our individual and collective needs.

"Black Lives Matter" and Social Justice

Many of us are unable to begin the process of self-examination because we're hung up on hot-button words or phrases. Politics, the media, and churches are rife with battles over phrases like "Black lives matter" and "social justice." It may help to briefly address these terms here.

Some see "Black lives matter" as an expression of truth needed to help us move past the disproportionate level of violence committed against Black Americans, while others see it as the dark epicenter of the liberal agenda—the first of many toppling dominoes that will lead us into a socialistic society of dystopian chaos. If you have concerns about the phrase "Black lives matter," you may wonder how we, the authors of this book, interpret it and whether we are aligned with the Black Lives Matter (BLM) movement.

To be clear, "Black lives matter" began as a hashtag after the tragic death of Trayvon Martin in 2012 and the subsequent jury acquittal of the man who shot him, George Zimmerman. It developed into something much bigger. The movement is hard to define, but the phrase is part of it, as is the official BLM organization and its networks that have arisen since the phrase was conceived.

While we do not fully support the Black Lives Matter organization or its political ideologies and objectives, we do affirm the truth of the statement "Black lives matter." Some Christians support BLM's positive attempts to raise awareness about racism, but the phrase is a sticking point for many conservatives and Christians despite the fact that respected leaders and organizations also affirm this expression as both true and worthy of repeating as a sign of empathy and openheartedness on the path to ending racism. Denominations that have publicly supported the truth of the statement include the Southern Baptist Convention,[3] Presbyterian Church (USA),[4] Assemblies of God, Church of God in Christ,[5] United Methodist Church,[6] and many more.

Ironically, almost every major white denomination mentioned either originated in response to the issue of slavery or experienced a major split over it. Southern Baptists were called Southern not just because they lived in the South but because they broke away from other Baptists who opposed slavery. This blatant racism within our nation's church history tragically mirrors the racism we will later explore in our American history. The church should have been a prophetic voice challenging slavery and racism, but instead it often was complicit and remains so today, mixing racism and nationalism with the gospel, even though they are incompatible with it.

Most of these denominations have publicly repented of their racist beginnings, something to remember when we discuss whether repentance is only for individuals. Even so, these histories still affect the demographics of churches in America, which remain largely segregated and divided over issues of race.

Black lives should matter as much as any other lives, but in this country, many Black people have experienced humiliations and violence that reveal otherwise. To affirm that Black lives matter does not mean we are critical race theorists, liberals, socialists, Marxists, social Marxists, or the lighters of virtue-signaling fires. We believe that both Black and white people are capable of committing crimes, that not all police are bad apples or brutal racists, and that the destruction of property and the harming of innocent life, of any color, are wrong.

We just don't believe that these things should be used as excuses to stop listening or addressing racism, especially as it affects the church. This leads us to another phrase that is often misapplied to this conversation: "social justice." It is all too common for anyone concerned about our nation's history on racism, racial inequities, or the concept of systemic racism to be labeled a "social justice warrior" or "social justician." To be clear, in Christian circles, these are not compliments.

We agree with pastor and New Testament professor Esau McCaulley, who said, "People keep warning us about the potential dangers of pursuing social justice while ignoring the absolute havoc the opposition to justice and ongoing racism has *already wreaked* on the unity, mission, and theological coherence of the church."[7] McCaulley addressed what we aim to explore in great detail: what in theology and history we are choosing to see and what we are choosing to ignore.

Modern discourse weaponizes hot-button terms and directs them toward an opponent, thus canceling their value in the eyes of anyone who might be tempted to listen to more than one side. Many Christians and conservatives see no need to listen to anyone who has been labeled a liberal, a social justice warrior, a critical race theorist (someone espousing CRT), and other pejorative terms. Attorney Justin Giboney, president of the AND Campaign, said, "Do you know what's more effective than creating statements condemning critical race theory? Actually dismantling racism so CRT is obsolete. Evangelicals still can't see that their lack of credibility on racial justice lends credence to the things they condemn."[8]

Giboney's insight reveals the tragic state of much of our thinking and discourse today. By directing our energies only against *anything* opposed to our viewpoints, we have little energy left to direct toward *something* of gospel substance, which renders us effective at *nothing* of value. We end up living in an either-or mindset in which only one conclusion can be correct and all others are utterly wrong. There is no room for nuance here. Real life doesn't work this way, but our modern conversations and ideologies most certainly do.

Many of us have become so reactive that we refuse to even hear a story or viewpoint other than those that affirm our ideological tribes or personal points of view. When we do this, we ignore not just one problem but two, and the one between our ears is the greater.

Changes in History, Hearts, or Systems?

Just as there may be hot-button phrases we need to hurdle to reach deeper understanding and more fruitful conversations on race, there are hot-button concepts that can hinder the right kind of thinking.

We will preview two of them here and expand on them in later chapters: (1) disputed versions of history, and (2) whether racism is a heart issue or a systems issue.

A Glimpse into Rewriting History

Conversations about race inflame many white conservatives because they are being told that someone is trying to rewrite history. For those who love this country and celebrate its founding, this can be especially insulting. But if our minds are open to gospel-driven change, we will be able to explore how our viewpoints may unknowingly be informed by errant historical narratives, especially concerning racism.

One such example is the Lost Cause, named after a book written in 1866, which sparked an ideological movement that has persisted for more than a century and a half. It was an effort to recast the Civil War narrative by portraying the Confederate cause as a just and noble one. In the aftermath of the war, Lost Cause proponents claimed that the secession of the Southern states wasn't about slavery but about protecting their way of life, including their Christian values.

The Lost Cause deified Southern military leaders such as Robert E. Lee and Nathan Bedford Forrest while characterizing Ulysses S. Grant as a hapless drunk and battlefield butcher. In truth, Grant, considered the premier military strategist of his time, was a surprisingly radical voice for racial equality as a two-term president during the Reconstruction era.

Today we lack understanding of the complex narrative regarding the Civil War and slavery that has informed modern history and the church, as well as recent events. Emerging from this limited view is a narrative that sums up slavery and Reconstruction in succinct, sanitized ways, blurring many of the facts about racism, discrimination, and the atrocities that set the foundation for race relations in America today. The events of the past are still haunting us—and it's not a liberal idea to admit it. It is a biblical one—again, Scripture calls us to take pleasure in understanding, not in merely expressing our opinions apart from hearing all sides.

We will engage in a deeper examination of the Lost Cause and other historical perspectives later. But this examination can benefit us only if we open our minds not to new ideas about our history but rather to old ones that ideologies like the Lost Cause have sought to distort and rewrite.

A Glimpse at Heart Transformation versus Systemic Change

Another hot-button concept that can hinder our thinking is whether racism is a heart issue or a systems issue. Some people believe that a heart change is the only way to end racism, while others believe it requires systemic change. The heart-change view is promoted on social media and proclaimed from pulpits around the nation. It asserts that everyone just needs Jesus, not racial equality—or that if we all get saved, racism will disappear without requiring us to listen, repent, or work together to repair our divisions. Those who embrace this view believe that racism exists only in the heart, and so long as you're a Christian who intends no harm, you can rest assured you're free of racism.

The systemic-change viewpoint asserts that despite legal and social progress toward racial equality, discrimination is still embedded in our judicial, governmental, and social systems in ways we may not realize or intend. For example, Black people experience a disproportionate number of traffic stops and searches, harsh drug-offense sentences, and police brutality.

Understanding the distinctions between these viewpoints, as

well as the various ways *system* is defined, will shape how we read the rest of this book.

The key distinction between the heart-change view and the systemic-change view lies in this simple statement: people have hearts, but systems do not.

Fortunately, we don't have to choose between hearts and systems. Both need to be addressed, just not through the same means. We need hearts to change, but we can't wait for heart change to occur before we address unjust systems. Martin Luther King Jr. said, "It may be true that the law [the system] cannot change the heart but it can restrain the heartless. It . . . cannot make a man love me but it can keep him from lynching me and I think that is pretty important, also."[9]

Some Americans, including Christians, defend our social, governmental, and justice systems as if the systems themselves are not inanimate—as if they have hearts. When the systems they consider sacred are questioned or criticized, they feel compelled to defend America, and even the gospel. Yet, as we'll learn, our country's founders intended our systems of governance to be examined and adjusted when necessary. Great freedom comes from choosing right responses toward people (from the heart) as well as right responses toward our systems (by taking action). But we first need to be clear about the distinction between the two.

Here is how pastor Osheta Moore, author of *Dear White Peacemakers*, described what it means to approach people and systems differently: "I've learned that systems of oppression detrimentally affect the ones who benefit from the oppression as much as the oppressed—in absolutely different ways, of course, but still devastating—and those systems are what I hope we turn our anger and fury towards, not each other. Never each other! But when it comes to those racist systems . . . I want to flip them over and destroy them like the tables in the temple. I think this is the hard work of the kingdom of God that we're called to in this moment."[10]

Separating systems from people *is* hard work, but it is the right work. The only way we can determine whether we may be ascribing a heart to a system that has none or responding in a heartless manner toward fellow image bearers of God who do have hearts is by examining how we truly think and react. Those who claim that America is too good to have widespread racism may believe they are defending America, but in their emotional responses, they end up defending racist aspects of our history and our systems as if they've forgotten that America is composed of people with hearts. For many conservative Christians, the systems have seemingly become more sacred than the people they are affecting, people who are made in the image of a sacred God. As Giboney attests, "Unwillingness to change systems that have historically disadvantaged your neighbor is conservatism [and certainly Christianity] in fatal error. Canceling all dissenting opinions and all physiological realities that complicate your narrative is progressive madness."[11]

We don't need to tear down our nation or history to address areas of concern within them, just as we don't need to sanctify or deify America's founders, history, or systems to honor them. In a later chapter, we'll explore a historical context for the founders' accomplishments that also acknowledges their grave misdeeds, the gravest of all being the enslavement and legalized abuse of Black Americans. The founders were people, and like all people, they were complex—not wholly good or bad. Binary, polarized thinking about the founders or anything else inevitably leads to extreme conclusions, but we don't have to stay there—in fact, staying there does more damage than we might think.

We don't want anyone to stop loving this nation, but we do want to cast a clear vision for what loving this nation *well*, according to the gospel, really entails. Historically and biblically, mixing nationalism with faith is dangerous, producing consequences we often fail to recognize because we're too caught up in what feels like patriotism—even if the original patriots would have objected to how we define it.

If discovering that America was and remains flawed shakes the foundation of our Christian faith, then we need to examine our foundation. For Christians, our allegiance is to God, who calls us to something infinitely higher than our nation or its founders. As preacher Charles Spurgeon pointed out, "Those hopes will surely fall to the ground which are built upon men who so soon lie under ground."[12]

For Christians, returning to a gospel lens, or a clearer understanding of the gospel, makes it easier to denounce racism in all its forms, beginning with ourselves and our own communities of faith. We can learn to hold multiple values and viewpoints in tension, no longer living as if one position obliterates the value of another. We can honor soldiers and law enforcement officers while also seeing the need for changing the systems within which they serve—systems created in moments of history when racial bias was not only accepted but was also enforced by these systems.

This way of thinking isn't just political; it is thoroughly Christian. When it comes to the choice of whether or not to engage the issue of racism, our perspective aligns with that of pastor and author Timothy Keller, who wrote, "Christians cannot pretend they can transcend politics and simply 'preach the Gospel.' Those who avoid all political discussions and engagement are essentially casting a vote for the social status quo. American churches in the early nineteenth century that did not speak out against slavery because that was what we would now call 'getting political' were actually supporting slavery by doing so. To not be political is to be political."[13]

Have you noticed how some of us complain that our ministers

are "getting political" only when something insults our own political viewpoints? Otherwise, what they're saying is just plain common sense, right? Such logic has even led some churches to justify hosting political rallies, though they still cry foul when those with differing viewpoints get political in church.

The late comedian George Carlin pointed out that when you're the one driving, "anyone going slower than you is an idiot . . . and anyone going faster than you is a maniac."[14] Bias is something we generally cannot detect in ourselves. We need outside help to see it. Like the apostle Peter, who insisted that Jesus shouldn't wash his feet, we all too easily become our own standard of righteousness. With racism or any other issue, we tend to think everyone else on the road is failing to meet the standard we deem correct.

Racism is something else we tend to recognize only in others. It's often difficult to recognize racist elements in our own ways of thinking. Statements like these make some white people feel uncomfortable, as if we are insinuating that they are, in fact, racist. The fear or anger (insult) of being labeled a racist keeps many from engaging in healthy conversations about race—as if doing so means admitting they're racists. We want to be clear that we are not calling you a racist. We repeat: we are *not* calling you a racist. (If you are using a highlighter, go ahead and use up half the marker here.)

If it feels as if everything you hear is indicting you as a racist, you may be caught in the "racism exists only in a person's heart" point of view, which explains why you might feel insulted. We can help you think outside your heart a bit because you may not be dealing with the actual nature of the problem, only how it affects you—specifically, your perceived guilt or innocence. The problem of racism is bigger than any one of us, whether we have contributed to it knowingly or unknowingly.

Author and pastor John Onwuchekwa points out that "when it comes to repairing past injustices, the chasm is *huge* and no one long jumps across. No single person, action, or institution can do all that needs to be done. A series of small successive steps are needed. However, let's never confuse *first steps* with *half measures*. First steps seek to address the very nature of the problem. . . . Half-measures often propose solutions that don't address the nature of the original problem. Rather, they provide a generous gesture to solve *a* problem (often a legitimate one), but not *the* problem."[15]

In the follow chapters, we aim to address not only the problem of racism but also the nature of the bigger problem—the way we view the gospel. To do that, we need to explore the gospel with new lenses, as well as our shared history that, like it or not, has brought us all to this place. As two friends of different races, we each had a difficult journey before we found healthier spaces in which to think, talk, and lead on matters of racism. At times we felt insulted for different reasons, mainly because we each have deeply held emotional viewpoints based on our own histories, perceptions, and experiences. But we learned that by doing our individual parts to address systemic racism, we're humbly empowered to move forward together. When we began being honest about our viewpoints and bringing them into alignment with the gospel, healthier changes began to happen in our lives.

In the next two chapters, we'll talk about how each of us has approached racial issues and handled the pitfalls we've faced. Instead of starting off with one of our conversations, we'll dive into our stories, sharing our hearts, our values, and our invitation to you to examine your life and history without insult or insecurity.

When we see ourselves as we really are, we can name the problems and face them together. What follows will be incredible.

CHAPTER 2

A Twenty-Dollar Life

Reggie's Story and the Heart
of the Individual

When I (Reggie) meet people who feel they have nothing to live for, I tell them my story. I tell them my life began at a value of only twenty dollars.

Remember the scene about the fourteen-year-old girl that we asked you to imagine in the previous chapter? That young girl was my mother. At fourteen she had a baby boy she named Keith. She continued to live at home with her parents, and they helped with the baby so she could attend school. But when she became pregnant again soon after, her parents decided they'd had enough.

When she came home from school the next day, she was surprised to hear the screams of her little infant coming from inside the house. When she opened the door, she found an empty house—no furniture, no appliances, nothing. Only her little baby. She never saw her parents again. They would never know that she was pregnant not just with one baby but with two, their second and third grandchildren.

After living in a crisis pregnancy center until she gave birth to the twins, she had two choices: give up her babies to the Tennessee Department of Children's Services so she could continue living at the center or launch out on her own. The choice was difficult, but she decided to leave the center with nothing but three children under the age of three. The only place she could find to live was a chicken coop on an abandoned farm on the outskirts of Knoxville, Tennessee.

She got up each morning at two thirty, walked her babies to a filthy gas-station bathroom to clean them up, and then carried them to a day-care facility where they would be safe, fed, and educated. The day care was her lifeline. She worked two full shifts as a waitress at two different restaurants to earn enough just to pay the day-care bill. After work, she'd pick up the kids, walk them back home to the chicken coop, put them to bed, and then get up at two thirty the next morning to repeat the process.

She and her babies lived in such horrific conditions that it wasn't long until she became sick and missed a few days of work. This one small shift in the razor-thin margins of her routine left her twenty dollars short on her day-care bill, the only way she could provide for her babies.

When a male "friend" learned of her dilemma, he offered her twenty dollars if she would sleep with him. She went through with it. She had been manipulated and used by a predator, but she felt she had no other choice. Soon she realized that she was pregnant with her fourth child.

That fourth child was me.

Realizing that she was unable to care for another baby in such difficult conditions, she reached out to a woman who had been her second- and tenth-grade teacher. The teacher and her husband, the school janitor, took the young woman and her children into their home and cared for them throughout her third pregnancy.

When she was ready to deliver her baby, in brokenness she told her teacher there was no way she could care for four little children. She wouldn't be able to keep them all safe and fed. With tears in her eyes, she asked the teacher a question that broke her heart as a young mother. Would the teacher and her husband adopt her new baby and raise him as their own?

It was a huge thing to ask, but this teacher had a big heart filled with love. Mr. and Mrs. Dabbs agreed to foster me, and eventually they adopted me as their son. They were the best parents a kid could have asked for.

It wasn't until I was in second grade that I learned that my real mom had given me up for adoption—and I still have no idea who my biological father is. Even at that young age, the challenges piled on top of me. It didn't help that I was a bigger kid (Fat Albert jokes were the norm)[1] who suffered from dyslexia, bullying, body shaming, and suicidal thoughts. But God was patient with me and intervened in my life with grace.

I eventually graduated high school and went to college, earning my degree from North Central University in Minneapolis, Minnesota. At that point, I began sharing my story of brokenness and hope with kids in public schools—and with teachers, who hold a special place in my heart. I met and married an incredible woman, Michele, who has stood by me throughout our crazy life together for almost forty years. She is Puerto Rican, so we know a thing or two about racial diversity in our home—and about the way people sometimes respond to racial diversity in the church. Our son, Dominic, is a young man of quiet strength and incredible character who remains our pride and joy. He works as an aerospace engineer.

I will never forget the time Dominic came home from kindergarten and said that a white student had asked him if he was always going to be dirty, or if he would ever get clean like the white kids. It was an innocent question, and we know that kids mean nothing by such things. They have to be taught to equate race with negative stereotypes.

Dominic's experience at school was a chance to begin teaching him that while everyone is different, we are all formed in God's image. What exactly does God look like? We won't fully know until we see him, but until then, he has given us a clue. When we see other people of all shapes, sizes, and colors, there is a divine resemblance because everyone has a little bit of God in them, since everyone is made in God's likeness.

For more than thirty years, I have been traveling the world and speaking at schools and events three hundred or more days a year. Somehow, a kid who entered the world through a twenty-dollar deal now spends his life telling millions of people every year that they are worth infinitely more than their shady pasts or impossible situations.

Racism has contributed many chapters to my story, most of which I've never shared publicly until now. Racism was part of my life even before I was old enough to realize it. A few weeks before I was born, my adoptive mom got sick and was admitted to the hospital. A white lady named Alice Jane Schaffer happened to visit the hospital at the same time. Alice Jane was a one of a kind—a female preacher at a time when that was rare. She was full of what can best be described as holy spunk. She and her first husband pastored a church in Knoxville. After her husband passed away, she remarried and became Alice Jane Blythe, which is why most who knew and loved her called her Sister Blythe.

Sister Blythe had come to the hospital to visit the church piano player, who was a patient there. However, she accidentally turned into the wrong room, the room of a teacher named Mrs. Dabbs. Being the person she was, Sister Blythe asked if she could pray for Mrs. Dabbs. If you had heard Sister Blythe pray, you would understand why both women were in tears by the time she said amen. My mom then asked her a tragic but necessary question: "Can Black people come to your church?"

Although hers was an all-white church, Sister Blythe's answer was a resounding yes.

As it turned out, the first Sunday Mr. and Mrs. Dabbs visited her church was the first Sunday after I was born and home from the hospital. Sister Blythe was surprised to see my mother holding a newborn baby. When they had first met, Mom didn't yet know she would be bringing me into her family. She was just as surprised as Sister Blythe!

Sister Blythe was emphatic, "Well, let's dedicate this little boy today!" And that's exactly what they did.

Years later, Sister Blythe revealed to me that when the service ended, 150 people left the church and never came back. In her words, they weren't missed. Sister Blythe lived above racism at a time when few Christians in the South did. Even so, it was sad that for so many believers, merely dedicating a Black baby in their church was an offense they were unwilling to endure.

A Father's Influence

Dad was in his late sixties when I joined the family, so he was fairly old to be fathering another little boy. Sadly, his own parents never got a chance to become old themselves. When Dad was about eight or nine years old, a drunk driver, who happened to be white, ran his parents down and killed them as they were walking home from church one Sunday. The driver never went to jail or faced any consequences, and Dad remembers a policeman saying, "Well, that's just two less niggers to worry about."

There was no justice, yet Dad somehow never let bitterness set up inside of him. I once asked him how, after all he had been through, he didn't hate. How could he keep telling us to never let hate win, to not focus on racism in everything we see, even though it was there? His answer seemed so simple: "Jesus."

Dad didn't mean that simply because of Jesus, there was no justification for feeling the pain of racism in his past. The harms inflicted by racism are like all unjust harms; they deserve justice. Walking in forgiveness toward others does not mean ignoring or excusing these harms. It does not free the guilty party from the demand for justice. It does not deny one's hurt. Forgiving does not mean forgetting. To truly forgive, we must remember. How can we forgive something we don't recall happening? Forgiving also doesn't mean trusting someone who hurt us—we can forgive and still maintain healthy boundaries. Neither is forgiveness the same as making amends (owning your wrongdoing), much less experiencing reconciliation (full restoration of a relationship).

My dad walked in forgiveness not because he gave up all demands for justice but because he *gave them over*. He knew that Jesus suffered the harshest judgment for all the wrongs the human race has ever committed. This means that not only did Christ willingly pay for the wrongs I have committed but also he paid for every wrong committed against me. Everyone can either accept his costly payment for our wrongs by grace or deal with the consequences ourselves. Dad learned that he could forgive those who had hurt him even if they never asked for his forgiveness or sought to make amends.

As a Black man, I have forgiven those who have wronged me, and I want to help other Black people forgive, but not in the falsely prescribed way of acting as if nothing ever happened or that racially motivated wrongs don't still happen today. I've heard many Christians use words like *forgiveness* and *racial reconciliation*, but it often sounds less like repentance and more like an excuse to toss off a halfhearted "sorry" so they can just move on. What I and my Black brothers and sisters are looking for instead is authentic, ongoing biblical healing that comes through honest confession and a courageous ownership of harm so we can love each other better moving forward.

Dad remembered his past, but he wasn't bitter, and he wasn't quick to take offense even when he had a right to. One time when he and his old friends were hanging out at the barbershop, an old white man was with them and made a racist comment. The man laughed and said he knew my dad was the one stealing their moonshine, but they could never catch him because "You people are too fast." I was there at the time—a thirteen-year-old boy in 1976 who was paying close attention to what was being said about my beloved father. Whether Dad actually took the moonshine, I'll never know, but I know he didn't seem offended by the man's slur. I couldn't understand how he just laughed and moved right past it.

When I asked him about it later, it was apparent that he had not just moved on but moved forward. Instead of stuffing his bitterness and moving on with life, he had allowed God to move him forward, away from bitterness and into a hate-free life not contingent on others' dealing with their own bitterness. Dad was born in 1911, so he lived during some difficult times in our nation's racial history. He acknowledged that back in those days, Black people had to be extremely careful where they went, how they spoke, and when and where they were seen by white people.

Dad could tell I wasn't satisfied with his answer. "I have chosen to teach you not to hate," he said, "because if I had hated, you wouldn't be who you have become today. You have a chance to do something I never got to do. I could only survive, but you can change it all." Looking back, I can see that he was right, but it hurts to think about all the injustices he had to endure over the years. He wasn't swallowing his offense as self-protection but truly had chosen not to allow such offenses to dominate his attitude or actions.

Dad never denied racism, but he didn't want it to be a reason for his kids to give up on how far we could go in life. He knew we would be tempted to think that white people were chosen over us—that being Black was a disadvantage. The truth is, there are disadvantages in being Black, but he knew that if we went down the dark road of bitterness, it would be hard to ever come back.

Now that I'm old enough to address these issues without getting caught up in anger and hate, I can see how focusing on racism could have hardened me when I was younger. Dad was right, but the time has come for us as a society and as a church to recognize that *not hating* is merely the beginning. God wants us to fully believe in and deploy the principles of honesty, confession, and forgiveness to help foster authentic healing and leave behind the cloud of stubbornness and apathy that hangs over our heads.

All Chocolate Is Good

Dad once told me that all people are like chocolate—some are white chocolate and some are dark chocolate, but hey, *all* chocolate is good. I often quote him when I open a school rally because it always gets a laugh. It also puts people at ease by gently acknowledging America's elephant in the room: race.

This analogy isn't just about skin color. All chocolate is good means that not all cops are racists. Not all football players who kneel during the national anthem are unpatriotic. Not all people concerned about racism are radical liberals. Not all white people are bad. Not all Black people are good.

All people have something in them that's good, but only as a distant echo of our divinely crafted origins as God's image bearers. We rarely do good things out of good hearts because pure goodness isn't in there. Even if we have good intentions, there is usually someone we hate—regardless of their flavor of chocolate—even if it's not about skin color. The liberal. The "woke" ones. The conservative. The social media troll.

Not being enslaved to hate was a gift my dad gave me, but he was just regifting it from God. This doesn't mean I don't get angry when the N-word is occasionally dropped near me on a plane or the countless times I hear it in public schools. I don't like being pulled over by a police cruiser and searched for no reason when I'm on my way to speak to fifty thousand people at a Christian festival, but it happens. Yes, these things are pretty commonplace in my life—and no, they shouldn't be.

This is why I feel now is the time to take my dad's message of being free from hate and put it to work changing hearts and systems. The stakes are high, but it will be impossible to begin addressing the issues if we can't learn how to get beyond the insult we all feel about racism. Getting beyond the insult does not mean trying really hard to be nice. It does not mean becoming the Christian "tone police" who worry more about hurting feelings than speaking truth.

Feelings may get hurt, but if we are willing to experience those feelings in a spirit of humility, teachability, and devotion to the gospel, hearts and systems can change as we allow our feelings to become catalysts for healing rather than harm. Hearts beat in the chests of individuals, so even though paying attention to their stories and needs won't be enough to end racism, it is the right place to begin.

The Parentheses of Individuals

As a Black man who often speaks to predominantly white audiences, I have a front-row seat to what I sometimes call "parentheses moments." Such moments typically don't take center stage, but they reveal a lot, especially when it comes to racism. *(Take note. Pay attention. There is something else you need to know. Don't skip this.)*

Parentheses moments always remind me of a quote often attributed to Dr. Martin Luther King Jr.: "In the end, we will remember not the words of our enemies but the silence of our friends."[2] Dr. King also said, "There comes a time when silence is betrayal."[3] I believe the silence of the church will truly haunt us in the end. When the narrative of overcoming racism is written, I fear many Christians will be in the parentheses instead of the main storyline.

(For one reason or another, many Christians did nothing to fight racism.)

There is no question this statement is true of our past, but it doesn't have to be true of our future. To change it—to move the church out of the parentheses—we need to rediscover the beliefs and experiences that were normal for Jesus and his followers. What was normal for them should also be normal for us, because, "Those who say they live in God should live their lives as Jesus did" (1 John 2:6 NLT).

When we think of racism as something that resides primarily in the past, we can miss the ways Jesus addressed it head-on, which is what he expects us to do as well. One well-known example of this is when Jesus traveled to the region of Samaria, a place Jews rarely ventured. He was resting near Jacob's well when "a [Samaritan] woman . . . came to draw water. Jesus said to her, 'Give me a drink.' *(For his disciples had gone away into the city to buy food.)* The . . . woman said to him, 'How is it that you, a Jew, ask for a drink from me, a woman of Samaria?'" (John 4:7–9, emphasis added). Next, the gospel writer inserted an important parenthetical statement to explain why she raised the issue of race: "*(For Jews have no dealings with Samaritans)*" (v. 9, emphasis added).

Boom. There it is. Racism in parentheses as plain as day. Racism was the backdrop everyone was aware of, and because Jews and Samaritans never spoke to one another and were divided on every issue imaginable, racism remained entrenched.

Until Jesus.

The animosity between Samaritans and Jews can't be overstated. Note that the woman was astonished that Jesus, a Jewish man, would even speak to her, much less request something from her. His act of requesting water was not one of entitlement, as if he were ordering her around like a servant. Quite the opposite. Exhausted from his travels, Jesus placed himself in a vulnerable position when he chose to sit by the well, acknowledging his physical need. He didn't tower over the woman physically or intimidate her.

Most Jewish people at the time would rather have died of thirst than ask a Samaritan for anything. Their racism wasn't subtle or cloaked but something they considered a mark of righteousness. They believed in their superiority and privilege based on their faith and their ancestry. But Jesus refused to play by the prevailing racial rules. Instead, he humbled himself and engaged the woman in conversation, listening as she shared her viewpoint. This was unheard of in both Jewish and Samaritan cultures.

She was a conversational mess, hopping from one topic to another. Her theology and view of God were not only wrong but also offensive to Jewish people. Yet Jesus didn't get caught up in biblical or cultural debates with her; he didn't rattle off a list of bullet points to correct every heretical viewpoint. He didn't attempt to dominate or cancel her value in any way. Neither did he shy away from her because the two of them were too far apart on the topics of religion and race (their politics). Instead, he leaned in and listened to her. Moved by genuine care for her well-being and a compassion for her situation, he desired most of all for her to experience healing.

Imagine if no one had engaged her because she was a Samaritan and her life was a mess. Actually, we don't have to imagine. Thousands of Jewish teachers and "good" religious people had never ventured into her village. The statement in parentheses tells us why: Racism and hatred were the norm for Jewish believers. They had no dealings with Samaritans. They believed they were the good guys in the story, and according to their scriptural and historical viewpoints that elevated Hebrews above other ethnicities, she was one of the bad guys.

No one except Jesus conversed with the woman, and the disciples weren't there to witness the exchange. These followers of Jesus were so committed to him that they preached the gospel, performed miracles, walked on water, and eventually became the Spirit-empowered launchpad of the church. And yet they appeared in the other parentheses of the story (John 4:8).

(For his disciples had gone away into the city to buy food.)

It wasn't uncommon for a few disciples to go into town to buy food for the rest, but this was a rare moment when Jesus sent them all. Although he sometimes spent time in solitude, that isn't what he was doing in this case. Instead, he was spending time in a place where Jews—including his disciples—never spent time so he could engage someone they would never engage. He was up for it, but he knew that his disciples were not. When they returned and witnessed Jesus and the woman talking, they "marveled" that he was speaking with her, but they didn't have the courage to ask him why (v. 27).

This gospel account was written by an eyewitness, the apostle John. He admitted that the disciples were shocked at what they saw, an obvious acknowledgment, or confession, of his racial bias. When he recorded this account many years later, he wrote it as a changed man. That, my friends, should give us hope that wherever we are on the continuum of explosive issues in our world today, we can change—and yes, even religious people who already follow Jesus can change.

Are you the kind of disciple Jesus might have to send elsewhere so he can bring healing in situations where racism is a reality? Would you be able to engage in such a conversation against a backdrop of social and political tensions and a woman's painful history, or would you be in Jesus' way? Would you be secretly offended to find Jesus openly addressing racial tensions and biases with the gospel?

Some might be insulted by such questions or quick to point out that "Jesus didn't talk to her about race. He just spoke the gospel!" But that isn't true. Issues of race and the gospel are not mutually exclusive. Consider carefully what Jesus said to her: "You worship what you do not know; we worship what we know, *for salvation is from the Jews*" (John 4:22, emphasis added). This statement and those that followed directly addressed racial and cultural divisions by discussing historical and theological differences between Jews and Samaritans. Yet Jesus never used these differences to shame or cancel the woman. Instead, he carefully chose words that invited her into a divinely scandalous relationship in which all she had done wrong in so many scandalous earthly relationships would no longer define her worth. Race wasn't the only issue Jesus was addressing, but it certainly wasn't omitted.

The only person on earth who already knew everything the woman had done—everything she was thinking and every misguided thing she would say—still chose to humble himself, listen to her views, and share the life-transforming truth of the gospel. He knew the wisdom of the Scriptures, which clearly states, "To answer before listening . . . is folly and shame" (Prov. 18:13 NIV). Jesus was the embodiment of all wisdom—and he listened first. He avoided the folly and shame we too often exhibit today.

But Aren't We All Just One Race?

It's hard to listen when we think that race is a topic that doesn't need to be mentioned. For many Christians, this is the case. The confusion or pushback arises from the idea that, ultimately, there is no such thing as white or Black people—no such thing as race—because we are all one human race.

This is absolutely true from a theological standpoint. The great preacher and activist John Perkins said, "For this wicked system of slavery to survive there had to be distinctions made between normal folks and this new breed of people that would be treated like animals. This is where the idea of race came into play. The truth is that there is no black race—and there is no white race. So the idea of 'racial reconciliation' is a false idea. It's a lie. It implies that there is more than one race. . . . God created only one race—the human race."[4]

We agree with Perkins, but some use this truth as a convenient excuse to disengage from dealing with racism rather than to engage it, as Perkins obviously intended. Or worse, they use it to accuse those who speak up for racial equity and justice of being racist themselves—of engaging in reverse racism. They sometimes quote the following verses to make their point:

> There is neither Jew nor Greek, there is neither slave nor free, there is no male and female, for you are all one in Christ Jesus.
> —Galatians 3:28

> After this I looked, and behold, a great multitude that no one could number, from every nation, from all tribes and peoples and languages, standing before the throne and before the Lamb, clothed in white robes, with palm branches in their hands, and crying out with a loud voice, "Salvation belongs to our God who sits on the throne, and to the Lamb!"
> —Revelation 7:9–10

Some use these passages, which cast such an incredible vision of the kingdom of God, to suggest that talking about race at all is watering down the gospel because there is only one human race.

We affirm that God has made only one race. However, we also make a distinction between ethnicity and race. Ethnicity is biblical, but race defined by skin color is not. Author and advocate Latasha Morrison states, "Despite the Bible's recognition of differing ethnic groups, there is no indication of race. Race, as we know it, is a political and social construct created by man for the purpose of asserting power and maintaining a hierarchy."[5] We must be careful not to hijack the biblical vision of a single race—the human race—and twist it into a "race isn't biblical" argument, especially as an excuse to ignore racism in our own back yards, or worse, in our own lives.

We cannot act as if America or the American church at large is living according to God's ways when few of our churches embody the racial and spiritual oneness described in Galatians or Revelation. This is why we must revisit the standards and promises of the gospel and apply them to our present contexts, not just our future or eternal ones. We should not wait for heaven to pursue or experience oneness in the body of Christ. Instead, we must fulfill the greater law of Christ, which calls us to "bear one another's burdens" (Gal. 6:2), something we can't do if we insist the burden of racism under which another believer suffers doesn't need to be acknowledged, or worse, that it doesn't exist.

Race may be a social construct, but we must combat social constructs that violate the basic tenets of the gospel, just as we do with other social constructs, many of which lead to horrific social evils. We are called to engage one another with grace and truth in all areas of culture that are misaligned with God's intentions. We are part of the alignment process.

In the incredible glimpse of God's fullness that the Revelation passage reveals is an acknowledgment of the cultural and ethnic differences we'll experience in heaven: "a great multitude . . . from every *nation*, from all *tribes* and *peoples* and *languages*" (7:9, emphasis added). Will there be one race in heaven? Yes, but perhaps a better way to say it is that there will be one *family* in heaven. "One Lord, one faith, one baptism" (Eph. 4:5). And, I believe, many colors.

We are called to pursue and live out the gospel in our communities to counteract the rise of skepticism, division, and contempt. We do this not by seeking to overthrow our opponents' ideologies but with authentic proof that the gospel is everything we claim it is, and more. This is why we should acknowledge our differences and not dismiss them; dismissing them sends the message that the Scriptures dismiss them as well. Instead, let's lean into the tension these differences bring, being willing to unpack the history of the social construct we call race, which has brought us to this point in time. We don't have to have the same skin color to be in the same family or live for the same mission.

Maintaining our diversity while living in unity requires abandoning what Latasha Morrison describes as a "color-blind approach to community."[6] In reference to the apostle Paul's statement in Galatians 3, that "there is neither Jew nor Greek," and that we are "all one in Christ," she writes, "Too many Christians believe that the ultimate goal should be seeing the world without color, and some even pretend to already be in this 'holy' place. But Paul wasn't suggesting that aspects of our . . . racial identity aren't important, that we should all meld together into one indistinguishable throng. In fact, Paul emphasized that unity can be found in diversity."[7]

Diversity is our reality, regardless of how we deal with it. Yet the beauty and honesty of the gospel provide a way to process our diversity. This gospel not only defines our true identities, but it also protects these identities from being overrun by the cultural elements around us. The gospel frees us to acknowledge, live within, and positively affect these elements rather than allowing them to rule us.

The Only Way Out Is Through

I am not *just* a Black man. I am many things. I am a son, a father, a husband. This is why I've always focused on other things besides my race, especially in my public and professional life. I am a man with a bigger story—and I need others to hear this story, even if race is one of the through lines. When we stop listening to others' stories and start talking about our own perspectives instead, we are trying to lead instead of learn. If we spend all of our energies trying to be understood rather than trying to understand, we're just looking for a way *around* the messy middle of these conversations—a way, like most are seeking, to make racism not our fault.

There is no way around racism. The only way out is *through*.

Whether we have contributed to racism or contributed nothing to its healing, we must get past the insult of assigning blame to others and move into listening to one another, regardless of our political or theological leanings. In the act of listening, we may hear things we need to apologize or make amends for and why *that* seems like such a scary thing to Christians is mind-boggling to me. The resistance of Christians to some of the basic principles of Christianity is where we must begin.

Racism is not just the fault of the individual. It is a fact of our brokenness that is spread throughout our history, our thought processes, and our systems in ways we often fail to recognize. Yet it is also *not* a default state of being—something that has always been and will always be. Someone somewhere chose it, and when we don't listen to those who suffer from it or engage in a biblical response to it, we continue to choose it as well, if only passively. The passive reactions of the many, what Dr. King described as "the silence of our friends," creates room for the active racism of a few—and for a system that supports them both. As Christian hip-hop artist Lecrae says, "If we built the walls on purpose, we need to tear down the walls on purpose."[8]

My dad, a Black man, tore down walls of racial bitterness on purpose. Sister Blythe, a white woman, tore down walls of racial bias on purpose. Dad didn't allow the racism he suffered to make him bitter. Sister Blythe didn't allow the culture around her to compromise her faith. She stood up for my Black family as the gospel calls us all to do. The nation and the church both have a long way to go, but these two champions model for us a glimpse of God's kingdom: they were very different, and yet they were one in Christ.

CHAPTER 3

A White Christian Moderate

John's Story and the Nature of Systems

Like Reggie, I (John) am from Tennessee. I am one of the few people who was actually born and raised in Nashville. With nearly one hundred people moving here every day, I am a rare native.

I attended kindergarten and first grade at two poor, racially diverse schools near Bordeaux, an area of town known for its gang activity. In second grade, my parents moved us closer to the Madison community and second-mortgaged our home to put my older sister, brother, and me (the baby) into private school—a mostly white school.

My dad was a public school teacher in Metro Nashville Public Schools for more than thirty years. He taught math before being promoted to assistant principal at a high school with students from more than thirty different language groups, which reflected the racial and cultural diversity of the community. Though he was one of the most joyful and upbeat people you would ever meet, Dad was tasked with handling most of the school's discipline issues. It was not uncommon for him to take drugs, guns, and other paraphernalia from students or receive tips from terrified students about dangerous developments in the school or community.

Dad always kept the confidence of any kid who shared information that might help keep the school safe. He felt so strongly about keeping confidences that an irate judge once threatened him with jail time for refusing to divulge a source. Dad appeared in court the next day with a toothbrush, something the judge had recommended he do if he remained unwilling to name his source. Fortunately, that judge was under the weather the following day, and another judge, who was more reasonable, heard the case and let my dad return home. We were all elated, but Dad was probably a little disappointed that he didn't get to add some time in the slammer to his storytelling portfolio. He was that kind of guy.

Most of my life, Dad worked two other jobs as a volunteer pastor and the owner-operator of a commercial lawn-care company. Ours was a family business, so all of us worked, including my mom. We mowed lawns at seven apartment complexes, often starting before 7:00 a.m. and not sitting down until the sun set. From age eleven through young adulthood, I worked long hours after school, over the summer, and during college breaks with a weed eater in my hands (or a weed whacker if you're a Northerner).

Some of my best memories are of walking with my dad to the truck at sundown, both of us sore, sunburned, and covered in sweat, grass, and grease. He would put his arm around my shoulder and say, "Son, you did the work of three grown men today, and I would pick you over them any day. I'm so proud of you!"

Dad passed away in 2017 from congestive heart failure at the age of sixty-seven, but I still have a handwritten note that he left on my church-office desk one morning that says, "Your dad loves you and is proud of you!" He told me every time he saw me, and he told everyone around us too, which was especially embarrassing in front of strangers at restaurants. Even so, I would give anything to be embarrassed just one more time. I miss him so much, but he left me with the gifts of a father's love and affirmation, something many generations of men never receive from their dads.

When I was about ten years old, Dad applied for a position as head principal at the largest high school in Tennessee at the time. After interviewing, he was selected as one of the final candidates, but he lost the job to a Black man because of an affirmative action policy. I was so disappointed, but I will never forget what Dad told me: since he and the other candidate were equally qualified and the school had a racially diverse student population, Metro Nashville Public Schools had made the right call.

Dad lost an opportunity, but he believed there were racial disparities in the public school system that needed correcting. All told, he didn't cling to his rights or scrape for his own advantage but instead entrusted himself to the Lord and chose an attitude of humility. Preferring others was the part he played in his community to make strides in the bigger fight for racial equity. My brother reminded me that Dad used to comment on how life for many of his Black students was different from ours simply because of their skin color. Dad believed this wasn't right, and he wanted to be part of the solution.

From second grade through graduation, I attended a private school. I loved school and ran for every class election I could. Eventually I became student council president as well as editor in chief of the school newspaper. (Nerd alert.) I joined every club, took every honors class available, and had the time of my life. Then God overwhelmed me with a full-ride scholarship to the University of Tennessee. With our deep Knoxville connections, both Reggie and I share a love of the Tennessee Vols.

It took a few years to figure things out in college (some call that being "undeclared"), but I eventually majored in history and minored in political science. Along the way I became a lifelong lover of history. I eventually earned a master's degree in curriculum and instruction, after which I taught high school and middle school history and math for several years, while also working part-time as a youth pastor at a small church.

I taught in a rural county school near the foothills of the Great Smoky Mountains on the edge of Appalachia, where almost every student was white. The city of Maryville, Tennessee, just a few miles away, was home to the Maryville Rebels, a wealthy high school and perennial state championship football powerhouse. Confederate flags abounded all over the city, as did many conversations with students and adults about what this flag means to our nation's past and present. More on that later.

In 2004, I was offered a full-time ministry position at a new church being planted just east of Nashville in a little town called Mount Juliet. Nearly two decades later, our family is still here. Around this time, I also felt compelled to write—perhaps as Alexander Hamilton in his titular musical, *like I was "running out of time."*[1] (With less notoriety, by the way.) I began writing books and accumulating piles of rejection letters from publishers. I was even inducted into the Who's Who of Unsolicited and Rejected Manuscript Submissions. It's prestigious.

Around 2009, I was hosting school and church rallies with my friend Reggie Dabbs when, after the prompting of my senior pastor and our mutual friend Andrew Wharton, Reggie asked me to help him write his first book. I had never considered working collaboratively, but I agreed, and with no literary agent or clue what we were doing, we wrote a manuscript and secured a publishing deal with a prominent Christian publisher.[2]

After that, I was asked to collaborate on other projects and was eventually signed by one of the best literary agents in the industry. There was no chance any of this should have happened, but God kept opening doors. All told, I have now authored, coauthored, or collaborated on more than twenty-five books, which is insane. For most books I write, I'm the "with" guy you've never heard of whose name is printed on the cover in tiny letters just below the bigger name of the author you have heard of. I love to write—and I love to help authors steward their messages and stories to the printed page.

Throughout this time, I continued serving as a pastor in Mount Juliet, eventually becoming the executive and teaching pastor at our church. I've had many incredible ministry experiences and built memories for a lifetime, but for many years I failed to realize how little I knew about the foundation of the gospel, and how that affected my perspectives on racism.

My version of the gospel came with a grace deficiency, and not the feel-good kind of grace most people think of when they hear the word. I thought I understood grace, but I often felt condemned and guilty, which drove me to work hard to make up for my shortcomings. But this cycle did not lead to freedom. I was constantly repenting of bad attitudes and behaviors, but I didn't have a foundational understanding of what needed to change on the inside. Because I relied more on good intentions and good works than trusting in grace, I lived my life striving rather than resting—and I thought all that striving would make me a better Christian.

It did not. It made me look impressive on the outside, but I was insecure and broken on the inside. To be clear, I was a Christian. It's just that my undiagnosed grace deficiency kept me from experiencing the joy and freedom God intended for me as a believer. I sang about grace, preached sermons about grace, wrote books about grace, and had conversations with friends like Reggie about grace. But my daily reality was consumed with worry, an incessant drive to work harder as if I were outrunning something, and crippling guilt over imperfections I kept hidden from everyone around me so they would think I was a really good Christian. I loved God, but I desperately needed the approval of people. My interactions were filled with subtle manipulations intended to make me look better than I was.

Most Christians would consider my struggles normal and my failings "acceptable" sins. It's not as if I was a drug addict, an abuser, or a racist, right? No harm, no foul. Besides, most people liked the John I was, the John who met their needs and served them well. My Christianity revolved around my performance and good intentions; I just couldn't see it. My fragile pride couldn't endure anyone insinuating that I might be missing the mark in any way, especially when it came to an issue as black and white as racism. I tried so hard to be a good Christian that I was convinced I couldn't be wrong in an area as blatantly sinful as that.

Then grace *really* happened. Through a series of conversations, journeys through Scripture, and many failures and hardships, I began to see that even though it looked as if I had everything together in all the ways that matter to most Christians, I was powerless to overcome the fear, anger, control, and need for people's approval that dominated every action and interaction of my life. This wasn't just the floaty, feel-good kind of grace; it required me to be honest about the true nature of my need. I had to let go of my confidence in being a good Christian with a good heart and good intentions, and I had to embrace reality: I was broken, unable to heal myself or change apart from the grace of Christ.

When I finally accepted that I was utterly broken yet utterly restored by grace and not by my good intentions or works, I was able to stop being so insulted by the idea that I might be contributing to racism in some way. This subtle but powerful transformation began to affect my life in unexpected ways.

I've already mentioned that my first reaction to hearing "Black lives matter" back in 2014 was "Don't all lives matter?" It was a normal reaction for a white Christian who couldn't conceive that he might have real issues with undetected sin in his life. But my wife helped me see things differently. God was at work in my heart as well, which is the only reason I was able to endure the insult I felt about my contribution to racism. Christ was already changing me, rooting my confidence in something much stronger than my knowledge, my good intentions, and my good works.

Colorblind Passivity

Like so many people—maybe like you—I came late to the game on the issue of racism. Until a few years ago, I lived most of my life as the quintessential white Christian moderate. I genuinely hated racism and never intended harm toward anyone because of a person's skin color. Yet Martin Luther King Jr. described me to a tee when he said, "The Negro's great stumbling block in the stride toward freedom is not the White Citizen's Council-er or the Ku Klux Klanner, but the white moderate who is more devoted to 'order' than to justice;

who prefers a negative peace which is the absence of tension to a positive peace which is the presence of justice."[3]

I have been part of the leadership vacuum in the white church, which has largely failed to address racism head on. The American church has not done its part to carry out God's "ministry of reconciliation" (2 Cor. 5:18) as it relates to race. As Christians, we are called "to do justly, to love mercy, and to walk humbly with [our] God" (Mic. 6:8 NKJV). So when we fail to walk justly, mercifully, or humbly on the path to racial justice, that path becomes overgrown with weeds and thorns.

The church's complicity, apathy, and disengagement have left a gaping hole in the influence we are supposed to have in the wider culture. In a video posted on Instagram, pastor and author Matt Chandler passionately decries this leadership vacuum and the church's squandered credibility to speak to racism.

> We really like Martin Luther King Jr. right now because he's dead. I have to believe that a Martin Luther King Jr. right now would be [considered] a liberal, Marxist, socialist that everyone despises, but we'll quote him now because he is not here to offend us. . . . The church led out in a very real way on the Civil Rights Movement in the 60s, but now, by and large, the church has refused to participate, which means that we have turned over . . . what is our inheritance to dark ideologies.
>
> When you say, "Hey, we're not going to get involved! Let's just preach the gospel," [it's] so hypocritical. . . . You don't just preach the gospel to sex trafficking. You don't just preach the gospel on the issue of life and abortion. No, you act! It's like this brain-broke disjoint that's got us acting absurd. And then critiquing this movement as being evil and dark when we have

given up our inheritance. You cannot point out all the flaws in this current movement while you have abandoned the [part you] were meant to play. You cannot . . . ignore the sorrow and lament of twelve to thirteen million image bearers in our country. You can't do that. We mourn with those who mourn. . . . This is our inheritance.[4]

Chandler's frustration isn't unfounded. The church as a whole seems to ignore these issues until there is a crisis so big that it can't be easily dismissed. Many church pulpits have remained silent on current events involving racism, even as we witness obvious biblical injustices play out on video. As we will explore later, the collective response of the white church seems to focus more on hot-button terms or counterbalancing injustices with false equivalencies ("What about the liberals?" "What about the socialists?") rather than humbly addressing these injustices or helping bring relief to people affected by them. As Chandler infers, instead of listening when someone speaks out about an injustice, we point out other injustices instead, which, ironically, is an act of injustice in itself.

This injustice was mine. As a citizen, a pastor, and a disciple of Christ, I failed to listen or respond when my Black brothers and sisters spoke out about how racism still affects them. I never set out to *not* listen, but the result was the same. I did not mourn with those who mourned. Instead, I thought of racism primarily in terms of the immoral actions of individuals—men in white sheets burning crosses, dropping the N-word, and making inappropriate jokes.

As a history teacher and a pastor, I was aware of the atrocities of the past, but not how the past intersects the present. I considered that to be a different story. I was happy to conclude that racism was something our nation had mostly moved beyond—well, besides a few rednecks and crazies out there. I was offended when I heard the occasional off-color comment or joke, though I rarely said so. My default state was colorblind passivity, which made me blind to many other injustices.

I was also naive about the concept of bias in the system (systemic or institutional racism). The topic not only seemed complex and political to me, but leading conservative voices were also declaring it taboo. And the race statistics people were slinging around seemed easy to manipulate, so how was I supposed to know whom to believe anymore? I hadn't been listening to real people or reading books or articles on the subject. I was too busy. So I had settled for simple conclusions about a complex issue.

Once I saw my brokenness and my need for grace and community, I became willing to listen and learn, to move past my defenses, justifications, and fears of being called a racist. Listening and learning took different forms. In addition to historical research, I humbly asked some Black friends if they might be willing to share their stories, and all of them agreed. These friends represent diverse backgrounds and experiences. Some are Southerners by birth, while others come from different parts of the country. Some have been in jail; others are in ministry. Some are rich, and some live paycheck to paycheck.

Although their stories are diverse, every single person has had a different experience living in this country than I have had, and it has absolutely been a matter of skin color. Most of them, at some point, have been called a racial slur, have been followed into a store unnecessarily under suspicion of theft, have had people cross the street to avoid passing them, have been accused of not being able to afford something expensive, and have either taught or been taught how to decrease the odds of senseless violence during everyday interactions with police.

The commonalities in their encounters with police were the most striking to me. At some point, all of these Black men have been questioned or searched by police without cause. One friend, a young man from a small rural town, was pulled over one day because he had just bought a car and had not yet registered it or obtained the proper license plate. He also had cash in the car at the time, along with two cell phones, since one of them had a service issue. The young man was asked to get out of his car, was searched, and was placed in the back of a police car while his car was searched for drugs. It was only after his white grandfather arrived at the scene that the police relented and let the young man go. Nothing the grandfather told the police was different from what the young Black man himself had already explained. His minor traffic violation did not merit all that he endured. Understandably, he was embarrassed, especially in a small town where everyone knew everyone else, that he had been detained and searched on the side of the road in plain sight for no valid reason.

Two years later, that same young Black man was riding in a car with too many passengers for the legal age limit. They were pulled over, but when the officer realized they were all on the football team and that the big game with their rival was coming up, he joked with them and let them go. After graduation and the end of the young man's football career, his interactions with police returned to the way they were the first time he was pulled over. To this day, as a married man with two small children, he still feels anxious just driving down the street. He religiously stays below the speed limit to decrease his chances of having other negative interactions with police.

Another friend with a history of crime in his distant past was called the N-word by police many times. They would sometimes catch him committing crimes with a group but release all the white guys who were with him and take him alone to jail. When he was a teenager, he and his white girlfriend were parked, doing what teenagers do, when a police car pulled up. The officers accused him of raping the white girl and used racial slurs as they forcefully took him into custody. The girl pleaded with them, insisting that he was her boyfriend, but they roughed him up anyway.

Another friend, who now works as a firefighter, had a job at a grocery store as a teenager. He had been on shift for two hours when a police officer approached him in one of the aisles. The young man assumed the officer was off duty and needed help finding something, but he quickly realized something else was going down. The officer knew his name and the description of his vehicle, as well as the kind of jacket he'd left on the front seat of his car. The officer had asked the young man's coworkers and the store's customer service managers for some of this information, which deeply embarrassed the young man. Apparently, he fit the description of a Black guy who had robbed a bank in another town nearby. The young man had to go down to the precinct with his parents and spend a lot of time and energy convincing the police that he was not a bank robber but was just a Black kid working in a grocery store.

This same young man was driving down the interstate with his father, who was asleep in the passenger seat, when he saw a police car fly past him on the other side of the median, heading in the opposite direction. Ten minutes later, an officer pulled him over for speeding. The young man knew the car would shake uncontrollably if it went even one mile per hour over seventy, so he was immediately suspicious of the officer's motive. He asked the officer if he was the same one who had sped past him in the opposite direction. He was. The young man then asked how the officer could have determined he was speeding from the other side of the road going the opposite way. The officer bluntly told him that he had paced the car, which was impossible. But before the young man could argue his case further, his dad, who was wide awake by this time, began saying over and over in a hushed tone, "Shut up and take the ticket!" So that's what he did. This young man's experience reinforced a lesson Black men learned in his father's generation: avoid speaking up for yourself with police, even when you've done nothing wrong.

These are just three examples of negative interactions with police. Each of these Black men has had good interactions with police as well, and they don't believe that all cops are bad or out to get Black men. This is why a systemic understanding of race is essential. These interactions also happened in different geographical areas from New Mexico to Tennessee, so this is not just a Southern issue.

Events like these could theoretically happen to white people as well, but they haven't happened to me or my white friends. I have been pulled over many times, especially when I was a younger man, for various infractions and misdemeanors—excessive speeding, driving without a license, and other shenanigans. But I have never once been stopped for no reason and searched.

The more I listened to my Black friends, the more aware I became of the need to take action. But I honestly didn't know what kind of action to take. Up to that point, I had thought not being a racist was enough. But I finally began to hear what many of my Black brothers and sisters had been saying for years: good intentions and neutral positions only reinforce a status quo that may benefit me as a white person, but not my Black friends.

The hard question I had to face was this: Did I really care about my Black friends in a way that was consistent with the humility and empathy that reflect the gospel?

Ultimately I realized that I need to become boldly, consistently vocal about what I believe and what I intend. That means being willing to proclaim that the gospel calls me to decry racism, with no what-abouts, buts, or other disclaimers attached. When I can't just say it and let it ride with no political or snarky cabooses in tow, I insult the people whose lives are affected by racism. I may think I care about them, but my words and my lack of action prove otherwise.

Sixteenth-century reformer Martin Luther addressed similar attitudes during the plague in 1527 when he said that a Christian should "act like a man who wants to help put out the burning city. What else is the epidemic but a fire which instead of consuming wood and straw devours life and body?"[5] Similarly, what else is racism but a fire that consumes the soul of our nation and the witness of the church? The nation burns and Black people are asking white Christians to come quickly and help, but our response is to deny that we've ever owned matches and therefore cannot be held responsible for the fire. We are more offended by the insinuation we might be racist than we are by the fact that racism exists.

I am the former white moderate who has decided to stop quibbling over whether I contributed to the fire so I can instead take my position holding the fire hose with my Black friends, Black theologians and historians, Black pastors, and other white people like me who have lived so far from the fire that we can barely smell the smoke. I have chosen to come closer.

Although I am no social media specialist, I have engaged the issue of racism on social media. More important, I have talked about this issue in Sunday messages and in videos that members of our church staff have produced to facilitate discussions with our congregation. I have also discussed racism extensively on my podcast. These seem like tiny drops in a huge ocean, but I had to start somewhere.

As I have become more vocal, white church members, Facebook

friends, pastors I barely know, and even family members have challenged me. Many of them have been deeply insulted that I am talking about racism, because, for some reason, they think I am calling them racists. I have actually gone out of my way to say that I am not calling anyone a racist, but repeatedly people have said to me, "I'm just so tired of everyone calling me a racist."

Church members have said things like "I'm not sure I can handle my pastor being a part of the Black Lives Matter movement," despite the fact that I have repeatedly emphasized that the statement "Black lives matter" is a biblical value I support without aligning myself with every ideological view of the Black Lives Matter organization. Nevertheless, it continues to create offense. Reggie also has taken heat for speaking out on his vast social media network, losing about twenty thousand followers after he posted quotes from Martin Luther King Jr. and Nelson Mandela, and for gently stating in biblical contexts that Black lives actually do matter.

Perhaps I was naive, but I hadn't anticipated that simply speaking out against racism would cause so many people to lump me in with those they consider radicals and socialists, not to mention liberals, the most damning slur that can be hurled by modern conservatives. Why are some of my white friends so easily triggered? Why do they feel they can't even talk about racism outside of certain engrained terms and perspectives, much less do anything about it?

Reggie and I believe that the trigger lies embedded in our way of thinking, especially in the church. The negative responses of white people should not be our greatest concern; the negative responses of Christians of any color are much more alarming. If the way we think about race isn't just about being white or Black but is more about being a Christian, perhaps we should evaluate how Christians in the early church in first-century Jerusalem responded to the social tensions they experienced. Have Christians always been so reactive to racial issues? Has arguing over hot-button terms been the go-to move since the beginning of the church?

Greek Widows Matter

The book of Acts chronicles the lives of early Christians, people of "the Way," as they were first called (Acts 9:2; 19:9; 24:14).[6] They lived in a culture that was hostile to their beliefs, but their way—*the Way*—wasn't characterized by hostility toward the people around them. Quite the opposite.

The persecution they suffered generally came from rival religious or governmental leaders who felt threatened by their explosive growth, their overwhelming influence on the culture, their selflessness toward one another as well as the poor and their enemies, and their willingness to suffer and die for a savior only some of them had met in person.

One great enemy of Christianity, the Roman emperor Julian (332–363 CE), lamented that Christianity had caused many to turn away from Roman gods. He said that "atheism [i.e., Christian faith] has been specially advanced through the loving service rendered to strangers, and through their care for the burial of the dead. It is a scandal that there is not a single Jew who is a beggar, and that the godless Galileans [Christian disciples] care not only for their own poor but for ours as well; while those who belong to us look in vain for the help that we should render them."[7]

Backtrack to the first century in Jerusalem, and you'll find that everything happening among people of the Way was undeniably attractive to those who were watching. Acts offers a beautiful description of the lives they lived together: "They devoted themselves to the apostles' teaching and the fellowship, to the breaking of bread and the prayers. And awe came upon every soul, and many wonders and signs were being done through the apostles. And all who believed were together and had all things in common. And they were selling their possessions and belongings and distributing the proceeds to all, as any had need. And day by day, attending the temple together and breaking bread in their homes, they received their food with glad and generous hearts, praising God and *having favor with all the people*. And the Lord added to their number day by day those who were being saved" (Acts 2:42–47, emphasis added).

"Having favor with all the people"—what a telling phrase. The believers described in Acts 2 weren't telling everyone what they wanted to hear; rather, they were showing everyone what life in the kingdom of God looks like. Yes, they gathered in the temple for worship, but they also broke bread in their homes daily. Sharing meals and doing life together was a sacred part of their process—a sacrament we can get behind!

Some of us today might get a little woozy over the part about "selling their possessions and belongings and distributing the proceeds to all, as any had need" because it smacks of socialism. But rest assured, the early Christians were not socialists. Sharing possessions was not a church-mandated program to ensure everyone had the same amount of wealth. Church leaders merely taught the people what Jesus had taught them—and the attitude with which they shared what they had "with glad and generous hearts" clearly reflected the spirit of his teachings.

There it is! Or perhaps better stated, there it was. Something happened in the early Christians that not only was genuine but also was joyful and generous. They cared for one another not because anyone coerced them but because they were filled with the Holy Spirit and were being changed from the inside out. Their numbers weren't growing because they started a church-growth campaign. They were simply choosing to follow God's ways. Yes, they were losing some possessions, but they were gaining so much more, and in it all, they were filled with gladness.

It's a beautiful picture, isn't it? It would be easy to assume that the people living in this almost-utopian community were Christian superheroes, immune to racism. Yet a mere four chapters later, we encounter a troubling, racially charged situation: "Now about this time, when the number of disciples was increasing, a complaint was made by the Hellenists (Greek-speaking Jews) against the [native] Hebrews, because their widows were being overlooked in the daily serving of food" (Acts 6:1 AMP).

This passage plainly states that ethnic discrimination was happening in God's church. How was this possible?

Even though they were being transformed by Christ and his ways of living, a sordid history of racial division was at work in their community. Ethnically, they were all Jewish, just from different sides of the Hebraic tracks. At this point, Luke had not yet written about what would become one of the central paradigms of the New Testament: God's command to Jews-made-Christians to share life with people they would normally have refused to speak with: Gentiles or, literally, the "ethnos." Today we are prone to overlook such overarching themes of the biblical story as we pick and choose isolated verses we can apply to living as good Christians.

There are obvious limitations to a direct comparison of the racial bias of the Hebrew Christians against the Greek-speaking Jewish Christians. For one thing, unlike ancestors of Blacks who were slaves to ancestors of whites, the Greek-speaking widows had not descended from ancestors who had once been slaves to the Hebrews. But Luke documented a very real ethnic division to reveal an important aspect of church history. This glimpse into the early church also invites us to pay attention to how believers responded when ethnic division occurred.

The church and its leaders didn't deny there was a problem because they never intended for one to arise. They didn't become defensive and insist that they genuinely never meant to harm anyone.

They didn't say, "None of us are racially biased. Bring us the volunteers who passed out the food. This is *their* sin, not a problem with the church!" They certainly didn't spiritualize the matter by saying, "Jesus told us that the gates of hell would not prevail against the church, so this is just a conspiracy of lies made up by those liberal Greeks who are watering down the gospel and causing trouble!"

Instead, they simply listened to the complaint, acknowledged the problem, and took practical steps to eradicate discrimination from their midst, regardless of who did it or how it got there. They owned the problem and the solutions together.

Their response is proof that we need not be personally or organizationally insulted that a human system might have flaws and need adjustments—as if human systems are synonymous with God's eternal kingdom. The early Christians' faith wasn't in a system (even a religious one) but in the grace of God that was transforming their broken lives.

An issue that in our day might spark protracted infighting, self-justification, finger-pointing, political reframing, and nationalistic-religious grandstanding was swiftly addressed in the early church because of a simple understanding that being in the wrong is the starting point of the human condition. Acknowledging a wrong and addressing it were considered normal and expected behaviors for Christians. Scripture offers no record of mass shaming of those brothers and sisters who brought the Greek widows' plight to the forefront, as if they were somehow setting aside the gospel to pursue matters of social justice.

When someone essentially said, "Greek widows matter," the response was not "Hebrew widows matter too!" That was already obvious, since the Hebrew widows were also receiving food in the distribution program. Neither did people say, "All widows matter!" The gospel and the nature of God revealed in Christ already confirmed this.

At the heart of the church's foundational beliefs was the understanding that in light of the human condition, believers needed to change not just at conversion but as a way of life. Repentance and change weren't reserved for overt acts of moral failure. The people of the Way knew they were moral failures. As a community, they saw a collective need that went deeper than the actions of a few individuals, though it didn't eclipse individual responsibility. Even so, they didn't hide behind individual responsibility to avoid addressing the need for community-level systemic change.

These early church leaders didn't fear being called racists. Instead, they humbly and joyfully embraced their identity as redeemed sinners who were experiencing real life change as they trusted God's Word, listened to God's Spirit, and lived honestly and authentically with God's people. These were God's ways, and they knew that apart from abiding in these ways, they could do nothing on their own that would be fulfilling, fruitful, or lasting.

Can you imagine the impression their mutual humility made on the people in their community who were trying to figure out what this new religion was all about? They learned that people of the Way were willing to humbly listen and wisely take the right action to resolve conflict.

Many people today are trying to figure out what Christians are all about. Sadly, if they view us only through a modern political or social media lens, it's no wonder they are often confused or even appalled. Just imagine how things might change if we were willing to adhere to the foundational tenets of our faith, beginning with a humble willingness to listen and change.

At the center of the Christian gospel is not defending Christian or Christian-adjacent systems but transforming human lives. Theologian John Piper writes, "Christians communicate a falsehood to unbelievers (who are also baffled!) when we act as if policies and laws that protect life and freedom are more precious than being a certain kind of person. The church is paying dearly, and will continue to pay, for our communicating this falsehood year after year."[8]

What exactly is this "certain kind of person" each of us is supposed to become? The humble, teachable, reasonable kind. The kind of people who can endure the insult of needing to change our attitudes and systems because we listen to the complaints of others without taking offense. The kind of people who don't just take positions but first and foremost assume biblical postures of mercy, justice, and humility—the posture of the one we claim to follow.

Again, we are not calling you a racist, but we are calling you a sinner who constantly needs the grace of a Savior. That is the essence—the good news—of our reality as Christians.

CHAPTER 4

WHEN WAS THE LAST TIME YOU CHANGED YOUR MIND?

"In the months after George Floyd was murdered, I got so many calls from white pastor friends," Reggie confided. "They're all good guys leading big churches where I've spoken many times."

"What did they say?" John asked.

"Most of them told me they had said nothing about racism in their churches since everything began blowing up," Reggie recalled in a matter-of-fact way.

"Nothing?"

"Yeah. That's why they were calling me. They knew they needed to say or do something, but they were afraid of saying or doing the wrong thing. They had all seen how some prominent white leaders have taken a beating on social media when they said the wrong thing, and they didn't want to be next."

At first John was offended that these church leaders hadn't said anything about what happened to George Floyd, but Reggie's reasons made sense. "I get it," John said. "It's overwhelming to suddenly feel like you need to say something very important that you know everyone is going to critique and attack. These days, some Christians and conservatives act like anyone who cares or speaks up about social justice must be social Marxists or some other scary-sounding term they've heard on social media. It's crazy because many of us are just Christians and ministers trying to rightly respond to what's happening."

"Yeah, but many Christian leaders don't know what's right here," Reggie pointed out. "There is just so much arguing and confusion over this stuff. Many of my white pastor friends were afraid that if they started talking about racial justice, they would lose all of the money out of their churches. They're good guys, but they didn't know what to say." He took a breath. "And I don't think they really knew if Jesus expected them to deal with this."

This was the heart of the issue, and they both knew it.

"I guess I get that too," John replied. "The insinuation that they should do something about racism upsets a lot of people because they consider themselves good, and good people could never be a part of racism."

"I think what people mean when they say they're good is a part of the problem," replied Reggie.

"You're right. It's like everyone avoids the issues by talking about having good hearts or saying we need heart change. Many Christians and conservatives seem to be using these heart concepts as something to hide behind so they don't have to pay attention to what's happening in the world."

"It also keeps them from having to do anything about it," Reggie said. "They're right that change has to start with the heart or eventually cause a change in the heart. Or else we're never going to get through it."

"That's a good point, as long as we don't stay there."

"Yeah," Reggie agreed, "we don't need to be Christians who say that hearts need to change, but only someone else's—or that after our hearts change, we don't need to change parts of the system too."

$$\bullet\ \bullet\ \bullet$$

As a Christian, I (John) used to seek comfort in the fact that when I sinned, my heart was still in the right place. It didn't feel right, but I wanted to believe that my actions weren't coming from a bad heart but rather from a momentary lapse in judgment. After all, Jesus was in my heart, so it had to be good, right?

This is a common Christian phenomenon: attempting to justify yourself, evaluating yourself by your intentions even as you judge others for their actions and attitudes. It doesn't work, which is why you feel so condemned when you try to justify yourself. When I felt especially guilty, Christian friends would often comfort me by saying something like, "It's okay. God knows your heart." It wasn't until later in life, and I mean after a decade and a half of full-time ministry, that I realized the truth: God's knowing my heart was indeed good news, but not for the reasons I thought.

Many say that racism isn't a skin problem but a sin problem. We certainly do have a sin problem, but some use this religious rhetoric as a smoke screen to avoid dealing with widespread systemic problems that go beyond the racist beliefs and actions of a few individuals. Confining racism to the extreme actions or beliefs of people we don't know conveniently places it in a theoretical category outside the realm of any responsibility we might have to engage it. From this perspective, racism occurs only when other "bad" people act out in racist ways.

Since we believe that our hearts are good and that racist people's hearts are bad, it becomes evident where change needs to happen: always in the hearts of others.

For me to see where heart change was needed most, a change had to take place in me—not just in my heart but in my ways of thinking.

A Change of Heart

White Christians who believe they are not acting in racist ways certainly believe in heart change; they just tend to assume their hearts are already in the right place *because* they're Christians. The truth is, being a Christian doesn't make anyone's heart right; rather, our hearts are justified by grace through faith in Christ's righteousness, and then we must keep them responsive to the ongoing change that only Christ can bring. The apostle Paul addresses this expectation when he writes, "Let God transform you into a new person by changing the way you think" (Rom. 12:2 NLT). Being a Christian doesn't remove the need for heart change; it creates the pathway by which it can occur.

If we assume our hearts are already in the right place, it's understandable why we might feel insulted at the idea of repenting for something we feel we haven't done. We think, *How can I repent of harming Black people or apologize to the Black church when I haven't done anything wrong? Shouldn't I feel remorse and apologize only for the things I have done?*

No, not exactly.

When it comes to racism, the modern church misses the lessons of the ancient church. Accepting without insult the daily need for authenticity, confession, and repentance is supposed to be normal for believers. God's plan of salvation was not just to forgive our individual sins but to continually redeem our fallen condition, which causes us to sin in the first place. We aren't just sinful because we do sinful things. Our sinful thoughts and actions don't come out of nowhere; they reflect a condition of sin within.

We connect the word *repent* with turning away from individual wrongs a person has committed, but this is not a full picture of repentance. The Greek word biblical writers use for the verb "repent" is *metanoeo*. Its most literal translation is "to change one's mind" or "to think differently." Repentance means turning from one direction to go in another. When it comes to repentance and racism, we will never be willing to turn around if we don't believe we should. And we can't change directions without first changing our minds.

The notion that our hearts are in the right place is sometimes described as the gospel of good intentions. It essentially says, "If I have good intentions—if I don't intend harm—harm cannot exist, and I cannot be held responsible for it." Sadly, I have lived by such a gospel. When it comes to justifying myself for avoiding the issue of racism in my own life, I am the chief of sinners.

The idea that I might have anything to repent of in connection with racism insulted me at first. But being offended was one of the best things that could have happened, because it began to dismantle the intricate scaffolding of self-righteousness within me that I never knew was there. And when that scaffolding fell, I fell hard with it. But I landed on the foundation of the gospel, something I thought I already understood but was missing in my life: grace.

I learned that I can't walk in daily grace when I don't think I need it every day. Grace is cheapened when I think my need for it isn't as great as the need of others who commit "big" sins, such as murder, adultery, or burning a cross in someone's yard. I realized I needed to wholeheartedly acknowledge the depths of my need for grace. The same realization prompted the repentant criminal who was crucified with Jesus to rebuke his mocking counterpart: "Do you not fear God, since you are under the same sentence of condemnation? And we indeed justly, for we are receiving the due reward of our deeds; but this man has done nothing wrong" (Luke 23:40–41). In other words, can't I see that what is happening around me (including racism) is tied to my state of brokenness in this world, a state I share with every other human? Can't I see that I need grace for every aspect of life, even those where I fancy myself well intentioned?

When we live by the gospel of good intentions rather than the gospel of grace, it is all too easy to justify whatever we do because we trust our good intentions. We feel we can trust that our hearts are good even when we mess up. We may not trust our good behavior to earn our way into heaven, but it isn't hard to justify everything else about our lives.

C. S. Lewis said, "Aim at Heaven and you will get earth 'thrown in': aim at earth and you will get neither."[1] If we accept grace for heaven but our own good intentions for earth, we will not experience the stuff of heaven in our earthly lives. This plays out every day in the experiences of countless Christians who essentially believe that through their own efforts they manage to be good people with good hearts, even when their lives bear little resemblance to those of believers in the early church.

I love this headline from a satirical Christian news site: "Calvinist Dog Corrects Owner: 'No One Is a Good Boy.'"[2] Jokes aside, the good news really does begin with wholeheartedly believing we are not good. We do have immeasurable value to God, just not what it takes to right the wrongs within ourselves. This is why Scripture repeatedly tells us that our hearts are not good (Jer. 17:9), and that we should "not lean on [our] own understanding" (Prov. 3:5). Yet we somehow think these scriptures apply only to our preconversion lives or to people outside the faith.

The challenge in accurately understanding repentance is that we see it primarily in terms of regretting our negative behaviors, which somehow happen in spite of our best intentions. We take corrective action only when we can clearly see our bad behavior. While it's true that intentions matter and actions follow repentance as evidence of faith (James 2:17), repentance starts with a change of mind. Thus, when white Christians repent of racism toward Black people and communities, we are merely changing our minds and acknowledging that we haven't always seen the fuller picture when it comes to the issue of race, and we are capable of faults and harms beyond our best intentions, actions, or goodness.

Why should it offend a Christian of any color to repent of harm that others, especially other Christians, have experienced because of our attitudes, actions, and inactions, even if we didn't intend harm? This should be just another Tuesday for any Christ follower who acknowledges that we have no good deed or good intention to stand on other than the kindness of God revealed through the grace of Christ, which consequently "is meant to lead [us] to repentance" (Rom. 2:4).

A Confession

I readily confess that I am a recovering Pharisee. You might think that means I was an uptight know-it-all who constantly critiqued and judged everyone else, but that wasn't my brand of Pharisee.

Even on my worst Pharisee days, most people considered me humble and kind—mainly because I tried very hard to be. Mine was less a problem of judging others and more a failure to judge myself through the lens of gospel truth. I thought of myself as an honest, well-intentioned guy, but I instinctively avoided the pain of being honest with God, myself, and others about my real brokenness. I viewed brokenness on a continuum of good to bad behavior, and compared to most people, I came out smelling like a rose. I wasn't *that* bad. I accepted a theology of grace for heaven, but on earth, I lived and died in the comparisons.

I was blind to the fact that I thought of myself as better than others. I tried to live a life pleasing to God and others, but I was riddled with guilt and insecurity. Despite an illusion of humility, I was a Pharisee, because deep inside I believed that grace wasn't enough to make me right with God. I unwittingly thought my own resources and efforts were also required.

Other people—the drug addict, the adulterer, and even the racist—needed grace way more than I did. After all, I worked so hard to please God, I figured that I knew better—and did better—than any of those people. But thinking that I knew better proved how little I knew about grace.

I believed I was saved by the grace of Christ, but I added my goodness to my daily walk with him. Any believer can unknowingly think as I did. My reactions to every issue we discuss in this book—from political upheaval to obsessive conspiracy thinking and endless battles with the liberal bogeyman—revealed what I really believed. So do yours. The lenses through which we see the world and our reactions to issues like racism reveal not just the values we assent to intellectually but the values we actually live by.

I have learned to recognize several warning lights that tell me

I might be drifting back into pharisaical patterns. The light that flashes brightest is when I find myself making detailed lists of all the reasons I am not in the wrong. I have tried this tactic in marriage many times when I've unintentionally hurt my wife. Yes, it's true that she is sometimes at fault as well (don't tell her I said that), but I know that when I head down the legalistic road of making a case for my innocence, it usually indicates I have stepped out of grace into self-justification. When I am in this state, I'm not listening to or loving my wife well. I approached racism the same way: Instead of walking in grace, I justified myself. I wasn't listening to Black individuals or communities, nor was I loving them well.

I am still a recovering Pharisee, but I have found that humbling myself and owning the hurt I have contributed to or caused, instead of fighting to the death over minutiae, aligns me with God's ways and connects me to his peace. This is the way of Christ—humbling ourselves and preferring others instead of clinging to our rights. He calls us to take the position of a servant and play a part in healing the wounds of others—especially when they point out how we have contributed to those wounds.

There's no point in yelling, "I didn't mean to!" "I don't see what you're seeing, so it must not exist!" or "What about what you did?" Doing so won't lead to peace in the relationship or healing for those we love. In contrast, the gospel of grace leads us toward peace, love, and healing as we daily acknowledge, prefer, and proclaim our allegiance to Christ over any earthly allegiance, however well intentioned it may be.

As I said earlier, we tend to judge others by their actions and attitudes, but we judge ourselves by our intentions. No wonder so many of us are offended—our judgment is based on intentions, not on the gospel. The gospel calls us to a better place, where Christ has taken the judgment for our sins and offers us his perpetual grace. In this place, humility overcomes defensiveness and self-justification, and understanding conquers the incessant demand to be understood before seeking to understand. Here we are open to the daily renewal of our minds—repentance.

When was the last time you changed your mind—about anything? I was a man with an unchanging mind toward certain topics. Then grace changed my mind by revealing the tragedy of my true condition, which led to discovering the joy of letting go of the illusion of my goodness and trusting fully in the true source of my salvation. As I lost confidence in my good intentions, I gained confidence in the concept that I might not see everything as clearly as I think I do—and the world won't implode if I admit I might be wrong. The truth is that having a changed mind opened up the world to me in ways that allowed me to better engage it with the gospel.

I saw that being open to changing the way we think should be normal for Christians. We need to listen to people—even our opponents—and respect their perspectives, even if we never share them. If I can't be open to hearing someone else's point of view because I'm already entrenched in my own, how can I fulfill the Great Commandment of Jesus—the commandment that overshadows and fulfills all the others—to love others as he loves me (John 13:34)?

Bee Stings and Apologies

Love is meant to be the radical calling card of those who follow Jesus. That is what compels us to "let your gentle spirit [your graciousness, unselfishness, mercy, tolerance, and patience] be known to all people" (Phil. 4:5 AMP). Note those last two words: *all people*. When it comes to having a gentle spirit, there's no escape clause that allows us to turn it off and on depending on whom we're dealing with. We don't have the option to be gracious, unselfish, merciful, tolerant, and patient with some but not others. Consider the opposites of these traits—disrespectful, self-centered, vengeful, intolerant, impatient. Such traits undermine the cause of Christ. Love calls us higher.

If I love you, I will listen to you. I will hear your hurt and not be quick to dismiss it or quibble over our different versions of the story. Instead of debating the validity of your wounds, I will be "quick to listen, slow to speak and slow to become angry" (James 1:19 NIV). If you say something I consider insulting, I will first attempt to absorb the offense, at least temporarily, so I can hear you. We may not agree in the end, but I will be reasonable and listen because I value you.

I will gladly lose so we can both experience the healing of Christ, just as Christ lost so that I could experience God's grace through his death and resurrection. When I am willing to die to myself in these ways, I experience the miracle of Christ's resurrection day after day in myself and in my relationships.

This is the "new and living way" (Heb. 10:20) to which we are called—a life of mutual humility and confession. The ancient apologist Tertullian said, "[People] for the most part either shun, or put off from day to day, this work [of confession] as an open exposure of themselves, being more mindful of their shame than of their health; like those who having contracted some malady [disease] in the more delicate parts of the body, avoid making their physicians privy to it, and so perish in their bashfulness."[3]

As believers, we shouldn't resist repentance; we should embrace it because we understand our state of being, not just our state of behavior. We affirm that our state of being needs to be continually renewed. The apostle Paul comments on this when he writes, "Be transformed by the renewal of your mind," or as we quoted earlier from the New Living Translation, "Let God transform you into a new person by *changing the way you think*" (Rom. 12:2, emphasis added). These are active present-tense words written to active Christians.

When the topic is racism, it should be normal for us to be open to listening and changing our minds because we no longer defensively think that someone is calling us racist. We understand that the conversation is not about us. Instead, we are fully aware that we are much worse than racists; we are sinners whose state of being precipitated the sacrificial death of the faultless Son of God. Since we own our fault and have already been freely forgiven for the most appalling of atrocities, why would we turn a blind eye or a deaf ear to another person's request to be heard? Why would we continue defending our own goodness, especially if the request is coming from fellow believers? We repent not just because we feel bad, though sometimes we do. We repent because we have no confidence in our ability to rescue or even mildly improve our state of being.

If we are willing to change the way we think and exercise humility and empathy toward others, what exactly are we apologizing for? For slavery? For the existence of racism? For the actions of hate groups?

While most Black people don't want strangers to walk up and apologize for slavery or racism, they do want white people to listen, absorb any offense, and avoid close-minded thinking about how our blemished past as a nation still affects our present. All people desire respect and empathy. We can be sorrowful about the pain inflicted, as well as mindful and repentant of any ways we may have unintentionally contributed to the pain. We can avoid the extremes that are ravaging families, churches, and politics—ways of seeing every situation and every person through purely black-and-white lenses. These ways do not reflect the explicit call of the gospel to humility and repentance as a lifestyle.

Reggie and I have a mutual friend who is a professional comedian and goes by the name Jonnie W. (You should look him up.) When COVID hit and Jonnie instantly lost much of his annual income, we told him we were sorry that this happened. Our "sorry" wasn't offered because we were to blame. We didn't create the coronavirus, and we didn't contribute to or intend any harm toward our friend. On the flip side, Jonnie didn't blame us for what had happened to him.[4]

In our experience, Black community leaders and Christians rarely place the blame for racism at the feet of contemporary white people. They just want empathy and progress. Instead, those of us in the white Christian community who proclaim ourselves forgiven spend our energies trying to prove that we aren't personally responsible for racism because we haven't done anything wrong. It just doesn't add up.

The apostle Peter captured the true spirit of what's required of us when he wrote, "Finally, *all of you*, have unity of mind, sympathy, brotherly love, a tender heart, and a humble mind" (1 Peter 3:8, emphasis added). Sadly, some Christians today disregard this admonition, mainly because political leaders and media pundits—not the gospel—have redefined our standards.

Here's one more scenario about what it means to apologize in situations where we are not necessarily completely or directly to blame. Let's say that bees stung a few guests who attended one of the outdoor church services we held during the COVID quarantine. As ministers, we would most definitely apologize for their pain, but our guests would not misconstrue the apology as an indication that we released bees on our visitors. That would be weird.

We also wouldn't say, "Look, what do you want us to do about it? We don't condone bee stinging here, so why do you want an apology from us? Even if it was someone's fault, we weren't directly in charge of checking the perimeter for bees, so blame the person who was responsible!" No, any of us who have ownership in the organization, along with a basic sense of gospel empathy toward our guests, would first care about the hurt that has been inflicted, regardless of its source, and then work to get rid of the bees in our "system." Any self-justification or blame shifting would be both immature and antithetical to the gospel.

Here's the point. The lack of concern among white Christians and their unwillingness to listen to or show empathy for Black people, along with the constant justifications and "what-abouts," are alarming indicators that we really don't care. *That* is the primary insult to many Black people who feel the sting of racism—and rightly so.

If we wouldn't treat visitors to our churches like this, why do we think it's okay to treat anyone that way? The call of Christ is to love everyone, including our enemies. We are to "do good to those who hate you, bless those who curse you, pray for those who abuse you" (Luke 6:27–28). If this is how we are to treat our enemies, how much more should we respond with love and compassion toward those who have suffered from racism and want our help to stop it? When we fail in this, white evangelicals are rightly blamed for our callous, self-justifying, nonempathetic reactions to the expressed pain of Black people.

In a 1967 speech against the ongoing war in Vietnam, Dr. Martin Luther King Jr. decried the failure of the revolutionary spirit of American democracy to uphold its own ideals, accommodating injustice instead. It's a dynamic that still feels relevant today, specifically in connection with the failures of the church in responding to racism. As Dr. King stated, "It is a sad fact that because of comfort, complacency, a morbid fear of communism, and our proneness to adjust to injustice, the Western nations that initiated so much of the revolutionary spirit of the modern world have now become the arch antirevolutionaries. This has driven many to feel that only Marxism has a revolutionary spirit. Therefore, communism is a judgment against our failure to make democracy real and follow through on the revolutions that we initiated. Our only hope today lies in our ability to recapture the revolutionary spirit and go out into a sometimes hostile world declaring eternal hostility to poverty, racism, and militarism."[5]

Just as Dr. King felt that the rise of communism was a judgment against America's failure to fully live out the revolutionary principles of democracy, the rise of cynicism, conspiracy thinking, and divisiveness, which have led to an unwillingness to listen and an insistence on arguing, constitutes a judgment against the church's failure to live out the revolutionary gospel principles of humility, compassion, and repentance.

Nonempathetic, intellectually immovable, haughty reactions that insult people in pain are inflaming racial tensions as much as the protestors we dehumanize and denounce. Again, though we do not support BLM as an organization, according to one study, 93 percent of BLM protests have been peaceful.[6] Yet most of our energies are expended condemning those who set city blocks aflame instead of engaging in gospel work to end racism, regardless of the actions of others—especially those who do not share our beliefs. When we use the actions of others as excuses for our inaction or negative reactions, we condemn and set fire to their value as humans, doing so under the flag of the one who created them.

We are not living up to the revolutionary promises of the gospel that the apostle Paul described as "the power of God for salvation [rescuing, restoring, healing] to everyone who believes, to the Jew first and also to the Greek" (Rom. 1:16). Ours is a gospel that bridges and transcends racial divides, but we have to let it rescue, restore, heal, and ultimately transform *us* before we can share it with anyone else.

The church's failure to live out the revolutionary truths of the gospel has damaged our role in perpetuating the cause of Christ. Christian hip-hop artist KB laments the fallout: "I've watched a surge of people I love walk away from Jesus in the last few years. . . . Just about *zero* have been lured away by Marxism, liberalism, or atheism. Almost all have 'shipwrecked' over the politicizing of Christianity and their church's apathy (hostility) [regarding] injustice."[7]

Apathy or hostility toward injustice—at least the kind of injustice that doesn't affect us directly—will continue to cause many spiritual shipwrecks unless and until we return to a foundational understanding of the gospel that transforms the way we think, live, and seek to love others. The gospel leaves no room for considering wokeness, liberalism, or any other ideology a valid reason not to exercise empathy, biblical justice, or a willingness to listen.

We must reevaluate what we're supposed to be fighting for so we can free ourselves from viewing our positions only in terms of what we're fighting against.

Considering Our Wrestling

Ask yourself the question *What do I fight for?* Many answers may emerge, but they are difficult to define apart from what you're fighting against, and it's all too easy to let the latter eclipse the former.

If we truly believe that "we do not wrestle against flesh and blood" (Eph. 6:12), perhaps we should evaluate how much of our energy is being expended mentally and verbally wrestling against people, people groups, or ideas that are different from our own. If we believe that God is in control of everything, including the church and our nation, why are we so recklessly out of control with our words, actions, and emotions?

If God's ways lead to peace, why are we perpetually on the offensive with a defensive attitude, as if God requires us to defend his kingdom against political and ideological opponents? How is it we remain blind to the ways all this fighting against flesh-and-blood people leaves us imprisoned behind heavy bars of anxiety, anger, depression, endless debates, contempt for those who disagree with us, and a general sense of outrage? When did it become permissible to disengage from God's ways as a pretext for defending his ways?

We must accept humble, grace-filled Christ following as a daily lifestyle and not just a turnstile we pass through on Sundays. If we settle for anything less than this, the gospel of peace is in danger of being perceived as little more than an errant political manifesto. Our lives are supposed to be the undeniable, attractive evidence of the good that Christ desires for all people, not evidence that God is a close-minded, loveless tyrant—like his followers.

Some are fighting harder against Black Lives Matter (or the liberals, the alt-right, the evangelicals, the Fox News anchors, the CNN anchors, the Catholics, the Democrats, the Republicans, etc.) than against racism itself. We're that distracted, and yet we lack the self-awareness to notice it.

You can pick your poison, but you can't pick how it poisons you.

Everything outside of a daily, humble acceptance of God's radical grace that leads to real repentance in our lives will poison us with anger, bitterness, self-righteousness, and a self-assurance that is unknowingly steeped in foolishness. This is why Scripture states, "Do you see a person wise in their own eyes? There is more hope for a fool than for them" (Prov. 26:12 NIV). When we are wise in our own eyes, almost by definition, we can't see it. We can't see that *the way* we're thinking is a bigger problem than *what* we're thinking.

Many people have asked Reggie and me, "What can be done right now to respond to these issues of racism?" Some, including Christians, have laughed at our answer: "Be willing to listen and change the way you think." The fact that being open to listening and changing one's mind has become laughable reveals a lot about the way we view our lives as Christians. Author and teacher Beth Moore says, "Nobody's never wrong. But those who cannot admit they are wrong will set out to prove others wronger."[8] She's right. We're so wrapped up in what we think is right and the good works that follow, that we somehow think believing rightly is a foregone conclusion. No matter how many good things we do, we must always allow our gospel belief in the person and work of Christ in us to continue shaping us.

People asked Jesus a question like the one people asked Reggie and me: "'What must we do, to be doing the works of God?' Jesus answered them, 'This is the work of God, that you believe in him whom he has sent" (John 6:28–29). Belief—the way we think—is not something to be laughed away; it is at the very heart of faith in Christ.

Yes, there is right and there is wrong. Yes, some causes are worth fighting for, and some are worth fighting against. But many of us are busier making definitive statements against something than we are listening to the ways of Christ in Scripture, the history and legacy of racism in the American experience, and the personal experiences of those who don't look like us. We are creating a self-centered and self-reinforcing narrative that suits our desired outcomes instead of listening. We stand for very little beyond the idea of standing against our opponents. Author Justin Giboney calls this an "opposition-based public witness."[9] We are defined by what we wrestle against.

But what if we stop to consider the ways we are wrestling? What if we ceased throwing punches at others as a way of being in this modern world? What if we considered the possibility of our wrongness not as an insult but as a reality of being human and an invitation to engage in the process of gospel change? If we did these things, Paul tells us what God wants to do in return: he wants to transform us into new people as we allow him to keep changing the ways we think. Just imagine what God could do in us if we all (present company included) offered our minds to him as open spaces he is invited to renovate and remodel.

This would not only change the story of racism that we're all contributing to in one way or another, it would also change the world, which was God's plan from the beginning.

CHAPTER 5

GETTING PAST THE IDEA OF
GETTING OVER THE PAST

Y ou know, John, I think many people believe that racism went
away with the civil rights laws in the sixties."

"Yeah, that reminds me of a quote by activist Bryan Stevenson:
'It's like the Civil Rights Movement [in America] was this three-day
carnival: On day one, Rosa Parks didn't give up her seat on a bus.
On day two, Dr. King led a march on Washington. And on day
three, we just changed all these laws.'"[1]

Reggie laughed out loud. "That's perfect! In the early 1990s,
I spoke at a high school in Texas and got a shocking reminder of
how active racism still is. It was a Monday morning, and I got there
early. The principal told me to go to the auditorium and get started
setting up. When I opened the door, the room was pitch-black.
This was before we had flashlights on our cell phones, so I began
looking for a light switch."

"I don't like where this is going."

"When the lights came on, the whole auditorium was still set up from a Ku Klux Klan rally the night before."

"No way! In the nineties?" John asked.

"Yep!" Reggie replied. "The principal came in behind me and said, 'Oh, sorry. I guess we forgot to tear all that down.' He didn't forget. He knew exactly what he was doing."

"What did you do?"

"I did what I had come there to do: I shared hope with those kids. It wasn't the only time that kind of thing happened. I remember another principal in North Carolina telling me that he had only brought me in because his superintendent had forced him to. He said that I wouldn't be able to relate to his students because not one of them was Black."

"I would be so mad!" John said in a raised voice.

"Yeah, but what good would that do? I just smiled and kept going. By the end of my talk, they had given me three standing ovations, which I don't care about, but it made quite the impression on the principal. Afterward, he wanted me to come back, but more importantly, he had at least begun to think differently about Black people and their interactions with white people."

John calmed down a bit. "I guess it has to start somewhere."

"I pray God lets it start with us. We must find a way to realize that racism is not just something in our past."

John thought about Reggie's words. "I think Christians are being told by some politically conservative leaders that we should be scared of everything we're hearing right now—that since racism is in the past, all the unrest today is nothing but a breakdown of law and order, and that the collapse of our society will follow if we allow our minds to entertain any talk of racial justice."

Reggie replied, "The bottom line is that there is no law that brings complete order, but there is a gospel that brings complete peace."

● ● ●

I (Reggie) attended Fulton High School in Knoxville, Tennessee, a school with a racially diverse population. I'm not a small guy, so I was recruited to play on the offensive line of our football team. I was also recruited to play saxophone in the marching band. I was both the on-field and off-field entertainment.

One night, our football team was riding the bus to play Cumberland County High School in Crossville, a town about forty-five minutes west of Knoxville. When we came to the edge of the town limits, our coach stopped the bus and pulled some of us off so that we could see a certain sign hanging on a tree just as we entered the city.

It read, "Nigger, don't let the sun set on you here."

Our bus was filled with a mix of both white with Black kids, and this was far from a veiled threat. Mind you, the year was 1981. Ronald Reagan (whom I loved) was the president, and Michael Jackson (whom I loved to listen to) was about to release *Thriller*. We weren't in Birmingham or Montgomery for a civil rights march in the 1960s. We were kids going to play football just down the road, but in a place that might as well have been a different planet.

And it was getting dark outside.

I share that story to illustrate the fact that racism is still alive and well. As we turn our attention to addressing the historical and current issues of racism within our systems and institutions, it's important to remember that the term *systemic racism* is not theoretical jargon.

As a Black man, I grew up in a fairly progressive city (Knoxville was mostly pro-Union during the Civil War), but even so, racism left an indelible mark on my life. By God's grace and my dad's wisdom, these memories never crystallized into hate within me, nor did they leave me feeling like a perpetual victim with a chip on my shoulder who always expects someone to apologize or take care of me. Such stereotypes are just distractions to keep people from really listening to the experiences of Black people in a nation we love—a nation renowned for freedom and justice, but that still had signs like the one publicly posted on the outskirts of a Southern town in the 1980s.

Technically, both federal and Tennessee state law prohibit attacking Black people (at any time of day) simply because they are present within city limits. But on that night, it would have been hard to convince the Black kids on our bus that the citizens of Crossville were interested in law and order when it came to our well-being. For those of us on the bus, that sign was a matter of life and death—it wasn't remotely theoretical. We all remembered people in our family histories who had been mistreated, forced to drink from different water fountains, beaten by policemen, raped by white men, sprayed with fire hoses, tear-gassed, or even lynched.

Our ancestors were slaves who were brought here against their will and were forced to work in horrible conditions with no hope of freedom. They were legally deemed property and declared in the US Constitution to be only three-fifths human. They weren't allowed to have legal marriages, name their own kids, or often even keep their own kids. Imagine someone ripping your baby from your arms and selling her to another plantation owner to make a few extra bucks.

The history of slavery and discrimination in America has largely been presented as if such horrors happened only long ago, but 1981 wasn't that long ago. Am I telling you this so you will feel bad about being white or feel angry because you are Black? Am I just trying to drudge up bad memories for the sake of getting everyone riled up? Am I supporting a political position or movement?

No, I'm just telling part of my story of being Black in America. Placing value on listening to people like me is where heart and mind change intersects the need for systemic change. Listening is only the beginning and certainly not all that needs to happen, but all that needs to happen certainly will not (and cannot) without first listening.

Sundown Towns

Couldn't my story from high school be just one experience of one guy in one backward town more than forty years ago? In the case of Crossville, Tennessee, in 1981, the sign that was posted at the city limits was no isolated act of a few misguided, immoral individuals. It was a visible expression and legacy of a very real, vast, and persistent component of racism known as "sundown towns."

Sundown towns were all-white communities that openly prohibited the presence of Black people, especially after dark. Route 66, the famed cross-country roadway that ostensibly welcomed all Americans to explore the nation's landmarks, was also a thoroughfare in many sundown towns. Signs like these and other racist tactics were commonplace, intended to intimidate Black people and discourage them from entering white spaces. A handbook known as *The Negro Motorist Green Book*, or simply the *Green Book*, was published to help Black travelers know where they could eat and sleep, as well as to warn them of sundown towns and other places to avoid.

Even after the Civil Rights Act of 1964 legally ended segregation in public places, some communities nevertheless found ways to maintain sundown-town-era practices. Author and scholar Candacy Taylor pointed out that to this day, "In Noel, Missouri, Somali immigrants say they are not welcome at Kathy's Kountry Kitchen, where even now servers wear T-shirts reading, 'I got caught eating at the KKK.' Stories like these are why the rosy hue of Route 66 nostalgia leaves a bitter chill in the souls of Black people."[2]

Research suggests there were thousands of sundown towns across the United States, but they were always more concentrated in the North than the South. As these towns proliferated, in addition to being warned against passing through them at night, Blacks were also prohibited from living in a sundown town and often suffered violence if they tried. Sociologist James Loewen noted that even long after it was legal for Black people to ride the same buses, go to work at the same businesses, and attend the same schools as whites, "Many sundown towns had not a single black household as late as the 2000 census, and some still openly exclude to this day."[3]

Our nation is governed by a network of local, state, and federal laws. Although federal laws apply at every level, there are sometimes huge discrepancies between the law of the land and how that law is enforced in countless local contexts. Plus, there always seem to be loopholes. In many cases, a violation of federal law in a small municipality isn't enough to make a blip on the national radar. Even when some sundown-town signs were taken down, the sentiments of white supremacy often remained. Locals knew enough to keep quiet about it to avoid attracting attention from the public at large—especially from those who supported racial equality. Such towns also made creative use of city ordinances, policing policies, and local judicial appointments to subvert federal law and maintain practices that amounted to racial terrorism toward Black people.

This meant that citizens could enact violence on Black people and expect to suffer no social or legal consequences.

This was considered law and order.

Just imagine how many God-fearing, church-attending Christians there were in Crossville, Tennessee, in 1981. Yet there was evidently so little concern about the overt sin of racism that none of them took action to remove a publicly posted threat to a bus with many Black kids onboard. Can you imagine the trouble these Christians might have faced had they taken the sign down? People might have had strong words for them, or worse—the same strong words and worse they had for the Black people who came through town. It was probably easier to just not rock the boat.

As the father of a Black son in his midtwenties, I am keenly aware of places and practices my son needs to avoid to reduce the odds of danger. Are my concerns overblown? Am I an alarmist? If you ask my friends and family, they will say that I rarely make a big deal about such things. Most Black people don't make a big deal.

Some people are content when we don't speak up about such things and even become offended when we do. However, they weren't on the bus when I entered Crossville in 1981. They also weren't on the plane a few months ago when a white passenger complained aloud multiple times that I had stolen his first-class seat because "Delta is going Black." I didn't say a thing, but the flight attendant certainly did.

"Sir," she said to the man, "I see here that you are a million-mile flyer with us, and we are grateful. But Mr. Dabbs—the gentleman you keep claiming has taken your seat—well, he is a 3.5 million-mile flyer. That is definitely his seat, so I'm going to have to ask you to stop harassing Mr. Dabbs."

He didn't say another word until the plane landed and we were both standing up to leave.

"So, what do you do for a living?" he asked.

"You know, sir," I replied, "you have forfeited the right to have a normal conversation with me. Maybe we can try again next time. Have a nice day."

At the end of the book, I will tell another plane story that ended differently than this one, but the guy in this story wasn't really interested in my life. He wanted to know how a Black man could have been successful enough to have more travel miles than a white man.

Was he just a crazy redneck? Perhaps, but the odds are that he was raised and continues to function in some sort of system or subculture that considers such thinking right and normal.

The Role of Anecdotal Evidence

What place should stories such as these have in our collective conversation about racism? After all, you may have stories of your own that differ from mine, so whose story should be believed and whose should be canceled? How do we weigh the value of anecdotal evidence when it comes to navigating conversations about the persistence of racism?

Anecdotal evidence is simply evidence based on anecdotes or stories. It is information that comes from the personal experiences of individuals rather than scholarly or research-based sources. Although there are differences between anecdotal and research-based information, we believe both are important. Favoring one to the detriment of the other is often what causes confusion and offense when discussing racist incidents, such as the personal stories I just shared. We must find a balance.

Some people won't accept historical evidence or modern statistics about racist policies because they "know a guy," Black or white, whose personal experiences differ from the data. Just peruse social media—everyone has a story. In our culture, personal experience is king. If we have one negative experience at a restaurant, we take to Yelp to let the world know that the restaurant is horrible. But someone else who visited the restaurant the same day takes to Yelp to let the world know how amazing it is. Five hundred other people do the same, and soon the restaurant has an aggregated score. The score is based on collective anecdotal evidence that creates a public narrative about the restaurant.

But there is also such a thing as a professional critical review. In the restaurant example, a food critic might dine in the establishment on multiple occasions over a period of time and order a wide variety of items from the menu. He or she considers factors the average patron does not, such as culinary trends, sanitation, atmosphere, or how knowledgeable the waitstaff are about ingredients used in various dishes. When the critic writes the review, he or she follows a rubric to determine whether the restaurant merits one star, five stars, or something between. Instead of relying on public opinion alone, readers can factor in the expertise of the food critic who specializes in assessing restaurants.

Both of these approaches have merit, but they work best when considered together.

In conversations about race, most people bring both types of evidence to the table, but they generally rely more heavily on their own experiences. Both John and I have heard from people of various races who have experienced bullying, teasing, or violence from people of other races. Such experiences can foster race-based impressions and biases that feel justified. After all, there is compelling anecdotal evidence that the way *people* act is the way *they* are, and thus, the way things are. Such experiences, especially when they happen in childhood, can leave lasting marks on a person's psyche and become an ongoing, even if unconscious, racial bias.

That's why we need to be willing to explore our biases by asking questions such as these: "Based on my past experiences, what conclusions have I drawn about Black people or white people as a whole? How do these biases affect the way I view current conversations on race? Do the things I think and say (or don't think or say) about racism sound like the things Jesus taught?"

If we can begin by being honest about what has informed our viewpoints and then use the gospel as a mirror to reveal where our viewpoints fail to reflect the teachings of Christ, we will be able to process not only our own experiences but the experiences of others as well. We can receive the truth of their experiences as equally valid to our own so that our emotions and experiences are no longer the defining perspective. At the same time, we will stop allowing one person or one group to be the only valid critics.

There are many examples of the ways people use the experiences or opinions of others whose viewpoints already align with their own as proof that their viewpoints are valid. So what does it look like to misuse or overapply anecdotal evidence? One example is the way some white Christians cite the stories and opinions of a successful Black person, like Dr. Ben Carson, as if his anecdotal experiences and conclusions are sufficient to discount the existence of modern systemic racism.

Dr. Carson is an accomplished Black surgeon and politician who grew up in severe poverty, worked extremely hard, and was able to overcome the incredible odds against him. His is an inspiring and noteworthy story. No one should dispute that he worked hard and overcame challenges. No one should dispute that other Black people have the potential to work hard and overcome challenges. No one should dispute that there are legal protections in place designed to prevent discrimination that might block minorities from being able to work hard as they try to overcome challenges. What we dispute is that Carson's experience is normative within Black communities and therefore constitutes an accurate indicator of whether systemic racism exists.

We need look no further than the leadership of the Republican and Democratic Parties to see that white leaders at Carson's level of success and influence far outnumber those of Black leaders. If Carson's story disproves systemic racism, why aren't many more leaders like Ben Carson rising through the ranks of our political parties? Seriously, what's the reason? If all things are equal, why aren't there more Ben Carsons out there?

Carson's experience is valid, but should his anecdotal evidence be used to nullify the research of historians, theologians, and other experts who have studied racism for decades? Doing so is an over-simplification of a complex issue, and yet it not only happens but also fuels unnecessary vitriol and dismissiveness.

We all come to the same table from different places—with pre-existing ways of seeing the world based on what we've seen in the world. This is why our anecdotal evidence seems foolproof to us, but anecdotal and research-based points from others are easy to dispute or dismiss. When we develop our viewpoints based solely on our anecdotal conclusions or the anecdotal conclusions of a few sources, we utilize a very small amount of the data and we bypass the path that could lead to well-balanced and accurate—albeit complex—conclusions.

One person's experience—even mine and yours—can't define the whole matter.

Beware

No individual Black person speaks for all Black people. No individual white person speaks for all white people. There isn't one Black community or one white community. There isn't one conservative community or one liberal community. The experiences of Black and white people, of conservatives and liberals, are as diverse as the people themselves, no matter what you hear in the news or on social media.

The same is true of Christians. While there are many members of the body of Christ, no single human being, organization, or church speaks for all of us. The only one who has that authority is Jesus. Beware of anyone who claims to speak for all Christians or who states what all Christians should believe on various matters, especially if they try to nullify your faith when you question or disagree with them. As believers, we should all adhere to Christian orthodoxy and ground ourselves in biblical teaching, but we should never bully or pressure others to accept one person's conclusions, especially when those conclusions overlook, oversimplify, or overamplify sound theology, historical complexities, and empathy.

Our polarized culture and public discourse both pressure us to be all-or-nothing thinkers. We are constantly being told, "If you don't fully agree with X, then you're not a 'real' Y!" This tactic is deployed on both sides of the political aisle and on all sides of the religious spectrum. In the months leading up to the 2020 presidential election, prominent conservative pastor John MacArthur stated that "any real, true believer" would vote for Donald Trump.[4] That's a call that MacArthur doesn't get to make. While we are called to live in authentic relationships, counseling and even correcting one another based on biblical truths and values, Christians do not have the option of declaring whose faith is or is not authentic based solely on the way people vote.

Doing so is not only unbiblical, since God is the only true judge of human hearts when it comes to salvation (James 4:12), but it also violates the principle of separation of church and state. There are reasons we need to maintain a safe distance between politics and faith, one of which is that religion in the service of politics is all too easily corrupted. This is why Jesus engaged the political structure of his day in terms of correcting the Pharisees and Sadducees for corrupting God's principles of justice toward people, and yet he did not speak out against the Romans and their many political foibles, which were contrary to God's ways. He engaged only when politics crossed into religion in a way that sullied God's ways among those who were supposed to be living them out by serving people, especially the poor and underprivileged. As Christian conservatives, this is one of the reasons that our efforts in this book are aimed more at calling Christian conservatives to align with our stated ideals of faith rather than just rail against radical liberal ideals that we don't necessarily share in the first place.

Our faith should inform everything we do, including the way we vote, but when those who desire our votes demand our allegiance to anyone or anything other than Christ, we are coasting fast into shallow waters with the imminent threat of running aground.

Author and pastor Timothy Keller puts it this way: "When it comes to taking political positions, voting, determining alliances and political involvement, the Christian has liberty of conscience. Christians cannot say to other Christians 'no Christian can vote for . . .' or 'every Christian must vote for. . . '"[5] We mustn't let the perspective of one person or one party dictate our broader perspective or be elevated as synonymous with the gospel perspective.

We need more than one kind of source. We need many.

The biblical principle is, "In an abundance of counselors there is safety" (Prov. 11:14). The point here is not about surrounding ourselves with many people who say the same things. Rather, this proverb speaks to seeking diverse viewpoints because an abundance of perspectives produces greater, not lesser, security. We need anecdotal evidence as well as research-based evidence. We need answers that do not sum things up succinctly to the detriment of understanding the complexity of the questions. We need to disengage from tactics that negate the acts of listening and engaging.

Navigating the What-Abouts

One diversionary tactic often employed against those who initiate conversations about racism is an endless string of what-abouts.

- What about abortion? How can you march for racism but not for the lives of the unborn?
- What about Black-on-Black crime in the inner cities? If you really believe Black lives matter, why have you never been up in arms about those lives?
- What about the sin of Black people being racist against white people?
- What about human trafficking? Poverty? Adoption? Ethnic cleansing in Africa and Asia?

The list goes on and on.

The fundamental assumption of those who use the what-about tactic is that since there are other matters just as important as racism, those who choose to address this issue but not the others are caught in hypocrisy.

We do affirm the importance of many other causes in addition to ending racism. We care deeply about feeding the poor, protecting those who are persecuted because of their ethnicity or religion, spreading the gospel, rescuing victims of human or sex trafficking, and countless other vital causes. We believe that all of God's people should engage in his work to bring healing and hope to those who suffer. However, it is a faulty, distracting logic to suggest that not engaging in all causes negates the need to engage in any one of them.

Take the example of Black racism toward whites. Racism flows between all races in some form or fashion. Is it wrong? Absolutely. But using its existence as an excuse *not* to address racism against Black people in the white community or in the church is akin to saying, "Sure, I stole the TV, but so did that other guy! Don't arrest me unless you're going to arrest him too!" Both thieves should be arrested, and each is responsible for his own crime. We also need to remember Jesus' words of caution that seem to apply here: demanding the removal of racist splinters in someone else's eye while overlooking the historical log of slavery and white supremacy in our own (Matt. 7:1–5).

All racism needs to end, but does refusing to listen to or acknowledge the historical and ongoing experiences of Black people in America contribute in any way to its decline? No, it does not. Which is why mutual humility is key. No matter who we are, our only effective move is to let right actions begin with us right now.

Sadly, the what-about diversion is interwoven in white evangelical culture in ways the average church attender may not realize. The finger is inevitably pointed away from white communities and toward problems in Black communities (such as drugs, Black-on-Black crime, and racism) as reasons not to acknowledge systemic racism. This is yet another expression of "I stole the TV, but so did that other guy!" It is a tactic we would never allow our children to get away with—using someone else's wrong as an excuse to dodge their own wrongs.

This tactic deflects to the issues we (whoever "we" may be) want to discuss, thus keeping *us* instead of *them* in charge of the narrative of racism, even though our collective history affects us, them, and everyone in between. This logic is yet another nod to white privilege, which includes the perceived ability to determine how the narrative is told. And yet the gospel calls us to so much more.

The point of this particular what-about tactic is to shame those who care about racism. People who employ this tactic are approaching these issues with a mindset of scarcity and fear rather than confidence and humility. This diversionary strategy has so many holes in it that it's hard to know how it holds water for anyone, but above all, it is illogical. Imagine condemning our country's founders for fighting England to gain independence because they failed to fight every other monarchial despot in the world to free those citizens as well.

Those who are quickest to use the what-about strategy often have a credibility issue. They don't hesitate to challenge others for failing to address various causes, even when they aren't doing anything to affect those causes either. In their zeal to point out the hypocrisy of others, they heap it on themselves, but often, they don't even notice or acknowledge their duplicity. Tunnel vision keeps them quickly moving to the next online takedown, the next virtue signaling of someone else's virtue signaling.

Virtue signaling is a modern pejorative term that refers to publicly expressing opinions or sentiments intended to display the moral correctness of one's position on an issue. Many people who speak out about racial justice are called out by others for virtue signaling. But again, the ones who are calling them out are also virtue signaling by publicly expressing their opinions about an injustice—in this case, someone's seemingly insincere virtue signaling. It is one of current society's most deeply veiled yet distracting what-abouts.

As it turns out, even Jesus dealt with what-abouts, and how he handled it is a good lesson for us. After his resurrection, Jesus made it clear that Peter, too, would suffer persecution and eventually martyrdom. It was heavy news, but it was meant to prepare him for what was to come. Even so, Peter did exactly what many of us do today: he pulled a what-about.

"When Peter saw him [John], he said to Jesus, 'Lord, *what about* this man?'" (John 21:21, emphasis added).

"How would John die?" was a fair question in an emotional moment. It's natural to inquire about someone else when the conversation feels heavy or uncomfortable. But Jesus redirected Peter to a healthier place.

"Jesus said to him, 'If it is my will that he remain until I come, what is that to you? You follow me!'" (v. 22).

Since we trust the grace of the gospel, we know that Christ's words to Peter were corrective but not condemning. They offered a blunt yet refreshing clarity: "Set your focus on my ways and my plans for your life."

Some people just want to get past our nation's difficult racist past. It can be hard to hear about the history and legacy of racism, and how it continues to affect individuals and systems today. But if we trust in the ways of Christ, we don't have to get caught up in the vast, endless realm of what-abouts or any other diversionary tactic. We can look into the past and the present with empathy, taking honest inventories that lead us past offense to healing and change.

Recovery

I (John) am participating in a yearlong Christian Twelve-Step recovery program. I am not an alcoholic or a drug addict, the only categories into which most people fit the idea of recovery. Even so, I'm unable to manage my brokenness in a way that heals me or frees me from its control. It is a brokenness not everyone understands or is willing to call brokenness.

My background as a third-generation pastor in a prominent evangelical denomination slanted toward the charismatic was rooted in a functional belief system of good works, though our stated theology said otherwise. In practice, as long as you were doing good things with all your might—which included praying longer, working harder, giving more, having more faith, worshiping harder (I still don't know what that means), and growing your church—you didn't need to examine the obvious contradiction between relying on good works and believing in a gospel that has nothing to do with your performance. Even kids got the message loud and clear. As one adult looking back noted: "I earned my way to church camp one year by memorizing verses about how I couldn't earn my way to heaven."

People with this mindset believe that grace alone through faith alone in Christ alone may get you to heaven, but hard work sustained by your good intentions and valiant efforts is what gets you God's good life on earth. As the Good Book says, "God helps those who help themselves," right? No, the Bible says no such thing. And although no one ever preached a gospel of good works in those terms (well, a few people did), the structure and pursuits of our religious value systems were clear: work hard and earn God's favor. So that's what I tried to do.

Everyone thought I was a successful youth minister, but after my students left high school, many of them struggled to keep trusting in Christ and living in authentic Christian community with others. Turns out, my relational leadership style, unbreakable loyalty to the people in our ministry, and good-boy Christianity—complete with the study of Greek texts, alliterated sermons points, and funny illustrations—were not strong enough spiritual foundations for my students. Knowledge and good works with a cursory nod to grace and sovereignty simply weren't enough to sustain them. They weren't even enough to sustain me!

I loved God and he loved me. I was going to heaven. My career as a writer was taking off, my marriage was healthy, and my life wasn't out of control. Even so, I was enslaved by worries, a desire for reputation, false humility, and an incessant need for the approval of certain people. When others seemed to be at odds with me (even when they weren't), I felt out of sorts and "unsafe." My way of life was broken. My system had fatal flaws. I had to be willing to take an inventory of my past and my beliefs to steady my present and move toward a healthier future.

For me, it began with learning to honestly see my issues and have the courage to name them. That's where it begins for the church and for our nation as well.

Inventory

"Hello, my name is John. I have a new life in Christ, and I'm in recovery for worry, the approval of people, control, and pride." If we were together, you would say, "Hi, John." We open each of our recovery meetings with interactions like this. The long list of issues from which I'm recovering changes somewhat from week to week, but I'm no longer surprised that I am completely broken, nor do I try to present any other version of myself except the one Christ is healing and redeeming every day. This is why I felt compelled to open my mind to the concept that I might not have been seeing the full, accurate picture about everything in life, including heated topics on racism.

The Twelve-Step recovery process is centered on learning to believe differently so we can examine the patterns in our past and understand the ways we've used unhealthy habits and coping skills to manage our brokenness in isolation. An essential part of the process is making a "fearless and searching moral inventory of ourselves," which is step 4 of the Twelve Steps. Completing the inventory requires an extended period of reflection as we look back over our lives and recall the beliefs, experiences, and relationships that have affected us most, for better or for worse. We write about our resentments, wrongs committed against us, wrongs we've committed against others, our sexual histories, and specific experiences and perceptions related to whatever issue brought us to recovery in the first place. Needless to say, it's intense.

Many friends who know and love me but misunderstand recovery aren't fond of the idea that I am taking an inventory of my past. They think I don't need it. "You shouldn't feel bad for your past," they say. "That's all behind you now. It's not like you did anything that bad. You intended the right things, and God has forgiven you, so you don't need to dig up all those painful memories. Don't be so hard on yourself!"

They mean well, and they are right on some points. God has forgiven me. My past faults don't define or control me, and I have always been mostly well intentioned. However, my friends aren't right on all points. The real problem isn't their desire to keep me from reliving the pain of my past; it's their assumption that reliving the pain is the purpose of taking an inventory. It is not.

In recovery, we don't take an inventory to dredge up the shame, anguish, and offense of every mistake or wound for the purpose of feeling dejected, condemned, and worthless. Instead, we take an inventory because we believe that through Christ, we never have to live the rest of our lives feeling dejected, condemned, and worthless about our past. With a right understanding of the gospel of grace, we are courageous enough to look clearly at the patterns of thought, attitude, and behavior that underlie our hurts, habits, and hang-ups. By doing so, we are able to break free of unhealthy patterns of the past. In contrast, most people who end up stuck in negative patterns are so wounded or dismissive of their stories that they would rather live with constant regret or deceptive self-justification than look back at whatever is causing those patterns. They're afraid to look where they've slipped.

This is why taking an inventory is not the first step of recovery. The earlier steps help us explore how broken our mindsets and patterns really are. By admitting this and accepting that repentance and change are normal practices for believers, we can fully embrace the truth that the gospel doesn't just get us to heaven but also transforms our lives on earth. This is why Reggie and I have written so extensively in these early chapters on gospel topics related to faith and racism. We can't just successfully jump into an honest inventory without doing the groundwork in these steps. And without an honest inventory, we can't fully realize what needs to change or how to pursue this change.

Whether or not we realize it or like it, our nation is taking an inventory of racism that includes evaluating our nation's past, our beliefs, and our patterns related to racial justice and discrimination.

The problem is, many in the church are like my well-meaning friends: they think that looking honestly at our past, the church's role in the story of racism, or areas of needed change among white Christians are all unnecessary actions that will lead only to fault-finding and condemnation. Like my friends, they don't realize that this is not the purpose of an inventory—not in the least. Tragically, when we as Christians reject any such inventory outright because of insult, pride, or the potential for loss of power, we forfeit our role in helping the church and our nation to heal from the wounds of racism as God intends.

Beginning an Inventory on Racism

Any honest inventory leads us to admit our hurts, habits, and hang-ups, including the sins and failures of our past—those we committed and those other people committed against us—so we can engage in forgiveness and repentance. We need to do this so that our lives and our nation can be healed and transformed. We must look past the sentiments of my well-meaning friends and questions like "Why dig up things like slavery when it's already in the past? Everyone today is equal, so there is no need to repent of the racism in the hearts of a few individuals, much less in our systems of church or government. Can't we all just get along? Everyone just needs Jesus! Why do we have to keep bringing this other stuff up again and again?"

Like my friends, many white Christians today misunderstand the necessity of acknowledging our nation's racist past. We recall the past not to heap condemnation on ourselves but as a necessary and humble first step that acknowledges our desire to be changed. As with all sin, God invites us to repent of our nation's racist past not because he wants to crush us but because he wants to set us free and give us hope. Jon Foreman, the frontman for Grammy Award–winning rock band Switchfoot, says, "For hope to mean anything, it must wrestle with pain. It must face the darkest parts of humanity with compassion and truth. True hope must provide answers and healing for the deepest wounds. Otherwise it is but a bandaid on the broken bones of our society. A well-intentioned pleasantry that actually does more harm than good. True hope is an awareness of a reality beneath the pain. Beneath the problem."[6]

The apostle Paul writes about this process of honesty leading to hope in his second letter to the church in Corinth. In his first letter, he was brutally honest about the need for the church to repent of their response to matters of sexual immorality. When the Corinthians were brave enough to admit their need for change, Paul wrote, "I rejoice, not because you were grieved, but because you were grieved into repenting. For you felt a godly grief, so that you suffered no loss through us. For godly grief produces a repentance that leads to salvation without regret, whereas worldly grief produces death" (2 Cor. 7:9–10).

Grief over sin leads to repentance, not to more guilt and shame. And repentance leads not just to conversion but also to continual transformation beyond any onetime response at an altar or a camp. (Remember, Paul was writing to believers, not unbelievers.) Through repentance, God continually rescues, restores, and heals the soul as we live by grace with God's people and according to God's ways. We "[suffer] no loss" when we grieve and repent of the past (v. 9). That means when we take a collective inventory regarding racism, we don't have to feel afraid or insulted because we think our personal integrity or our nation's history is being attacked. We can listen and respond "without regret" because we know that Christ is already redeeming and transforming us in the process.

For Christians, taking inventories that lead to repentance is not about restoring salvation but about restoring a right relationship with God and with people. It is a daily process. We don't examine our faults and repent out of fear that God has abandoned us because of our sin. We take an honest look at our lives and repent because we trust that God loves us and longs to free us from the negative consequences of sin. We can repent of the sins of slavery and racism—in our nation's past and present—even though we did not engage in slavery or create the systems that perpetuate racism. We repent because we long for the restoration of godly relationships among people of all races who share one nation and are members of one church. Taking an inventory requires that we stop trying so hard to ignore or bury our nation's past. It requires a fearless honesty that leads to restoration without regret.

From this point forward, we'll focus on taking an honest inventory of our past, our beliefs, and our patterns of thought, attitude, and behavior as they relate to systemic racism in our nation and the church.

"

PART 2

TAKING HISTORICAL AND THEOLOGICAL INVENTORIES

"

CHAPTER 6

LANGUAGE, LAWS, AND LEGACY

I want to hear more about this recovery program you've been in." Reggie could tell that John's Twelve-Step journey affected many of their conversations about racism.

"Man, I've been on a journey of change for a while, but God knew that this program was my next step. It's been life changing."

"I guess when I think of recovery, I think of alcoholics and drug addicts," Reggie admitted. His honesty was refreshing.

John chuckled. "Yeah, that's what most people think. Many of my Twelve-Step friends struggle with alcohol and drug addictions, too, but the bottom line is that worry, the need for people's approval, anger, and control are just as much life-controlling issues for me as substance addiction is for some of them. Many Christians live with the same issues I have and act like doing so is normal. But I had to ask myself if I really thought this is what God intended for my life—to look successful on the outside but fight constantly against insecurity within."

Reggie sighed. "Bro, I spend my life telling people all over the world how much they are truly loved by God, and that he wants them to be free. They love what I say, but I see so many that never find a way to truly rest in his love. They live controlled by worry, fear, anxiety, and guilt."

"That was me," John interjected. "Worry and fear used to dominate my mind, which caused me to work harder to outrun my insecurities. When you do that, you begin to have confidence in how hard you're trying, which ironically can make you prideful at the same time—a broken person convinced you're fine. You can't even listen to those who don't already think and talk like you do."

"That's the thing," said Reggie. "Being controlled by those negative things doesn't just affect the way you feel; it affects the way you listen, speak, and respond. You don't even realize that you shut down or blow up when certain terms are used."

"Yes!" John exclaimed. "That's why it's hard for people to know why I see this systemic racism issue differently now. I'm no longer defending my own ideas and terms to the same degree. I realize now that if people freak out when I mention systemic racism, it's usually because they can't get past the words. That's how I got hung up on the phrase 'Black lives matter.' I was caught up in the word game."

Reggie said, "It does kind of feel like we're disputing terms or laws but not actually talking with people about racism."

"Yep, exactly. For me, it's not just because someone convinced me of all the facts, it's because somewhere deep inside, I began to see that my pride was a life-controlling issue that kept me from listening to viewpoints different from my own, especially if they pointed out that I had a role to play in making things better. I had to be honest with myself. I had to take an inventory."

Reggie paused. "Man, that sounds like what the whole church needs to do with this racism conversation—get past our language issues and take an honest inventory about what went on in our past so we can deal with what's really going on in our thoughts and actions today."

● ● ●

As we begin our inventory, it will be helpful to address one of the issues that keeps us from having healthy conversations about race: the words people are using. With the advent of social media, we have become a society built on words more than anything else. We now argue over terms, often forgetting about the issues at hand.

This is certainly the case with racism.

Now that we understand racism is not just a social issue or a sin issue but a gospel issue, we'll begin our inventory by addressing a key term that stops many people in their logical tracks: *systemic racism*.

Our Language Issues with Systemic Racism

Systemic racism is a hot-button term because some people feel it is not only undefinable and divisive but also creates a victim mentality. Yet denying the systemic nature of racism is undeniably one of the biggest roadblocks to healing the wound of racism, especially if we're unwilling to even entertain engaging in an inventory of the past or our beliefs about race. The term often keeps white people from being able to listen well or to speak helpfully about racism because they're too busy arguing about whether systemic racism exists and, if so, in what ways. Above all, some people think that if we acknowledge systemic racism, we are calling ourselves a nation of racists, which is not the case.

Systemic racism (also known as institutional or structural racism) refers to inequitable processes in our social fabric that adversely affect people of color. These processes can exist in any institution or system of power, including places of employment, government agencies, social services, and churches. Advocates for racial justice would say that a school system demonstrates systemic racism when it zones a higher percentage of Black students into the most overcrowded and underresourced schools with the least qualified teachers, while white students in the same community are zoned into newer facilities with smaller classroom sizes and better qualified teachers. No one may have intentionally zoned Black kids into lower quality schools, and there may be additional factors at play besides racial ones, but even so, there is a pattern of inequity.

The school-system example demonstrates why it's so important for us not to think of sin and repentance solely in connection with individual actions. If we assume the problem can be traced to a racist school superintendent or school-board member (and yes, they do exist), we will fail to address racism as it exists in the complex systems the superintendent and board member inherited and in which they continue to serve.

Many white conservative evangelicals believe that civil rights laws have already addressed any systemic racism that once existed. Done and done. If the law says there can be no discrimination and yet racism persists, an individual or a group of racists must be to blame. Those who hold this view might say, "The law declares (and has declared for years now) that racial discrimination is illegal and that everyone in this nation is equal. Therefore, there's no such thing as systemic racism. Slavery, racism, and violating people's rights are illegal, so it's time to move on and stop dividing the nation."

This view highlights the need to explore what we mean by "system" and "systemic"—we need to name and keep naming in specific terms what we are exploring, as any inventory would do.

When we use the term *systemic racism*, we are referring to many components in a complex patchwork made up of the law, history, individual and cultural perceptions, social strata and patterns (conscious or otherwise), power structures that have existed for generations, and more. No single component constitutes an entire system (as we are referring to it), and it would be impossible to list all of its parts. "The system" is a reflection of many variables that contribute to the whole of our social structures and interactions. Even though all of the components of a system can't necessarily be fully demarcated in one complete sentence or paragraph, most can still be addressed.

The term *system* can refer to this larger, complex conglomeration of many components, but it can also refer to its various parts. Thus, we can address different systems within the larger system, including the Constitution; local, state, and federal laws; the government; the church; policing; housing policies; hiring trends; or even the way the government of a small town functions, which is extremely complex with many variables. Sometimes we will say "the system," and sometimes we will say "the system of government" or a community's "local system." If we can be open to this broader definition of *systemic*, perhaps we can bypass wasting energy debating the term rather than trying to positively discuss, much less address, issues of racism.

For many, language is closely connected to legality, which is the next component of our inventory.

Our Legal Issues with Systemic Racism

Over and over, those who deny the existence of systemic racism in our nation refer to language from the Constitution, the Civil Rights Act of 1964, and other legal documents as evidence that we no longer have a systemic problem that is bigger or more deeply embedded in our society than the immoral acts of individuals. The law is a crucial component of our systems, but it cannot fully compose or correct them.

Though the system is complex, our nation's founders knew that its legal and constitutional components were important. That is why they designed laws and a system of government that would be adjustable, not static. The concept of the balance of powers among the executive, legislative, and judicial branches is based on the need for constant accountability. The founders knew that the lifeblood of any sustainable system of government could not reside merely in the well-intentioned hearts or actions of individuals. In their own history, these men were all too familiar with the instability that arises when a government or social system functions at the whims of a monarch or a small group of landowners.

Our laws and our leaders are important, but our system of government was always intended to be more complex and malleable than either, something the founders foresaw and for which they prepared. Thus, we can't just claim, "The law has ended systemic racism." There is much more to the system than just the law.

From the outset of our constitutional form of government, there was tension between the stated law of the land and the applied law of the land, especially as it was applied or enforced with certain people groups, including categories of gender and race. We must not forget that although the Constitution spoke eloquently of freedom for all, it excluded women from voting and defined Blacks as three-fifths of a human being. These were systemic problems that needed attention. The system—in this case, the constitutional and legal structures and their enforcement—was very much in need of adjustments.

Contrary to what some think today, making adjustments to our systems of governance is not a violation of those systems. This is how it was intended to work. The need to make changes was embedded in the earliest visions of those who founded our republic. Near the end of George Washington's second term as president, most Americans wanted him to keep on serving until his death, much like a king. His decision not to run for a third term wasn't just out of humility. It was informed by a deep belief that even a good "king" should not remain in power indefinitely in a healthy democratic system. Washington attempted to downgrade the public's faith in what we seem to be most defensive about today: who leads the system and how that seemingly perfect system is preserved.

Washington knew that neither leaders nor systems of government are perfect, and that both need continual change. He acknowledged as much in his farewell address when he said, "The basis of our political systems is the right of the people to make and to *alter* their constitutions of government."[1] Constitutions need altering not because systems are evil but because they are inanimate and incapable of perfection. Ongoing adjustments keep systems useful and good for the people they are intended to serve and protect.

Components of the system must continue to breathe and adapt. For example, we celebrate July 4, 1776, as our nation's Independence Day, but it was just the day independence was declared. It wasn't until 1783, after several years of war with Britain, that independence was fully realized, and of course only for white males. The point is that the declaration was part of the systemic equation that had to adapt to fulfill its intent.

In much the same way, the Emancipation Proclamation of 1863 declared an end to slavery, but it required two more years of bloody conflict in the Civil War before it was fully realized as the law of the land. Yet even after the war had ended, slavery was legal according to the Constitution. (The Thirteenth Amendment had been passed, but not yet ratified.) This is a prime example of a time in our history when the governing system was at odds with itself. (An executive order contradicted a constitutional protection.) This should not surprise us because we know that the system is inanimate and doesn't have a heart. It is constantly balancing its various components, which is why the term *systemic racism* shouldn't offend us. The parts of any system need constant adjustment. In the case of slavery, members of Congress agreed that the constitutional system needed adjustment, so on December 6, 1865, they ratified the Thirteenth Amendment to abolish slavery.

Many today believe this ended systemic racism in the United States. However, it led to other forms of legalized racism as local and state leaders found ways to disadvantage the former slaves the amendment was intended to protect. The Thirteenth Amendment stated that "neither slavery nor involuntary servitude, except as a punishment for crime whereof the party shall have been duly convicted, shall exist within the United States, or any place subject to their jurisdiction."[2] One key phrase, "except as a punishment for crime" was the fly in the ointment.

In the South, that phrase inspired a host of new laws known as Black Codes. These were throwbacks to the slave codes Southern states had long used to control every aspect of slaves' lives, which included denying slaves the right to legally marry, name their own children, and be protected from rape, beatings, and lynching.

Among a host of regulations, Black Code laws made it illegal for slaves to be unemployed or stand around on property that wasn't theirs. (Few freed slaves owned property.) The Mississippi State Legislature made the terms clear in a vagrancy law passed in 1865:

> Be it further enacted, that all freedmen, free Negroes, and mulattoes in this state over the age of eighteen years found on the second Monday in January 1866, or thereafter, with no lawful employment or business . . . shall be deemed vagrants; and, on conviction thereof, shall be fined in the sum of not exceeding, in the case of a freedman, free Negro, or mulatto, $150, . . . and *imprisoned at the discretion of the court*. . . . And in case any freedman, free Negro, or mulatto shall fail [to pay the fine] for five days . . . it shall be, and is hereby made, the duty of the sheriff of the proper county *to hire out said freedman, free Negro, or mulatto to any person who will, for the shortest period of service, pay said fine or forfeiture and all costs.*[3]

From 1865 to 1866, Black Codes reestablished slavery without technically violating constitutional law. The law—part of a system that has no heart—was essentially neutralized by technicalities it was unable to foresee or prevent. It is the job of people—who do have hearts—to interpret, enforce, and adapt the letter of the law to reflect the spirit of the law. That is systemic change.

In the case of the Thirteenth Amendment, the letter of the law hijacked the spirit of the law, opening the door for the Black Codes, a backward system of law and order that allowed Black men and women to be arrested for almost any infraction. Under this system, simply being a Black American became a criminal offense. Without jobs, Black people couldn't repay the fines they incurred, which led to mass incarceration, another system of slavery in which Black people became property of the state to work off their sentences. Let this sink in. Even though the Emancipation Proclamation and the Thirteenth Amendment were legal, systemic changes, Black Codes made it technically legal for whites to arrest, charge, sentence, and send Black people back to the same plantations where they had been slaves. Ironically, society owed Black people a greater debt than the legally contrived debt to society that they were forced to pay.

Although the Thirteenth Amendment was a good law, an exception allowing slavery as a "punishment for crime" led to a host of bad laws embodied in the Black Codes. While laws have an essential role in our governing systems, laws alone can never guarantee those systems will be free of racism.

When we speak of systemic issues, including systemic racism, we are speaking of issues that go beyond the law, including how our laws and systems of government are perceived, interpreted, and enforced. This means we must pursue systemic changes while simultaneously pursuing heart changes. Both are essential for lasting and meaningful change.

When Congress agreed that the South's response to the Thirteenth Amendment created a problem, they enacted further systemic change by passing the Civil Rights Act of 1866, which was vetoed by President Johnson. However, Congress overrode his veto and then also reenacted the law in 1870 to help enforce the Fourteenth Amendment, which was passed in 1866 but was not ratified by the states until 1868. Among other things, these legislative acts guaranteed the protection of civil rights for freed slaves, rendering the Black Codes null and void. Congress was able to act because the founders before them had realized what many of us fail to accept today: the intention of the law is not always upheld in practice, even when there is nothing technically illegal going on. For this reason, laws are designed to be adjusted, not to remain static. The Black Codes would not be the last instance in which the law or an enforcer of the law in our nation would come up short in recognizing or fixing systemic problems.

Law and Order for Whom?

Why is it important to understand that the law is part of a system of government but doesn't constitute the entire system? Because many Christians and conservatives today bank everything on the idea that law and order is the chief aim of a democratic and just society. Yet as we have seen, something that's technically legal can still be far from just. Our history demonstrates that the status quo of an orderly society can be maintained to protect one people group more than others.

Despite amendments to the law, the white ruling class in the South, as well as many whites in the North, considered themselves superior to Blacks. That was their real problem. And they bolstered this mindset with errant interpretations of Scripture. From their point of view, it seemed prudent to value legality not just above justice but also above righteousness.

Most white people in the post–Civil War South didn't protest the Black Code laws because they didn't perceive them as injustices, and they weren't adversely affected by them. They were comfortable in their belief that white people were superior, and their Black counterparts were less than human.

During the War of Independence from Britain, white Americans had been willing to die for the constitutional principles of freedom and justice. In the Civil War, Southern whites seceded from the

Union, citing the same principles. Yet when it came to defending freedom and justice for Black slaves, they felt justified in ignoring these principles.

Would we have thought or acted differently had we lived back then? We might hope so, but it's doubtful. Our patterns of thought and behavior, like those of white people in earlier times, reflect the commonplace cultural norms of our time. If we aren't willing to think and act differently now, it's unlikely we would have been willing to think and act differently then. Events in recent years reveal how little our hearts and our systems have changed.

For example, in 2018 many Christians supported President Trump's unapologetic statement that the United States should admit more immigrants from countries like Norway, not from "shithole countries" like Haiti.[4] It wasn't hard to see the subtext—Norway is predominantly white and wealthy, and Haiti is predominantly Black and impoverished. Those supporting the statement may not have been openly endorsing racism, but neither were they affirming the gospel Jesus lived and preached, a gospel in which the values of humility, grace, and receiving "the least of these" leave no room for white supremacy or racism of any kind.

Pause for a moment and take note of whether you are more offended that Christian authors used the term *shithole* than you are by the fact that we're quoting Donald Trump, a powerful politician almost unequivocally endorsed by white evangelical Christians. As Christians, too many of us are more insulted by the idea that anything we've supported is racist than we are by whether it actually is. The most alarming issue is not the fact that a prominent politician could say such a thing but that Christians could defend and even celebrate it with no qualms about its incompatibility with the gospel.

Was it illegal to make such a statement? No. But did this

statement, which conservative Christians widely supported (or at least didn't decry), reveal a problem in the hearts of individuals and in our system of government? We think so. Supporting such a statement shows a disconnect between rightness declared and rightness delivered, between what is legal and what should be normal behavior for Christians.

The death of twenty-six-year-old Breonna Taylor is a more tragic example of how far from flawless the law is. On September 23, 2020, plainclothes officers in Louisville, Kentucky, executed a no-knock warrant signed by a judge. The officers allegedly knocked first and announced themselves as police, but Breonna's boyfriend, Kenneth Walker, said he never heard them. What he did hear was a battering ram knocking down the apartment door. Walker assumed the armed men in plain clothes were intruders and fired his legally owned weapon at the police. The officers collectively fired thirty-two shots in return, six of which hit Breonna in the hallway of her own apartment. She bled to death in that hallway.

Compounding the tragedy is the fact that what the officers did wasn't illegal. Kentucky law allowed police to execute the no-knock warrant and enter the apartment without warning. The castle doctrine (or Stand Your Ground law) also made it legal for Breonna's boyfriend to fire in self-defense. And because the officers were fired upon, it was legal for them to fire back at Walker.

A grand jury found that no one who fired a gun at a person was guilty of any crime. The only person indicted was an officer charged with wanton endangerment for firing several shots through a wall into another apartment, where no one was injured. The law made it easier to indict someone for shooting a wall than for shooting an unarmed person in her apartment.

After the incident, local and state lawmakers banned no-knock warrants in Louisville. Even so, rioting occurred in the city after all of the officers were cleared of wrongdoing in Taylor's death. The Black residents of Louisville couldn't understand how it could be considered just for police to shoot Breonna Taylor in her home when she committed no crime.

It is tragic and wrong that Breonna Taylor was killed.

It is tragic and wrong that two Louisville police officers doing their jobs were shot as well.

It is tragic and wrong that while most of the protests that erupted around the nation were peaceful, there were isolated incidents of violence, looting, and rioting.

It is tragic and wrong that so many of us feel that nothing needs to be addressed in the law enforcement and justice systems that contributed to Breonna Taylor's death.

As fathers, neither of us can imagine our children being gunned down by police in our homes even though they committed no crime, or that we would have no recourse or justice because the law allowed it. This is a systemic problem, even if you don't like the term *systemic*. Our laws and systems of government are meant to serve us, not the other way around. We also serve an eternal king whose gospel empowers us to be humble enough to recognize when change may be needed and courageous enough to call for that change, regardless of the political fallout.

Yet even when the law is changed to correct an injustice, it cannot fully resolve every systemic issue. As Christians and as citizens, we should anticipate the need to engage in evaluating and adjusting any system that serves us and those around us. We are the heart of the system.

Ironically, one of the best ways we can affect the system today is to examine how the past is still affecting it.

Our Legacy Issues with Systemic Racism

The final component of our inventory in this chapter requires us to address the prevalent sentiment today that what happened in the past should stay in the past. Most people acknowledge the horrors of slavery and racial discrimination in the nineteenth and twentieth centuries. Most people also acknowledge, often with many whatabouts and other caveats, the tragedy of racial violence today. Even so, many of these people disengage from healthy conversation on race when it turns to history, because they cannot see any valid ways the atrocities of our past could affect or be connected to our present racial issues.

The truth is, historical events and perspectives affect our present-day systemic issues because history leaves a legacy. Our inventory will be much easier to navigate if we can view historical legacy as a component of systemic racism.

Like all systemic issues, systemic racism is defined not just by present reality but also by the ongoing legacy of historical issues. Imagine that two teams are running a marathon, but one team is given a forty-minute head start. Thirty minutes in, the organizers of the race acknowledge that giving a head start to one team isn't right, so they allow the second team to join the race. At this point, no one would stand up and say, "Now the race is completely fair. Everyone can run at the same pace, so no one should cry foul!" Sure, both teams can now run at the same pace, but the second team is still disadvantaged because the organizers decided to give the other team a head start. The injustice may be in the past, but the legacy of that decision for the second team is ongoing.

Just as our nation still feels the cultural and political legacies of World War II, including ongoing tensions with communistic regimes, a military presence in Europe, the creation of the United Nations, and a host of other issues, we also continue to live with the legacy perpetuated by centuries of slavery and legally sanctioned racism. Acknowledging this legacy does not mean we ignore the progress we've made as a nation, but refusing to acknowledge it can hinder us from making more progress.

There is a lot of heated discussion these days about history being erased or rewritten, especially when it comes to monuments being vandalized or torn down. Regardless of how we feel about preserving or destroying monuments, we may be unaware that as a nation, we tend to pick and choose the parts of history we want to collectively remember and the parts we would like to forget.

The events of September 11, 2001, remain etched in our nation's collective consciousness. Thousands of lives were senselessly lost that day, and our hearts continue to mourn for those who died, regardless of their race. Pearl Harbor is another tragedy that remains in our national memory not only as a moment to lament but also as a moment to honor those who gave their lives in an existential battle against ruthless enemies.

We are told that Americans should never forget Pearl Harbor or September 11, 2001, and we shouldn't. Yet it is somehow unpatriotic to remember and honor other historical events that equally affected the lives of Americans. When they are mentioned, some people become angry that liberal troublemakers are drudging up the past instead of letting it go and moving on. One example is the Tulsa Race Massacre.

On May 30, 1921, violence erupted in Tulsa, Oklahoma, in response to the brutal lynching of a Black man named Dick Rowland *after* he had been arrested by police. Charges against him were later dropped, but the greatest of injustices had already been inflicted, and Black citizens were understandably outraged. On June 1, the local government deputized many white men of the city, and the mob descended on the Greenwood district, wreaking havoc on the Black community there. In a span of twenty-four hours, these "deputies" had burned thirty-five city blocks to the ground, including schools, churches, and more than twelve hundred homes. What was even more tragic, was that several hundred Black residents lost their lives and more than eight hundred were injured. "Not one of these criminal acts was then or ever has been prosecuted or punished by government at any level: municipal, county, state, or federal."[5]

Many white Americans have never heard of this event, or they know of it only as the Tulsa Race Riot, not the Tulsa Race Massacre. Calling it a riot places the blame on those who protested the lynching of a man in police custody, not on the people who lynched him or those who destroyed hundreds of Black lives.

Many Americans have also never heard of Juneteenth, a national holiday commemorating the end of slavery, or Japanese internment camps during World War II. Parts of the history of our nation have been whitewashed, even if inadvertently. Yet these events and many others are as much part of our history as the events our nation chooses to remember.

We should beware when someone tells us what we can "never forget" and what we should "never mention," because these events from our past affect our present in ways we don't necessarily realize. They are legacies that have an ongoing impact on our systems. It's curious that certain historical events are downplayed, questioned, and even denied, while others are celebrated—seemingly with no cognitive dissonance. For people of color, this contributes to the feeling that their histories—and their lives—matter less than other historical events that bolster the national narrative of patriotism and progress.

Perhaps the most effective way to understand this is to imagine something in your family's history that negatively affected your family's legacy. It might have been a bankruptcy, a death, or a natural disaster that changed your family from that point forward. Now imagine that you're in the middle of sharing this event with someone when that person abruptly cuts you off and says, "Sorry, but I don't think that really happened. Besides, that was so long ago, you really need to stop dwelling on the past. My past was hard too." This is essentially how many Christians have responded to the atrocity-ridden history of Black people and to their descendants, who remember, lament, and remain affected by its ongoing legacy.

As an indirect comparison, some people today deny that the Holocaust occurred, despite photographic, anecdotal, and government-owned video evidence to the contrary. But most people not only acknowledge that it happened but also are respectful and moved over the savage, inhumane way the Nazis slaughtered millions of Jews and other classes of people they targeted for elimination. Descendants of death-camp victims would be deeply insulted if someone told them they need to stop using their family's tragedy as a crutch and get on with their lives.

If such a sentiment sounds extreme and unbelievable to you, just peruse the comments on social media. An alarming number of people not only deny the history of Black Americans but also shame them for wanting to acknowledge the ongoing effects of hundreds of years of enslavement, followed by more than one hundred years of injustice as the nation refused to honor its Constitution.

We need to understand that Black Americans who descended from slaves carry the burden of a tragic legacy. Their not-so-distant ancestors were either brought here on slave ships against their will or were born into a horrific system of abuse and dehumanization. We must refuse to neutralize their history with spurious theories about how most slaves were treated well by their masters, or by focusing on other parts of American history that lament or celebrate something less ugly or seemingly more patriotic.

Both positive and negative aspects of history constitute our legacy as a nation.

These historical legacies, along with the language we accept or reject and the laws we institute and adjust, deeply affect our systems. As the path to healing and recovery leads us through honest inventories, we can feel more secure as we encounter ideas like systemic racism and listen to their merits without dismissing them outright. We can also acknowledge the progress we've made in addressing racism while also realizing that this progress does not mean we have arrived. This will position us to explore more openly the ways our history has affected hearts and systems in our past—in our nation and the church—and how it continues to inform hearts and systems in our present.

CHAPTER 7

THE HISTORICAL LEGACY OF SLAVERY IN THE CHURCH AND THE NATION

As a white kid raised in the South and a pastor who also taught in public school, I've had a front-row seat to the way some white people in the South think about slavery."

"That's right," said Reggie, "I sometimes forget that you were a teacher."

"Yeah, I taught history and political science in East Tennessee—like on the edge of Appalachia."

"Bro, since I'm from Knoxville, I speak in some of those more remote areas near the mountains, so I get that it can be a different world."

"And from what I've seen," John replied, "compared to a larger metropolitan area like Nashville, many white people in both areas view racism in similar ways."

"That's interesting. I would assume the views would be different in more rural areas."

"Obviously, my anecdotal experiences don't prove anything, but they are interesting." John paused to remember. "I think what I most vividly recall over the years is how people, including a number of my students, thought of slavery and the Civil War. The way many of them viewed those four hundred years might still be affecting our lives today."

"I agree. And the sad part is that people in church don't seem to think much different on these things than the general public." Reggie's voice was somber.

"That's probably because even as we study the way slavery and racism affected our nation and its systems, there is a parallel storyline that's sometimes hard to admit."

"And what's that?" asked Reggie.

"Well, when God's people should have been positively addressing the issue of slavery, the church was often complicit in it. This isn't the whole story of slavery and racism, but it deserves to be mentioned. And when slavery finally ended and our nation needed the church to step up and speak the right things, other leaders—politicians—took the lead instead."

"I'll give you two guesses how that worked out," Reggie quipped.

● ● ●

Until the seventeenth century, it was a long-standing theological belief that Christians were not permitted to enslave one another, certainly a belief the Bible substantiates. Some have argued otherwise, citing scriptures about slaves obeying their masters, but such a viewpoint is based on an incomplete understanding of the biblical context of slavery.

Slavery in the Old Testament was often the result of one nation conquering another, or a person working to pay off a debt. While the ownership of people degraded their humanity and often denied slaves basic rights, it's important to note that it was not generally based on skin color. In the New Testament era, the same kinds of slavery continued, sometimes as a punishment for a crime, but it was also not uncommon for prominent Roman households to have doctors and teachers as slaves. However, the status of these slaves often differed from what we think of as slavery today—degrading people based on the color of their skin, which supposedly proves their human inferiority, and denying them basic human rights.

We point out this distinction not to suggest that ancient slavery was somehow better or more acceptable than modern slavery but only to emphasize that in modern times, skin color became the basis for American slavery. Once that domino fell, slavers used skin color to justify degrading people they considered inferior or subhuman.

Again, ancient slavery often included a component of indentured servitude, in which enslaved people worked to pay off debts and regain their freedom. Chattel slavery, on the other hand, refers to the permanent ownership of enslaved people simply because of their race, including their children and children's children, with no hope of regaining their freedom. According to the Abolition Project, "Chattel slavery was supported and made legal by European governments and monarchs. This type of enslavement was practised in European colonies, from the sixteenth century onwards."[1] While elements of chattel slavery certainly existed in antiquity along with other types of slavery, as the Abolition Project attests, European colonies adopted a form of slavery based exclusively on race. Chattel slavery was practiced in various parts of the world, including Central and South America, but nowhere did it have as great an impact on the establishment of a democratic society as it did in the United States.

The Early Failures of the Church

In the early years of the American colonies, it was far from a foregone conclusion that all Black people would be slaves. There were free Blacks living and working in the colonies. But as the need for labor skyrocketed, colonists found their solution in slavery, a convenient decision for their own enrichment and devastating for the 12.5 million Africans enslaved during the transatlantic slave trade.[2]

At this pivotal moment, the church should have been a prophetic voice decrying the evils of slavery. Christians had generally placed limits on slavery, albeit antiquated and misguided ones, such as drawing the line at enslaving other Christians. But that changed in 1667 when the Virginia General Assembly adopted a statute that declared, "The conferring of baptism does not alter the condition of the person as to his bondage or freedom."[3]

The church should have opposed this unjust law, but it chose prosperity over obedience to the ways of Christ instead. Now, white Christians could own slaves and even baptize them—which meant accepting them as brothers and sisters in Christ—but they could also mistreat them. When Black slaves converted to the Christian faith, they had to acknowledge that their new freedom in Christ did not grant them freedom from their earthly owners.

In justifying slavery, Christians overlooked the apostle Paul's letter to Philemon, in which he pleaded for the emancipation of a slave named Onesimus, who likely owed a debt to Philemon that

Paul offered to pay. Instead, slave-holding Christians cherry-picked Paul's other statements on slavery, took them out of context, and used them as justification for their form of chattel slavery, which was certainly prohibited in Scripture. We see this reflected in the Old Testament commandment not to mistreat foreigners and sojourners (Ex. 22:21) but to "love them as yourself" (Lev. 19:34 NIV). We also see it in the extensive New Testament narrative about sharing life in Christ across ethnic and national lines—a challenging call to the early Jewish believers to love and have communion in Christ with the "ethnos," or Gentiles. Paul's words to the Galatians summed up God's revolutionary directive to break down ethnic barriers through the gospel: "There is neither Jew nor Gentile, neither slave nor free, nor is there male and female, for you are all one in Christ Jesus" (Gal. 3:28 NIV).

Instead of responding with humility and repentance to the radical call of Scripture to spiritual freedom and ethnic inclusion, white American slaveholders twisted Scripture to justify their system of chattel slavery. They were convinced the Bible provided divine evidence that white people were superior to Black people, which meant the principles of Scripture could be applied differently to slaves. The atrocities they subsequently committed were somehow permissible in their minds—including rape and murder, the separation of children from their parents, and savage beatings of Black men, women, and children.

As Austin Channing Brown puts it, "Slavery was no accident. We didn't trip and fall into Black subjugation. . . . Every bit of it was on purpose."[4] The purposeful part is bad enough, but realizing that many enslavers claimed to be doing God's work adds grave insult to the unspeakable injury of American chattel slavery. The twisting of biblical principles contributed to the failure of the church to cry out against slavery. This failure is a terrible stain on the American Christian witness and a tragic legacy that continues to affect racial conversations today. In 1845, abolitionist and statesman Frederick Douglass acknowledged the dichotomy between the tenets of biblical Christianity and slaveholding Christianity when he wrote, "What I have said respecting and against religion, I mean strictly to apply to the *slaveholding religion* of this land, and with no possible reference to Christianity proper; for, between the Christianity of this land, and the Christianity of Christ, I recognize the widest, possible difference. . . . I love the pure, peaceable, and impartial Christianity of Christ: I therefore hate the corrupt, slaveholding, women-whipping, cradle-plundering, partial and hypocritical Christianity of this land."[5]

As American Christians, what are we to do with such disturbing facts about our history? We are to listen, learn, and lament along with those who rightfully mourn the atrocities in our history. We must at least begin there, though certainly not end there. There is so much good work to be done, but if we won't listen or lament with humility, then we can't begin the work we should be doing.

Historian Jemar Tisby calls all Christians to "discern the difference between complicit Christianity and courageous Christianity."[6] Our nation's white founders and Christians of their time chose to be complicit, but we can choose courage. As citizens of the kingdom of God, our primary allegiance is to the God of the Israelites, a people who also suffered at the hands of brutal slave masters. Throughout Scripture, God repeatedly called them to remember their painful history in Egypt. In one example God instructed the Israelites to say to the priests when presenting a firstfruits offering of gratitude, "The Egyptians mistreated us and made us suffer, subjecting us to harsh labor. Then we cried out to the LORD, the God of our ancestors, and the LORD heard our voice and saw our misery, toil and oppression.

So the LORD brought us out of Egypt with a mighty hand and an outstretched arm, with great terror and with signs and wonders" (Deut. 26:6–8 NIV). God didn't tell Israel to "get over it" because they were no longer enslaved. Rather, he called them to remember their pain as well as their triumphs, because both were part of a healthy, humble national and spiritual consciousness.

We must remember the suffering of the men and women who lived and died enslaved, including the violence they endured before ever reaching our shores. Each of the ships that brought enslaved Africans to this country was loaded with hundreds of human beings, including children, shackled in cramped cargo holds where they lay almost piled on top of one another during a voyage that lasted months. With each wave the ships crested, their waste flowed up and down on them. Children endured the same conditions as the adults. Women were routinely raped. Men were killed on a whim, and the only reason not to kill them was to exploit them for profit after landing in the New World.

Author Austin Channing Brown states, "We have not thoroughly assessed the bodies snatched from dirt and sand to be chained in a cell. We have not reckoned with the horrendous, violent mass kidnapping that we call the Middle Passage."[7] She is right. We have not undertaken this assessment as a nation. The inventory is disturbing but necessary. It is estimated that over the course of four hundred years, more than ten million Africans were forcibly brought to the Americas, with another two million dying from disease, starvation, beatings, or other perils along the way.[8]

In today's age of statistics and metrics, it is all too easy to hear staggering numbers such as these without registering an emotional response. To put these numbers into context, imagine that the cities of New York and Dallas were invaded by foreign mercenaries, their entire populations trafficked into lifelong, inescapable slavery. Also imagine that in the process, the population of the entire Houston metropolitan area was murdered. The scope and scale of the loss of African lives exceeds any other tragedy in American history. This is the historical legacy of most Black people in America, and many feel that their history is routinely disregarded, downgraded, or dismissed.

Whether we like it or not, the history of our country is one we all share. We don't have the option of omitting centuries of slavery and racism from our collective past. The gospel calls us as American Christians to be willing to lament the dark realities of our past and honor the truth of our history as we listen to our Black brothers and sisters and acknowledge how its legacy still affects them.

If our ways of thinking have caused us to overlook the complicity of the American church in racism, we may have overlooked a host of other elements of racism in our history and culture. We began this chapter with a brief history of the American church on matters of race because our ways of relating to the gospel rightly or wrongly affect the ways we relate to everything else in this world. But many political and governmental leaders also contributed to the systems of slavery and racism in our nation. Our inventory takes us next to the early years of the republic and the years immediately following the abolition of slavery.

The Legacy of Missed Opportunities and Leadership Vacuums

Mirroring the churches they attended, the American founders failed to collectively address slavery at a time when ending it could have changed everything. From the beginning of our country, slavery was a hotly debated issue that ebbed and flowed on the national political stage. Many of the founders claimed to oppose slavery, yet they still owned slaves. Their hypocrisy reveals the opportunity they missed to lead the nation where the church should already have led it. But there was too much money and power to lose.

In spite of their failure to oppose slavery in practice, the founders were well aware that they were building a nation on a powder keg that would likely explode one day. Terms like "the peculiar institution"[9] were eventually coined as euphemistic references to slavery. There are some hints that Thomas Jefferson, a slave owner himself, expressed negative sentiments about slavery. He certainly opposed it in the new western territories that were being added to the Union. Tragically, however, he did nothing to end slavery in his own state of Virginia, whose economy relied on slave labor. Like so many of America's founders, he didn't know how to maintain his economic standing, as well as the economic standing of a growing nation, without subjugating Black people.

There were powerful opponents to slavery, however. Jefferson's political nemesis and Federalist counterpart Alexander Hamilton falls into this category. Born and raised on the island of Saint Croix in the Caribbean, Hamilton expressed what historian Ron Chernow characterized as "an unwavering belief in the genetic equality of blacks and whites—unlike Jefferson, for instance, who regarded blacks as innately inferior."[10]

Hamilton's views were progressive for his day, but he wasn't alone. As early as 1775, various groups in the North and the South, including the Philadelphia Quakers, were launching antislavery societies and organizations. Slavery was not a foregone conclusion or a universal belief during that period.

Just as there is racial tension today, there was tension at that time concerning what was right and wrong. We get a clear picture of that tension in Benjamin Franklin. As a young man, Franklin brokered the sale of slaves, including his own. But later in life when he was troubled by his conscience, he changed his mind about slavery and became the president of Pennsylvania's abolition society.[11] He went from buying and selling slaves to working to end slavery.

Franklin's change of heart and behavior certainly doesn't negate his slaveholding past, but neither does his past negate his conversion to the abolitionist cause. To understand Franklin and the role he played in our history, we need to understand and hold both realities in tension. This tension is one of the legacies of our history, and we can't resolve it without humbly listening and being willing to think differently.

Benjamin Franklin is not someone we can categorize as entirely good or entirely evil. He was a flawed human being and subject to the same evils as the rest of us. When he participated in slavery, he engaged in an act that today would not only disqualify him from leadership but also land him in jail. And yet it did not disqualify him from leadership in the eighteenth century. Franklin's contributions to democracy and, in his early days, to perpetuating slavery are both true, which means his story is complex.

Complexity and nuance are difficult to discuss in our context, which is characterized by polarization and extremist thinking. What is not complex is the fact that despite the rhetoric about freedom and liberty for all and the privately expressed good intentions of some, the founders' acceptance of slavery was immoral. The practice of slavery was not forced on them. They chose it and systematized it, even though some of them clearly knew better. Too many of those who had qualms either disregarded them or trusted in their good intentions, which is why we mustn't place too much confidence in our good intentions. "There is a way that appears to be right, but in the end it leads to death" (Prov. 14:12 NIV).

Austin Channing Brown writes,

We have not been honest about all of America's complicity—about the wealth the South earned on the backs of the enslaved, or the wealth the North gained through the production of enslaved hands. We have not fully understood the status symbol that owning bodies offered. We have not confronted the humanity, the emotions, the heartbeats of the multiple generations who were born into slavery and died in it, who never tasted freedom on America's land.

The same goes for the Civil War. We have refused to honestly confront the fact that so many were willing to die in order to hold the freedom of others in their hands. We have refused to acknowledge slavery's role at all, preferring to boil things down to the far more palatable "states' rights." We have not confessed that the end of slavery was so bitterly resented, the rise of Jim Crow became inevitable—and with it, a belief in Black inferiority that lives on in hearts and minds today.[12]

The bottom line was that the founders were afraid to address the issue of slavery because they believed their fledgling nation's emerging economy couldn't withstand such a cataclysmic change. At that time, the democratic republic that became the United States was more a political experiment than a political superpower. In spite of the growing crack in our foundation, generations of Americans simply continued to build on it, until the whole structure of our national life came toppling down in a bloody civil war.

England, the nation from which we fought to gain our independence, outlawed the slave trade in 1807 and abolished slavery altogether in 1833. American leaders were behind the times, and yet abolitionists abounded. This discussion wasn't flying under the radar of American thought. From the beginning, our country's founders and leaders knew that slavery was a ticking time bomb; they just kept tossing it from one generation of leaders to the next, hoping that it wouldn't explode in their hands. And then one day, it finally exploded in the hands of Abraham Lincoln.

Lincoln is revered today as the Great Emancipator, the leader whose wisdom helped preserve the Union. But as popular as he is in American history, he was one of the most hated men of his time. We see evidence of this in the Southern states' response to his first campaign for president. Lincoln's election in November of 1860 was the tipping point for civil war. On December 20, South Carolina seceded from the Union, followed by other Southern states. Four months later, Confederate troops fired on Union forces at Fort Sumter, igniting the Civil War.

The South was convinced that Lincoln's aim was to abolish slavery, even though the evidence then and now unfortunately does not point to that conclusion. Lincoln was apparently more concerned with preventing slavery from spreading into the western territories, whose populations had increased to levels sufficient to apply for statehood. This was the hot issue of the day, affecting the delicate balance of power in Congress between slave states and free states. A political firestorm swirled as both sides jockeyed for more political ground by seeking to add free states or slave states to their respective rosters. The nation was steeped in divisiveness, conspiracy, and suspicion when the Civil War broke out mere weeks after Lincoln took office in March of 1861.

By the end of his first term and four years into the Civil War,

Lincoln, a Republican, sensed the difficulty he faced in seeking reelection. He decided to cross the aisle and bring a Southern Democrat onto his ticket as vice president in the hope of creating a more cohesive political coalition and as a signal of his desire to bring unity and peace to a divided nation. Unfortunately, Lincoln chose Andrew Johnson, a man who was the antithesis of Lincoln in character and political philosophy. Following Lincoln's assassination in the spring of 1865, Johnson became president of the United States at a crucial moment when the nation needed a leader to guide it through the difficult period of Reconstruction. Johnson's self-focused leadership did more damage than good in rebuilding a nation free from the fetters of slavery. His presidency contributed to the painful legacy we're still dealing with today.

Johnson did his best to muck up the works of Reconstruction by overtly opposing the progress his predecessor had made and many Reconstruction policies Congress passed, including the Fourteenth Amendment, the Civil Rights Act of 1866, and Freedmen's Bureau bills. Instead of echoing his predecessor's gracious tone, President Johnson relied on racially charged vitriol to challenge all legislation, even vetoing the Civil Rights Act. Congress passed it anyway by overriding his veto.

In 1865, Johnson said, "White men alone must manage the South." In 1867, during his annual address to Congress, he wrote, "No independent government of any form has ever been successful in their [Blacks'] hands. On the contrary, wherever they have been left to their own devices they have shown a constant tendency to relapse into barbarism."[13] According to historian Eric Foner, it was "probably the most blatantly racist pronouncement ever to appear in an official state paper of an American president."[14]

Andrew Johnson's legacy reiterates how the complexities of

systemic issues go beyond the technicalities of the law. The nation was already divided over issues of race, but he exacerbated those divisions at a time when the president should have been fostering a sense of unity. The church compounded the damage he inflicted by not speaking the right message or inviting the right kinds of conversations in the cultural milieu of the day. Many Christians in the South agreed with his viewpoints instead of the gospel; after all, very few religious leaders were courageously helping their congregations connect the dots of the gospel and racial justice.

By 1868, President Johnson was an embattled leader and his own worst enemy, yet many Christians looked past his ridiculous leadership because they agreed with his errant viewpoints on race. He often gave speeches while intoxicated and had fits of narcissistic rage, making the nation's woes entirely about himself. He constantly attempted to churn up his supporters with baseless claims of assassination attempts and grand conspiracies. At one point, he posed the question, "Who, I ask, has suffered more for the Union than I have?" As historian Jon Meacham commented, "Lincoln, for one, comes to mind."[15] Despite Johnson's feckless leadership and grandstanding, Republicans in Congress advanced legislation on behalf of Black people set free by the Emancipation Proclamation. Unfortunately, the cause of racial equality was hindered by a system rife with prejudice that teemed with true believers in the religion of white supremacy, which was also married to their Christian religion. This sullied union created an environment where unbiblical cruelty and the widespread support of Southern white supremacists, even though they were unfit leaders, were viewed as righteous actions.

On the practical side, the abolition of slavery resulted in an almost unfathomable shift in an economic system whose infrastructure and commercial vigor had been built on the backs of slaves.

Slave labor was the foundation for the explosive economic growth of a nation so young.

Lincoln was assassinated a mere forty-two days after his reelection, and the hope for a unified and speedy implementation of basic rights for millions of emancipated Black citizens died with him. Johnson was eventually impeached but served out his term as an unelected president, leaving office on March 4, 1869. His unfortunate legacy of racism added yet another obstacle on the road to equality for Black citizens, making the journey much longer and harder than it should have been. The white church also exacerbated the pain of that journey for Black Americans. White Christians were living in the legacy of a generation of believers before them who failed to courageously address the evils of slavery and racism when our nation began. Refusing to subjectively examine the past makes it harder to see how that legacy affects our ways of thinking today. Biases can become fixtures and systems can become sacred.

How can we face up to this legacy and overcome the biases embedded in our systems that come from following errant human leaders instead of following Christ?

God's Man versus God's Ways

Many Christians living downstream of the legacy of their past chose to follow bad political leaders rather than sound doctrine, but we don't have to repeat their mistakes. We must first stop chalking up our errant attitudes and actions to God's sovereign will when it suits us to do so. Let's not forget that church and political leaders early in America's history offered seemingly foolproof biblical arguments for an unbiblical thing: chattel slavery.

While the American church has often failed to speak out on the immorality of racism, throughout history we have frequently spoken out in favor of earthly leaders, even proclaiming them God's man (or woman) for the job. We aren't qualified to grant such endorsements, but we do so anyway, even quoting scriptures—such as "[God] removes kings and sets up kings" (Dan. 2:21)—to justify our view that God has placed our preferred politician in power.

When one of our leaders comes under fire for saying or doing something that runs counter to our faith, it is all too easy to fall back on scriptures that not only elevate God's sovereignty above the actions or choices of humans but also justify and offer divine approval of sinful actions. We may say something like "I know that he/she says some pretty crazy things, but God put him/her into office for such a time as this! Besides, what about those liberal Democrats?"

What we don't seem to acknowledge is that if this view of God's sovereignty is true—that our political leaders assume positions of power according to God's will and without human involvement in the process—then Reagan, the Bushes, and Trump were not the only ones who were God's men "for such a time as this" (Est. 4:14), but so were Carter, Clinton, and Obama.

Some in the conservative camp point out that God placed evil kings like Nebuchadnezzar in power but surrounded them with faithful believers such as Daniel, Shadrach, Meshach, and Abednego. Since God sometimes uses evil people for his purposes, they argue, we can be at rest when leaders who promise to defend our faith speak and lead in ways that run counter to our faith.

In a technical sense, this is true: God does use leaders and nations to accomplish his will. However, this analogy is far from flawless. First of all, Daniel and his three friends were taken captive as slaves, not as citizens. They did not vote Nebuchadnezzar into office by means of an established democratic process. Rather, they were human spoils of war who, by God's design, were eventually elevated to positions of influence under their totalitarian conquerors.

Second, and most important, while Daniel and his friends served their captors admirably and were even used by God to influence them, they refused to comply with edicts that violated the ways of God. Daniel's defiance of the ungodly king landed him in a den of lions, and his three friends ended up in a fiery furnace. In both cases, God expected his servants to remain true to his ways rather than using his sovereignty as an excuse for accommodating wickedness.

God's expectations of us are the same today, even if we live downstream of the destructive legacies of slavery and racism that still exist in our culture. The American church may have missed opportunities to speak out against racism throughout our founding and again during Reconstruction, but we mustn't chalk up this failure to divine sovereignty. Yes, God is sovereign, but he also expects his people to follow his ways in all situations. Abdicating this responsibility throughout our nation's history created space for the worst kinds of leaders to exert influence at the most inopportune times, influence God intended the church to have instead.

The good news is that God is not done with us. We are not confined by these legacies. Our greatest legacy is the grace of God that is working in us to make all things new. Instead of rewriting the history of our nation, let's continue an honest inventory of slavery and racism, accepting the truth of our tragedies and bringing our wounds to Christ so that we can be transformed. As our ways of thinking change, we'll move toward a better legacy for future generations.

CHAPTER 8

REWRITING HISTORY

As a white kid growing up in the South," John recalled, "I was taught that racism is wrong and that we should try not to acknowledge color to avoid racism. I don't remember anyone actually saying this, but that was the lesson I learned one way or another."

Reggie laughed. "Funny you say that, but I was kind of taught the same thing. Dad gave us talks about racism, but we tried to not address it outside of these private conversations."

"Our teachers at school and church weren't actively teaching us to be racist; in fact, we were told that racism was wrong. Yet from a historical perspective, everything they did teach made it seem like slavery and racism were things of the distant past that needed to be forgotten." John paused to reflect. "I do remember many people, especially friends from childhood, who felt that slavery 'wasn't as bad as people say it is.' Some even went as far as saying that it was a good situation for those who were enslaved because they were treated well, had a purpose, and were basically members of the slaveholders' families."

"Bro, tell me that ain't true."

"It was, but I think I know where those kinds of ideas came from."

"Where?"

"Well, when I began teaching history near the foothills of the Smoky Mountains in East Tennessee, I routinely heard this same sanitized narrative about slavery from my students. We all know that what kids say is often what they've heard at home, so my students were just repeating a perspective that was apparently important enough to be talked about in their homes. It was common to hear kids tell me that they were wearing Confederate-flag belt buckles or T-shirts not out of hate but out of a desire to preserve their Southern heritage."

"Bro," Reggie replied, "could you imagine that German students would pin swastikas on their shirts claiming it wasn't out of hate but to preserve their German heritage?"

"Exactly! But you know that such a comparison would be considered very offensive to many white Southerners because the atrocities of the Holocaust somehow seem like something worth acknowledging, but not the atrocities of slavery."

"That is a very true statement. How did you reach your students?"

"Well, I'm not sure I did, but I tried something that points to the historical reason they thought the way they did. I would say, 'I can accept that you want to preserve and honor your heritage, and I can tell that it means a lot to you. So if the cause of the Confederacy is so very dear to your heart and your family legacy, surely you will have no trouble naming five Confederate generals who fought in the war.'"

Reggie laughed. "Let me guess . . . crickets."

"Yep." John chuckled. "But they could all name one general—Robert E. Lee. They didn't know it, but there was a specific reason they did: the Lost Cause."

• • •

As we continue our honest inventory on racism, we come to a pivotal narrative that affects much of the conversation about racism today, though we may not be aware of it. As many people debate the issue of Confederate monuments being vandalized and torn down, decrying these actions as the rewriting of history, another rewriting of history has taken place that is often unacknowledged. It represents legacy-based ideas we hold dear, which are passed down to us through family or the history we were taught.

In 1866, Virginia Confederate and journalist Edward Alfred Pollard wrote a book titled *The Lost Cause: A New Southern History of the War of the Confederates*. Pollard openly claimed his work was a new history, and that's exactly what it was. It whitewashed and simplified the complex causes of the Civil War, preying upon the wounded consciousness of a Southern society utterly decimated by five years of brutal warfare that left their countryside and their economic systems in utter disarray. Instead of seeing in their own inventory the truth—that social upheaval was the inevitable outcome of the "peculiar institution" of slavery that many of the founders had foreseen and tried to delay or avoid through many compromises and conflicts less severe than war—Southerners were fed a different story to soften the ideological blow. The powder keg had exploded, and slavery was the chief cause. But the Lost Cause instigated a seismic shift in the narrative, and we are still feeling the aftershocks more than one hundred and fifty years later.

Pollard was not alone in this effort. Virginia lawyer Jubal Early and former Confederate president Jefferson Davis were other leading voices in fostering this new perspective on the war and its aftermath. These ideas resonated with Southerners and white people around the nation, resulting in an ongoing war of ideas that Pollard himself dubbed "the Lost Cause."

It is important to note that the idea of Pollard and others attempting to rewrite history is not a construct of contemporary historians. The book title was Pollard's idea, and his book was published to advance a popular revisionist set of ideas that accomplished at least one of Pollard's original goals: to rewrite the history of the Civil War in the minds of future Southerners and perhaps even Americans in general.

Pollard's ideas centered on white superiority and a special sense of nobility and victimization ascribed to the South and its way of life. According to historian Jon Meacham, "The question was no longer slavery, but white supremacy, which Pollard described as the 'true cause of the war' and the 'true hope of the South.'"[1]

Here is how historian Jemar Tisby describes the fundamentals of the Lost Cause:

[It is] a narrative about southern society and the Confederate cause invented after the Civil War to make meaning of the devastating military defeat for southern white Americans. The Lost Cause mythologized the white, pre–Civil War South as a virtuous, patriotic group of tight-knit Christian communities. According to the Lost Cause narrative, the South wanted nothing more than to be left alone to preserve its idyllic civilization, but it was attacked by the aggressive, godless North, who swooped in to disrupt a stable society, calling for emancipation and inviting the intrusion of the federal government into small-town, rural life. Confederates reluctantly roused themselves to the battlefield not because of bloodlust or a nefarious desire to subjugate Black people but because outsiders had threatened their way of life and because honor demanded a reaction. Even today, the Lost Cause mythology functions as an alternative history that leads to public disputes over monuments, flags, and the memory surrounding the Civil War, the Confederacy, and slavery.[2]

As Meacham infers, the Lost Cause claimed that the real causes of the war were not what they seemed. Pollard and those who perpetuate this narrative today came up with some key ideas upon which this ideology would rest, including the beatification of Robert E. Lee, the claim that states' rights rather than slavery was the cause of the war, and the demonization of Ulysses S. Grant.

The Beatification of Robert E. Lee

One of the components of the Lost Cause narrative was the elevation of Robert E. Lee to a level of nobility just shy of sainthood. Lee was esteemed not only as a military genius but also as a man of unimpeachable Christian character. A seemingly small yet decisively critical element of the Lost Cause was to link it with Christianity. In effect, the Southern story was rewritten as a kind of holy narrative. University of Mississippi historian Charles Reagan Wilson writes about this in his book *Baptized in Blood*: "R. Lin Cave, a [Confederate] chaplain . . . praised [Lee's] . . . 'reverence for all things holy.' . . . In an understatement, one minister commented that Lee was pure enough to have founded a religion."[3]

In many ways, that's exactly what happened, except that others founded the religion in Lee's name. In the minds of those who advanced the Lost Cause, Robert E. Lee was reimagined not just as a brilliant military leader but as the unjustly conquered savior of the South. That was the storyline implanted deep into the Southern psyche, eventually seeping into the national consciousness as well.

Following his death of a stroke in 1870, Southern and Northern newspapers lionized Robert E. Lee. Commenting on the incongruity between the portrayals and the man himself, abolitionist and statesman Frederick Douglass wrote, "We can scarcely take up a newspaper that is not filled with *nauseating* flatteries of the late Robert E. Lee. . . . It would seem from this that the soldier who kills the most men in battle, even in a bad cause, is the greatest Christian, and entitled to the highest place in heaven."[4]

Lee was lauded for reluctantly taking up arms to defend his beloved Virginia against an aggressive federal government (even though the South fired on the North, opening the eastern theater of the war). Lee was a decorated United States military officer who had fought valiantly in the Mexican-American War and had taken an oath, established in 1787, to "support and defend the Constitution" and "obey the orders of the President of the United States."[5] When the Civil War ignited in April of 1861, Abraham Lincoln asked him to lead the Union forces, a request he denied, despite his solemn oath as an obedient soldier in the United States Army.

As the legendary status of Robert E. Lee has continued to morph in the century and a half since his death, it is often alleged that he either didn't own slaves or set them free. The truth is, Lee owned three or four families of slaves that he inherited after the death of his mother. Later, he inherited another 189 slaves following the death of his father-in-law, George Washington Parke Custis, in 1857. It was actually Custis's will, not Lee's kindheartedness, that stipulated that these slaves were to be set free within five years of his death.[6] Lee took full advantage of his short window as a slave owner and worked the slaves extremely hard in an effort to pay off debts before he was forced to set them free. Fearing that five years wasn't enough time, he unsuccessfully petitioned state courts to extend their term of servitude.

For an indication of his treatment of Black people, we can point to the fact that three of Lee's slaves, Wesley Norris, Norris's sister Mary, and their cousin George Parks, escaped in 1859, fleeing to Maryland before being caught and returned to Lee's estate in Arlington, Virginia (a requirement of the Fugitive Slave Act of 1850). Norris later recalled,

> [General Lee] told us he would teach us a lesson we never would forget; he then ordered us to the barn, where, in his presence, we were tied firmly to posts by a Mr. Gwin, our overseer, who was ordered by Gen. Lee to strip us to the waist and give us fifty lashes each, excepting my sister, who received but twenty; we were accordingly stripped to the skin by the overseer, who, however, had sufficient humanity to decline whipping us; accordingly Dick Williams, a county constable, was called in, who gave us the number of lashes ordered; Gen. Lee, in the meantime, stood by, and frequently enjoined Williams to lay it on well, an injunction which he did not fail to heed; not satisfied with simply lacerating our naked flesh, Gen. Lee then ordered the overseer to thoroughly wash our backs with brine, which was done.[7]

Writer Sean Kane concludes, "Robert E. Lee owned slaves. He managed even more. When defied, he did not hesitate to use violence typical of the institution of slavery, the cornerstone of the cause for which he chose to fight."[8]

As two men raised in the South, we were both taught a different view of Lee than what these historical and scholarly records show.

Now we know why: the "system" in which we lived—in this case, cultural perceptions and the legacy of ideas passed down through multiple generations—affected what we were taught.

This isn't the only element of the Lost Cause we recognize in our upbringing. To this day, many in the South argue over the true cause of the Civil War, another intentional feature of Pollard's Lost Cause narrative.

Swapping Out Slavery for States' Rights

Another hallmark of the ongoing Lost Cause narrative is the claim that the Confederacy fought not over the issue of slavery but over the issue of states' rights. According to the narrative, Southern states were merely protecting themselves from Northern aggression. This line of thinking persisted in the national consciousness into the twentieth century, evidenced in popular books and motion pictures, such as *Gone with the Wind*.

The written declarations of secession that Southern states formally presented to the US government leave no doubt that slavery was at the center of the debate. In 1861, the state of Mississippi declared, "Our position is thoroughly identified with the institution of slavery—the greatest material interest of the world." It also accused the Union of "[advocating] negro equality, socially and politically, and [promoting] insurrection and incendiarism in our midst."[9]

South Carolina echoed these sentiments, justifying its secession because of "an increasing hostility on the part of the non-slaveholding States to the institution of slavery." Georgia followed suit, stating, "The question of slavery was the great difficulty in the way of the formation of the Constitution. While the subordination and the political and social inequality of the African race was fully conceded by all, it was plainly apparent that slavery would soon disappear."[10]

As these declarations demonstrate with unapologetic clarity, the Civil War was absolutely fought over slavery and against the backdrop of the Confederate states' foundational belief in white supremacy. Any claims of states' rights or an overreach of federal power as the true causes of the Civil War are a fabrication. The real issue was the ownership of Black Americans as property. That was the heart of the matter about which Southern states were clamoring, in the firm belief that their constitutional rights had been violated. The fact that so many Americans today still believe that slavery wasn't the central issue in the Civil War is testament to the effectiveness of the Lost Cause narrative.

Like all good fiction, this narrative established a sympathetic hero who faced a major challenge to life and limb outside of his control. In this case, the hero, Robert E. Lee, confronted the aggression of the North to deny Southern states their rights. Every story needs a villain, so the Lost Cause apologists chose the military leader who bested their hero in real life: Ulysses S. Grant. For this part of their reboot of history, the details of Lee's defeat and the man who brought it about required many revisions.

The Demonization of Ulysses S. Grant

A third component of the Lost Cause narrative was reframing why Confederate military forces lost. The new narrative suggested that Southern forces weren't actually bested by superior military skill but were overcome by the vast, well-funded Union forces, which were, nevertheless, inferior in terms of skill, training, strategy, and above all else, honor. The story of the South evolved into the heroic tale of a small number of noblemen bullied by barbarians from the North, who wanted to rob the South of their genteel and industrious way of life.

If Robert E. Lee was the hero in the Lost Cause narrative, then no other man fit the role of villain better than the victorious Union general Ulysses S. Grant. Even into the 1980s and 1990s, those of us who grew up in the South were taught in college that Grant wasn't much of a military mind but was a drunk and a butcher who had no other strategy rolling around between his ears than sending a succession of young soldiers to their deaths until the Confederacy eventually ran out of bullets with which to shoot them. No esteem was ascribed to Grant's success as a Union general or his military acumen, which played a key role in preserving the nation he later served as a two-term president.

The truth about Ulysses S. Grant differs considerably from the Lost Cause narrative. In his own time and into the late nineteenth century, historians considered Grant to be among the "front rank" of US presidents, along with George Washington, Thomas Jefferson, and Abraham Lincoln.[11] Frederick Douglass considered Grant as influential as Lincoln, if not more so: "May we not justly say . . . that the liberty which Mr. Lincoln declared with his pen General Grant made effectual with his sword—by his skill in leading the Union armies to final victory?" Douglass considered Grant to be "the vigilant, firm, impartial, and wise protector of my race."[12]

Grant was an alcoholic, but more in a clinical sense than a destructive one. With the help of a few people, namely his close friend and chief aid General John Rawlins, he dealt with this demon throughout his life, but there is little historical evidence that it ever affected his official duties or his family. Despite the fact that he faced much hardship, poverty, and failure in his life, those who knew him considered him a thoughtful, humble, and deeply principled man and leader.

Comparatively speaking, Grant treated Black people much differently than his counterpart, Lee. Lost Cause narrators sometimes claim that Grant was a slave owner, no different from the Southerners against whom he fought the war. The reality was that his wife, Julia, was the daughter of Southern slave owners, the Dent family. Grant, on the other hand, was born into a family of abolitionists. There was no love lost between a young Grant and the father of his bride, Colonel Frederick Dent, a Confederate to the core.

Once Ulysses and Julia were married, Colonel Dent gifted his daughter four slaves for her use, though he never transferred legal ownership to her because he didn't want his son-in-law to become their master under Missouri law. Grant had made it clear that he would set them free.[13] Among the peers of the Dent family, Grant was known as someone who opposed the institution of slavery and treated Black people with kindness, paying them wages and even working alongside them in the fields.[14] This infuriated his fellow white citizens who considered such things an affront to their (white supremacist) sensibilities.

The only hint of truth in the accusation that Grant owned slaves may be that in 1859 his father-in-law transferred to him ownership of a thirty-five-year-old mulatto slave named William Jones, perhaps as a gift. Grant filed papers in the circuit court of Saint Louis to emancipate William. Grant was poor at the time, so setting William free also meant forfeiting potential financial gain from William's labor or from selling him to another slave owner. It was a bold action that didn't earn Grant any friends, but it clearly demonstrated where he stood on the issue of slavery.[15]

In terms of his ability as a military commander, Grant was one of the first generals of his time to manage and implement a cohesive strategy across multiple armies and on multiple fronts, including innovative supply lines and modern communication processes. He managed millions of men and dollars in a way that none of his contemporaries, including Lee, were capable of doing. Historian Ron Chernow writes, "In summarizing his salient qualities [in 1885], *The New York Times* foresaw that in future generations 'if a great soldier is indomitable in purpose and exhaustless in courage, endurance, and equanimity; if he is free from vanity and pettiness, if he is unpretentious, truthful, frank, constant, generous to friends, magnanimous to foes, and patriotic to the core, of him it will be said, "He is like Grant."'"[16]

Even in his lifetime, Grant was aware of the impact the Lost Cause narrative would likely have on his legacy. Though it is doubtful he could have known it would eventually erase most of his honorable accomplishments, including those he enacted as president, such as ratifying the Fourteenth and Fifteenth Amendments and using the military to put down the Ku Klux Klan. Feeling the growing sentiment of the Lost Cause in his own time, he said, "The Southern generals were seen as models of chivalry and valor—our generals were venal, incompetent, coarse . . . Everything that our opponents did was perfect. Lee was a demigod, Jackson [Stonewall] was a demigod, while our generals were brutal butchers."[17]

In terms of Grant's presidency, his administration was beset with scandals various members of his cabinet and other political appointees perpetuated, but certainly no more than modern administrations. Beyond that, Grant's dealings with Native Americans left his legacy with a justified black eye, but in terms of the Lost Cause, this issue is rarely cited as a reason for denigrating him. After all, white supremacy is no respecter of persons of color, be it Black people or brown people from indigenous nations.

Grant's tarnished legacy, Lee's sanctification, and the martyr-dom narrative of the noble South were all components in a war of ideas (misinformation, to be exact) that continues to this day on new cultural battlefields.

The Monumental Rewriting of History

In the aftermath of George Floyd's killing on May 25, 2020, statues and monuments around the nation and the world became battlefields in this perpetual war of ideas. Protesters defaced or tore down many of them,[18] which sparked a cycle of counterprotests. This war of ideas reveals the heart of the issue we are addressing in this book, as well as the ongoing legacy of the Lost Cause narrative.

One statue in Richmond, Virginia, at the epicenter of this battle valiantly depicts on horseback the hero of the Lost Cause, Robert E. Lee. Following George Floyd's death, the governor of Virginia vowed to have it removed from public lands, but a lawsuit prevented this from happening. Months later, a circuit judge ruled that the monu-ment could be removed, citing the testimony of expert witnesses who "described a post-war South where the white citizenry wanted to impose and state unapologetically their continued belief in the validity and honor of their 'Lost Cause,' and thereby vindicate their way of life and their former Confederacy." The judge added, "It was out of this backdrop that the erection of the Lee Monument took place."[19] The statue was erected not to honor history but to sustain a legacy of white supremacy that the Confederacy fought to preserve.

Many people are disturbed and insulted when protestors in

cities across the United States tear down or demand the removal of monuments to various Confederate leaders. Opponents of this desecration cry foul, as if the nation's history is being rewritten. What they fail to realize is that most of those monuments were erected for the express purpose of rewriting history.

Nearly three decades after the Civil War, organizations such as the United Daughters of the Confederacy began to spring up in the 1890s, lobbying for new legislation to honor Confederate leaders and ideals and for funds to build monuments to commemorate the heroes of the new war narrative. It's important to note that thousands of monuments were erected not immediately after the war but decades later during the height of the Jim Crow era, and their purpose was not to preserve heritage or memorialize the dead but to promote the Lost Cause narrative.

At the time of this writing, a bronzed bust of Confederate General Nathan Bedford Forrest still stands in the Tennessee State Capitol building in Nashville. Forrest, a Confederate hero, was the first Grand Wizard of the Ku Klux Klan. He was in command at the Battle of Fort Pillow, where more than three hundred Black Union soldiers on their knees were denied the right to surrender in battle—a human right both sides agreed on. Instead, they were butchered on the spot, a warning to other Blacks not to run away and fight for the North.

There is evidence that, late in life, Forrest repented of his inhumane crimes of racism. While this is encouraging and certainly what we as Christians should hope for with anyone enslaved by sin, the bust of Forrest at the Tennessee Capitol does not depict repentance for butchering Black soldiers in the Civil War or terrorizing Black people when Forrest was in the KKK. Instead, he is depicted as a regal figure in his Confederate uniform at his highest rank.

If you think the bust of Nathan Bedford Forrest is a relic of a bygone era, you're mistaken. The Tennessee State Legislature approved its creation in 1987—more than one hundred and fifty years after the end of the Civil War. This is a blatant display of racism still active in our systems of government and politics, and we must not turn a blind eye to such displays.

Another monument commemorating a Civil War battle was erected in New Orleans in the 1890s, thirty years after the Civil War. It was torn down in 2017, despite much protest. However, the monument's inscription revealed the not-so-subtle intentions of such edifices: "United States troops took over the state government and reinstated the usurpers, but the national election, November 1876, recognized white supremacy in the South and gave us our state."

This inscription reveals the truth: Confederate monuments are not about history. They are about what they've always claimed to be about: perpetuating a narrative that sustains a legacy of racism and white supremacy.

Erecting monuments on battlefields where soldiers lost their lives is one thing, but erecting monuments to the ideals of white supremacy in public spaces is another thing entirely. The history of the Confederacy can be rightly remembered at battlefields, cemeteries, and museums, but to honor them in full regalia in public spaces we all share is to honor what they fought for. We must handle this part of our history with care. That isn't to say we should feel bad about our family histories—we can't choose the families into which we are born, and we don't have to denounce them for their mistakes. We can acknowledge our family trees and our families' misdeeds—this tension is healthy. Since the white coauthor of this book has ancestors who fought for both the North and the South, we acknowledge this complex heritage.

We must recognize the difference between propaganda and personal history, and become aware of the ways propaganda has changed how people view slavery, the Civil War, and the ongoing legacy of these atrocities. As attorney and advocate Bryan Stevenson attests, "The North won the Civil War, but the South won the narrative war." Tragically, the authors of the Lost Cause succeeded. In an interview with *CBS This Morning*, Stevenson went on to say, "[White people in the South] weren't required to repudiate and acknowledge the wrongfulness of bigotry and slavery. They actually glorified that era, and that created a century where black people were pulled out of their homes, beaten, drowned, hanged in this era of terrorism, but we haven't talked about it."[20]

Another significant thing to note about that monument from New Orleans is the date. The year 1876 was a turning point in the postwar era, something we need to keep in mind to understand how white supremacy continued to thrive, especially in the South.

The *Real* Lost Cause

President Grant's two terms in office were far from easy, but his replacing the racist and ineffectual Andrew Johnson marked the beginning of the Reconstruction era Lincoln had envisioned. During Grant's tenure at the helm of the nation, the Fourteenth and Fifteenth Amendments to the Constitution were adopted, making the federal government, rather than the states, primarily responsible for protecting the human and civil rights of Black Americans. And Grant took the enforcement of these rights seriously.

The new legislation created new life among Black communities in the South. Black men seized the opportunity to vote, electing many Black men to various state legislatures and Congress. Public schooling was afforded to Black children, and institutions of higher education opened to Black adults. For a few years, Lincoln's hopeful experiment seemed to be working.

However, white supremacists in the South who felt threatened by the advancements of their former slaves began to take matters into their own hands. They organized the Ku Klux Klan in the mid-1860s and, over the following years, engaged in nefarious endeavors to terrorize and intimidate Black people to force them into submission and prevent them from assuming any position of power or becoming upwardly mobile. Horrifying stories of brutality began to surface, including accounts of lynchings and the slaughter of hundreds of Black voters who dared to show up at polling stations to exercise their constitutional right to vote.

When these attacks arose during Grant's first term as president, he mobilized the United States military under the command of his former Civil War comrade and most trusted general William Tecumseh Sherman. Sherman was not nearly as progressive on the issue of Reconstruction or racial equality as Grant, but orders were orders. Union soldiers became an occupying force in the South to keep the peace and enforce Reconstruction policies. It was an aggressive strategy, but it proved effective in tracking down and arresting members of the KKK and others who violated the law. For a brief time, Reconstruction advanced Lincoln's vision for what life could become for Black citizens in a post–Civil War America.

Maintaining this vision long-term, however, presented a number of challenges. For one thing, sustaining an occupying force in the South was expensive, costing the nation and taxpayers millions of dollars each year. In addition, many Northerners who may have been intellectually opposed to slavery were not really sold on equal rights for Black people in practice. Racism was still alive and well in America. As political scandals plagued Grant's cabinet and staff, his political and operational capital began to wane. Toward the end of Grant's second term, it looked as if national support was also waning for his efforts to keep white supremacists in line in the South.

Everything came to a head in 1876, when Republican Rutherford B. Hayes and Democrat Samuel Tilden found themselves embroiled in a disputed election. (Sound familiar?) The nation fell into political chaos that lasted for months. As the Republican candidate and the supposed successor to Lincoln and Grant, Hayes was expected to continue to champion Reconstruction. On the other hand, it was feared that an administration under Tilden would signal the end of Reconstruction.

As composer Lin-Manuel Miranda wrote in the musical *Hamilton*, no one was in the room where it happened, but what happened next set back the cause of civil rights another hundred years. In some obscure, smoked-filled chamber, unelected party officials struck a bone-chilling compromise to resolve the disputed election. The Southern Democrats agreed to allow Hayes to claim the presidency on one condition: that he remove Union troops from the South.

Hayes feared that a Tilden election would end Reconstruction, but ironically, his own election did. Hayes became president under the guise of protecting the rights of former slaves, but he eliminated the only means of doing so—Union troops.

Immediately, life for Black people in the South descended into renewed chaos and terror. Southern states passed discriminatory legislation that came to be known as Jim Crow laws, which enforced strict racist and segregationist policies. Without the Union army present to enforce the Constitution, white supremacists engaged in violent campaigns to retake control of their communities. As the New Orleans monument commemorated, 1876 was the year that white supremacy was restored to the South, and freedom became the real lost cause for Blacks for another 120 years.

Lynching once again became commonplace in the South. There was no justice for Black Americans in state and local law enforcement or judicial systems, and the federal government turned a blind eye. In another ironic twist, many of our modern patriotic traditions emerged during this time. In 1892, for example, the Pledge of Allegiance was written with a key phrase lauding our national value of "liberty and justice for all."

By the 1910s and 1920s, Jim Crow—the violent, governmental enforcement of the Lost Cause narrative—had become an accepted way of life and thinking across the nation. In 1915, President Woodrow Wilson hosted a White House viewing of a silent movie called *The Birth of a Nation* and praised its merits. It was an overtly racist film with white actors in blackface portraying Black men as sexually aggressive buffoons who were a threat to white society, and to white women in particular. It also portrayed the actions of the KKK as noble efforts to recapture and protect white culture. The film reverberated throughout the nation, causing many white supremacists to dust off their hidden sheets and go public.

In 1925, some thirty thousand KKK members marched on Washington, DC, in proud racist regalia, representing a staggering number of federal, state, and local officials who had no qualms about parading their views on white supremacy. Slavery had been abolished, but racism was still very much alive, even bolstered by new and growing pseudoscientific theories about the intellectual and moral superiority of the white race.

The Klan grew in political clout at an astounding rate. American political-history scholar David H. Bennett notes why it appealed to so many, writing, "The Klan offered structure, position, and brotherhood to many restive or disoriented men from small towns and big cities in the America of the 1920s."[21] All told, eleven US governors were open Klansmen, along with sixteen US senators. It is estimated that more than seventy-five House members were also members of the Klan, as well as future justice of the Supreme Court Hugo Black.[22]

It's not hard to imagine the impact these men had on our systems of government. Civil rights leaders just a few decades later weren't fighting only for equality; they were fighting against this long-established, finely tuned system of racist mindsets and policies that were technically illegal and openly practiced for nearly one hundred years.

All of this, and more, was a consequence of abandoning Reconstruction reforms and accepting a passive attitude toward racism that soon reverted to normalizing violence toward Black people. It was a state of affairs against which leaders such as Ulysses S. Grant would have fought, especially at a time when the cause of "liberty and justice for all" might otherwise have been greatly advanced.

As technology progressed, ideology regressed. In 1935, sociologist and activist W. E. B. Du Bois summed up this dissonance between the progression of modern technology and the regression of race relations: "If the Reconstruction of the Southern states, from slavery to free labor, and from aristocracy to industrial democracy, had been conceived as a major national program of America, whose accomplishment at any price was well worth the effort, we should be living today in a different world."[23] As the nation advanced, the cause of racial justice and equity declined. American society's energy for industrialization and technological progress was seemingly endless, but its collective energy to keep working to heal the wounds of slavery after the Civil War had faded back in 1876. A fresh and ever-growing infusion of energy in the form of white supremacy took its place not only in the national and political spheres of influence but also in the church.

A Legacy and Lessons for the Church

While there were exceptions, the American church was mostly complicit in Jim Crow practices. During Reconstruction and the Jim Crow era that followed, most Southerners identified as Bible-believing Christians, but their errant views of Scripture allowed them to defend slavery, horrific violence, and the systemic oppression of Black people.

Membership in the Ku Klux Klan sounds pretty extreme to most of us today, but it was normal for many in the early twentieth century, including those in the church. In the North alone, KKK membership in the 1920s and 1930s is estimated to have been between three and five million, and the Klan claimed to have forty thousand ministers in its ranks.[24]

Between 1877 and 1950 in the twelve Southern states, there were more than 4,400 documented lynchings.[25] Terrifying accounts of the brutal lynching of Black men and women—pregnant women as well—sometimes occurred on the grounds of Black churches to further intimidate and destabilize family and social structures in the Black community. After all, law enforcement and judicial officials were also members of the Klan. According to some accounts, body parts were hacked from screaming victims and passed around among onlookers as souvenirs. Many of these onlookers considered themselves to be Christians.

How was such an overt violation of Christian faith possible in our grandparents' generation? Historian Jemar Tisby points out, "The majority stance of the American church was avoidance, turning a blind eye to the practice. It's not that members of every white church participated in lynching, but the practice could not have endured without the relative silence, if not outright support, of one of the most significant institutions in America—the Christian church."[26]

Ultimately, the church's complicity with slavery and its aftermath was possible because ordinary people mixed their desires for power, social standing, and wealth with their Christianity to the point that they could no longer tell the difference between what God wanted and what they wanted.

At the very least, Christians should have been openly condemning racism and violence against Black people. In not speaking up for what was right or speaking out against what was wrong, an ostensibly Christian nation lost its moral voice, even as it thumped the Bible in defense of its own misguided morality.

The larger lesson for us today concerns the slow descent of faith, awareness, and decency when God's righteousness and justice are not valued above our own advancement or comfort. For our white forebears, white supremacy and all it entailed seemed right in the moment, even marching with the KKK, or worse. Their faith was so compromised by racist lies that they believed they loved and followed God's ways even while terrorizing Black men and women made in his image. At best, they turned a blind eye to racial injustice—for decades.

Surely if it was possible for our grandparents' generation to be deceived in such ways, it is possible for us to be deceived as well—to mix misguided notions with our faith, producing a toxic brew we don't realize we're drinking until we're so drunk on it that we can no longer tell the difference between the two.

Is it possible to mean well yet think in ways that don't support the well-being of others? Is it possible that there are deeper reasons in our hearts and our systems for the ongoing segregation of Black and white people in our churches? Is it possible that our reactions to the words "Black lives matter" aren't just happening in a vacuum but reflect a vast array of historical and cultural elements embedded in our inventory of our nation and the church?

Are we willing to keep leaning into this inventory so we can better understand how our history has contributed to the legacy of systemic racism?

CHAPTER 9

WHITE PRIVILEGE AND THE LIBERAL BOGEYMAN

I don't think anything inflames people in these conversations more than the term *white privilege*." Reggie knew that even bringing up the subject with John could lead to awkward places.

"Man, I've had the same experience," John said. "People get so angry! I used to struggle with the term, too, until I researched what it means and what it doesn't mean."

Reggie took a breath. "Right, a lot of people seem to think it means calling all white people racist or telling them they should feel guilty for being white."

"Or," John added, "that white people haven't worked hard in their lives."

"Right. The bottom line is that neither of us comes from a wealthy family, and both of our parents worked hard to provide for our families. These things have nothing to do with white privilege."

"Exactly," John replied. "I've heard a lot of conservative commentators talk about it in those terms, and that's all it takes for many people to feel offended and stop listening, without learning what the term actually means."

• • •

So far our inventory has revealed a number of ways the church and our nation missed opportunities to engage racism rightly, which inflicted countless wounds for Black people in America. As the gospel reveals, friends and true community can help wounded people navigate their painful experiences toward a place of perspective and healing where they can begin to function in healthier ways. But those who want to help must be invited, and they will be invited only under certain conditions: they must genuinely care about the individual's past experiences and present well-being, be willing to listen with patience and empathy, and refuse to demand immediate healing.

Yes, individuals make their own decisions, but it is inaccurate to assume that those decisions are made in a vacuum or on an even playing field. Some Americans rise above their circumstances to achieve "the American dream" we all aspire to. Some families, Black and white, struggle with poverty and work hard to make as much as they can of the opportunities afforded them. Many Black families work just as hard as others but are still trying to overcome a four-hundred-year-old generational legacy of slavery and discrimination that denied their ancestors the freedom white people enjoyed.

This brings us to another term of offense: *white privilege*.

Defining White Privilege

Many assume that the term *white privilege* is a recent creation, but researcher Peggy McIntosh used it more than thirty years ago to describe "an invisible package of unearned assets that I [a white person] can count on cashing in each day . . . like an invisible weightless knapsack of special provisions, maps, passports, codebooks, visas, clothes, tools, and blank checks."[1] Conceptually, it represents inherited systems that afford privileges to the majority culture in ways its members don't necessarily recognize.

This definition is important to note because so many Christians and conservatives have wrongly characterized the concept of white privilege as racist. They argue that holding members of an entire race accountable for something they can't help (being white) or for atrocities committed against Black people long before they were born is itself racist. But white privilege isn't about blaming white people for being white or for our nation's racist past. Ironically, many conservatives demonstrate white privilege, as McIntosh defines it, by attempting to dictate how the term and the narrative on racism should be defined and then insisting that white privilege doesn't actually exist.

Outside of far-right circles, white privilege simply means that regardless of the state in which white people find themselves—rich or poor—they don't have added disadvantages related to the color of their skin.

That's it.

White privilege does not mean that white people are responsible for slavery or racism. Nor does it contend that all white people are rich, that they haven't worked hard to get where they are in life, or that they were given extra things they don't deserve.

The idea of added disadvantage is important because it addresses another misconception about white privilege, which is that the grand-parents, parents, and families of many white people were just as poor as anyone else; they simply worked hard to get ahead. So it's insulting to ascribe to them any sort of privilege. But we can remove this stinger from the term *white privilege* when we realize that it addresses only the *added* disadvantage of race, and the elements of status or socioeconomics that might fit within the general concept of privilege.

However, a good gospel question we need to ask ourselves as Christians is "Do I really believe I deserve every good thing in my life?" American exceptionalism and meritocracy—the ideas that we can and should pull ourselves up by our bootstraps, and that we earn everything we have—would respond yes. But the gospel clearly says no.

Humility reminds us of God's words to the Israelites: "Beware lest you say in your heart, *'My power and the might of my hand have gotten me this wealth.'* You shall remember the LORD your God, for it is he who gives you power to get wealth, that he may confirm his covenant that he swore to your fathers, as it is this day" (Deut. 8:17–18, emphasis added).

Martin Luther King Jr. also cautioned against the illusion that we all have equal access to opportunity. "It's all right to tell a man to lift himself by his own bootstraps, but it is cruel jest to say to a bootless man that he ought to lift himself by his own bootstraps."[2] Dr. King was speaking not of work ethic but of the reality that life in America is often different for people who are not white. (We've explored some of the historical origins of this reality.)

We don't have to deny the existence of white privilege because we think it's an indictment. It's not an indictment; it is simply a reality. It is a legacy most white people have been privileged to avoid acknowledging or addressing. Those of us who are white have had the privilege of choosing not to talk about racism in our churches or around our tables because it hasn't affected our lives in the ways it has affected the lives of millions of Black people. The fact that it hasn't is also a privilege.

So if white privilege does exist as we have defined it, what then? There is nothing for white people to be insulted about, nothing to feel guilty about, and nothing to get up in arms about. Instead, our gospel disposition of humility and openness can keep us from becoming derailed by semantics.

We know white people in ministry settings who feel that the semantics—or the rules—of acceptable language are constantly changing. To them, using terms such as white privilege is little more than a nod to political correctness. Even if they wanted to speak rightly, they resent that the terms continue to vary. For example, they point out that Black people used to prefer being called Negroes, then blacks (with a lowercase *b*), then Afro-Americans, then African-Americans, and now it's Blacks again (only with a capital *B*). Who can keep up?

In view of the historically easier paths white people have had in getting hired, securing desired housing, pursuing educational opportunities, and more, our frustration over terms is yet another reflection of white privilege. Many white people see this ever-changing set of rules as an obstacle that prevents them from getting on with life. They just want a predictable set of rules they can follow without having to listen and understand issues that don't affect them, especially when they can't dictate the narrative. There is often little awareness or consideration that Black people have a legitimate right to determine the evolution of terms that affect them.

In one church where this issue was raised at a staff meeting, a younger staff member said, "It's not our decision what someone wants to be called. Yes, things are going to continue to change over time, but as a mom with young children, I've decided with my husband that in our home it honors God to always be mindful of the words we use. We may have to keep listening and preferring others, but is that such a bad way to live?"

Her wisdom echoes the admonition of the apostle Paul: "Do not let any unwholesome talk come out of your mouths, but *only* what is helpful for building others up according to *their* needs, that it may benefit those who listen" (Eph. 4:29 NIV, emphasis added). Many of us use this scripture only to warn our children about curse words, but the application is much broader. Other versions translate the word *unwholesome* as "worthless."

In essence, avoid speaking worthless words.

We believe that bickering over the inconvenience of keeping up with terms qualifies as a worthless endeavor. Instead, as Christians, we have the opportunity to take Paul's admonition to heart and speak only what is helpful for building others up according to their needs and for their benefit. Doing so would change the entire conversation about race—or, better said, we'd have actual conversations about race rather than dueling monologues. And we'd stop allowing disputes over words to eclipse the ways of Christ.

The Scare Tactics of Racial Terminology

We've seen how misunderstandings over words like *white privilege* can derail our progress in talking honestly and openly about race. But other words can have the same effect. One example is equating any talk of white privilege or systemic racism with extreme ideologies like socialism, communism, or Marxism. When we are repeatedly told that our nation will descend into socialism or communism if we engage in certain social issues or terms, it's no wonder we resist engaging in conversations about race. That is often the goal of conservative pundits and leaders who tether racism to radical ideologies: to shut down the conversation. Sadly, most people don't seem to question whether the claims are valid. Scare tactics like these keep us from listening to what others have to say about issues such as white privilege.

All too often, in our view, conservative religious and political leaders have used terms such as *liberal* or *socialist* as bogeymen to scare their constituents into voting, donating, or thinking the way they want them to. This is political and spiritual manipulation. We understand how insulting this may sound, but the truth is, these tactics are standard practice in nearly every political debate or pundit commentary, and sometimes even in the pulpit.

In many of the conversations we've had with conservative political and religious leaders, the word *liberal* is dropped into the exchange like an atom bomb that instantly turns any nuance or complexity in the conversation into a mushroom cloud. Just calling someone a liberal saves a lot of time and energy, which is why it happens in so many conversations, whether on television, podcasts, radio, or in person.

Another term used in much the same way is *woke*. Many conservatives who rail against woke culture warn other conservatives to beware of those who are exploring matters of racial justice, even from a biblical perspective. The irony is that counterwokeness permeates much of conservative culture. Many conservatives are so obsessively woke to their opponents' wokeness that they're more afraid of being liberal or woke than they are of failing to adhere to gospel truths.

It doesn't have to be this way. We can break free from this mindset by remembering the tone and instruction of Scripture. After all, "to answer before listening—that is folly and shame" (Prov. 18:13 NIV). It is also folly and shame for conservatism, but we can change that by refusing to accept or perpetuate these scare tactics, and by embracing a humbler state of mind and heart. Paul is clear about this state: "Let your gentle spirit [your graciousness, unselfishness, mercy, tolerance, and patience] be known to all people" (Phil. 4:5 AMP).

"All people" includes the liberals, the woke ones, and the socialists, especially if you're not one of them.

Yes, liberal voices have their own tactics, but as we've pointed out, we're not liberals. So for the purposes of this book, we're more concerned with holding our own tribe accountable. The errant tactics of another tribe do not dismiss or excuse our own. To think they do is not only unbiblical but also childish.

Earlier we mentioned a common scare tactic some conservative leaders use to shut down conversations about racism. They follow a predictable sequence that involves using the terms *liberal* or *socialist* and then tethering conversations about white privilege or racial justice to them before launching into falsely equivalent stories to illustrate the connection and the tragic outcomes.

One popular conservative voice, a Canadian professor named Jordan Peterson, demonstrated this tactic with precision. In an open forum in which he was asked about white privilege, he responded, "I think the idea of white privilege is absolutely reprehensible." During the applause that followed, he added something very important that the audience didn't seem to hear: "And it's not because white people aren't privileged." In this one sentence, he acknowledged the validity of the concept of white privilege, but only for a second. He continued, "Most people have privileges of all sorts, and you should be grateful for your privileges and work to deserve them."[3]

Peterson acknowledged that people can possess privileges before they work to earn them, meaning that people can have certain advantages through no merit of their own. Why did he acknowledge this? Because it is an undeniable fact of history, sociology, and culture.

The hitch is his quick turn to the next part. "The idea that you can target an ethnic group with a collective crime, regardless of the specific innocence or guilt of the constituent elements of that group, there is absolutely nothing that's more racist than that. It's absolutely abhorrent." Another eruption of applause. The deed was done. He swiftly pivoted from acknowledging that white privilege exists to making an intellectual leap—that white privilege is a socialist concept (specifically Marxist, as we will see) meant to hold a race responsible for "a collective crime." This is a leap we do not make, and no one we're reading or studying is making this leap. Holding white people collectively responsible for racism is not at all the point of acknowledging and addressing white privilege. However, the threat of that idea alone is menacing enough to keep some white people from even considering the actual definition of white privilege.

Peterson then launched into a history lesson about Russian kulaks in the 1920s. Kulaks were prosperous peasants who owned land and were leaders in their villages.[4] Peterson skipped over a complicated history to suggest that the kulaks were "virtually all killed or raped and or robbed by the collectivists" because they had wealth, which made them criminals in the eyes of the collectivists. Do you see what he did there? By tethering the concept of white privilege to Bolshevik-era Marxists, followed by a story of class-based ethnic cleansing, he made it clear that no one in their right mind in a democratic society would entertain the concept of white privilege, even if the definition is quite different from what he implied.

This is just one example of the scare tactic routinely used to link legitimate racial issues, such as white privilege and systemic racism, to bogeyman terms like *liberalism* or *socialism* and their tragic outcomes, including rape, starvation, and concentration camps.

Neither of us align ourselves with liberalism or socialism, but we do want to point out that there is nothing scary about the words *liberal* or *socialist*. They can't hurt you—they're just words. Understanding the meaning of these terms is the best way—the biblical way—to protect ourselves from any negative effects of their ideologies. If we curb our reactions to these terms long enough to listen, we can avoid being manipulated by those who may be using scare tactics to control thoughtful engagement.

Again, we are not supporters of socialism, but for the sake of understanding, whether or not we realize it, elements of socialism already exist in America and affect our daily lives. Social Security is a socialistic program, as is Medicare, government-funded and mandated public education, a standing army, and federal highway systems. These do not make our nation a mirror image of Soviet Russia or communist China. Not all socialism is created equal, and acting as if it is generates undue, albeit effective, fear. There are so many differences between the United States and Russia and China historically and politically that it is hard to know where to begin.

One significant difference is that Soviet Marxism was more class based than race based and certainly wasn't adopted as a replacement for chattel-based slavery. Furthermore, Russia didn't descend into Marxism from an existing democracy with a long-standing constitution, a system of checks and balances, a bill of rights, a tradition of the peaceful transition of power, term limits for political leaders, or the like. As in China, Russian socialist extremists overthrew monarchial and imperialistic dynasties that had inflicted centuries of abuse on their subjects. This is nothing like our history. This is not to say that the United States is immune from threat. However, comparing conversations about racism to what happened in Russia and China is at best intellectually and historically irresponsible. Nevertheless, it has proved effective in keeping people from listening and engaging the issue at hand: the ongoing legacy of racism in America.

This knee-jerk, fear-based tactic of connecting socialism with racial-justice movements was repeatedly used throughout midtwentieth century to deter Americans from addressing racism. It is the ideological equivalent of hitching a wagon full of explosives to a relief vehicle full of needed supplies.

A 1930s poster[5] from the Birmingham, Alabama, branch of the Ku Klux Klan issued this warning: "NEGROES BEWARE. DO NOT ATTEND COMMUNIST MEETINGS. Paid organizers for the communists are only trying to get negroes in trouble. Alabama is a good place for good negroes to live in, but it is a bad place for negroes who believe in SOCIAL EQUALITY. The Ku Klux Klan Is Watching You. TAKE HEED. Tell the communist leaders to leave. Report all communist meetings to the Ku Klux Klan. Post Office Box 651, Birmingham, Alabama. Communism will not be tolerated. KU KLUX KLAN RIDES AGAIN."

The scare tactic here is far from subtle. There's no doubt about why the Ku Klux Klan would use communism to generate fear. While it is certainly a possibility that there were communists in Birmingham during the 1930s, the mere threat of communism was enough to deter any conversations about racial equality. As we noted in chapter 3, in his 1967 speech on the war in Vietnam, Dr. Martin Luther King Jr. addressed the "morbid fear of communism" as one of the ways we have failed to invoke America's "revolutionary spirit" and take action against racism.[6] The ploy is still effective in derailing conversations about social justice today.

Rising above the Scare Tactics

To be clear, no one becomes a Marxist accidentally. Doing so would require intentionally denying Christ, calling for equal distribution of all citizens' assets, and openly working to destroy democracy and capitalism. These are not actions one falls into unaware. If we can rise above the scare tactics, we may address racial issues with more empathy and engagement.

The odds are that our Christian friends, family members, or pastors who are trying to positively address the issue of racism are not communists, radicals, Marxists, or social Marxists (another term that really scares people into avoiding these conversations), especially if they claim they are not. Real adherents of these tribes have no trouble proclaiming their allegiances, so it's probably a little silly to think otherwise of people who do not. Someone planted these

197

suspicious ideas in our heads—and they are the ones we should probably be wary of.

We began this book talking about being willing to examine not only the topics that make us uncomfortable but also how we process and respond to them. Our reactions may seem instinctive, but as we have seen, they may also be conditioned. In this chapter, we have highlighted some of the tactics people use to keep us from listening and engaging in conversations about terms like *white privilege*. Even if well-meaning people employ these tactics innocently or authentically, they can still derail the conversations we need to have about race. If we can avoid getting swept up in the funnel cloud of controversy regarding terms, perhaps we can play a part in ending the tornado of racism. After all, Christ has equipped us to take honest inventories and courageous action. May no fear of terms or ideas deter us from this heroic vision of the gospel.

CHAPTER 10

WHEN GOD AND COUNTRY DON'T GO TOGETHER

I think what alarms me the most about the viewpoints I'm hearing from many conservatives and Christians these days is that there is very little separation between their politics and their religion." John tried not to sound judgy, knowing that Reggie had influence and friends in a lot of conservative and Christian circles.

"What do you mean?" Reggie asked.

"I mean that people talk about America like it's an embodiment of Christianity."

"I don't know if they mean to do it, but people do seem to do that." Reggie wasn't trying to disparage anyone; he was just being honest.

"It scares me from a historical standpoint," John admitted.

"Why is that?" Reggie replied.

"Well, I don't mean to nerd out on you, but anytime in history that a nation put itself in the position of God's kingdom, its leaders had a hard time not acting like God."

• • •

A person may not accidentally stumble into Marxism or socialism, but believe it or not, one *can* inadvertently stumble into fascism. While socialism requires a series of intentional moves away from democracy and Christianity, fascist ideologies can be subtly integrated into them over time so that eventually, people begin to believe that the authoritarian system or leader they have granted power to also has God's seal of approval.

Fascism is an authoritarian ideology characterized by ultranationalism and dictatorial power that leads to forced, often violent, suppression of any opposition and a strong regimentation of society and the economy. To be clear, one doesn't have to be a dictator to exert fascistic or dictatorial power. Fascist ideology can exist even where a fascist regime hasn't secured power.

Basic political science teaches that socialism is the far left of liberalism, while fascism is the far right of conservatism. Many of the recent social posts and conversations among conservatives include a certain quote that originated from a former World War I U-boat commander named Martin Niemöller. Niemöller welcomed Adolf Hitler at the beginning of his ascendency to power in the 1930s but eventually opposed him because he foresaw the logical end of his nationalistic rhetoric and tactics. Niemöller's quote is often posted to warn conservatives about the rise of liberalism and its influence on American society: "First they came for the socialists, and I did not speak out—because I was not a socialist. Then they came for the trade unionists, and I did not speak out—because I was not a trade unionist. Then they came for the Jews, and I did not speak out—because I was not a Jew. Then they came for me—and there was no one left to speak for me."[1]

The irony of conservatives using this quote is that Hitler wasn't a liberal but rather a conservative, just of the extreme sort.

German citizens of the 1920s and 1930s were manipulated on a mass scale by the basic tenets of extreme far-right thinking. Among other elements, fascism combines religion with nationalism, deifying an ideology and its resulting systems. Once deified, the systems must be fiercely protected at all costs because they now seem sacred, even if they violate sacred principles. The definitions of right and wrong are slowly reworked in the foundry of time and extreme rhetoric, which is why it is possible not to realize that you now consider something to be right that was once easily considered wrong. This is how it took only a little over a decade for the Germans to look the other way—and often openly support—the systematic discrimination, disenfranchisement, and ultimate extermination of millions of Jews. They thought they were supporting the right way of thinking.

Fascistic thinking aims to convince those under its influence that there are dangerous "others" in political, racial, or ideological groups who are plotting to take away the rights or possessions that we, the "real" citizens, enjoy. Nazis targeted and persecuted Jews, but it is significant that the Nazis took notes from American systems of racism, specifically the way we had successfully codified racial discrimination into law. Nazis praised the United States' antimiscegenation legislation, which outlawed interracial marriages in thirty of the forty-eight states. Adolf Hitler spoke highly of our successful implementation of Jim Crow laws, which had disenfranchised and terrorized Blacks in the same way he eventually succeeded in disenfranchising and terrorizing Jews by successfully building the German Third Reich.

Yale Law School professor James Whitman wrote, "In *Mein Kampf*, Hitler called America the 'one state' making progress toward the creation of the kind of order he wanted for Germany. In 1935, the *National Socialist Handbook on Law and Legislation*, a basic guide for Nazis as they built their new society, would declare that the United States had achieved the 'fundamental recognition' of the need for a race state."[2]

It has also been said that the Nazis were befuddled when the United States so strongly opposed Hitler's Nazi regime in World War II.[3] After all, Hitler felt that the two nations were very much aligned in their ideologies concerning race—and on many fronts, they were. Yet most Americans today would not conceive of the idea that there was an element of racism in our nation that mirrored Fascist Nazism. Again, this is why certain elements of fascism are so dangerous—they can sound like patriotic rhetoric but with dark undertones we must be diligent to recognize.

Hitler targeted Jews. Italian dictator Mussolini targeted Slavs, Croats, and Jews. Fascism's paradigm is that you target someone—it is the ultimate governmental form of opposition-based thinking. Today there are world leaders who employ similar tactics. New York University professor Ruth Ben-Ghiat explores the rise of these same fascistic ideas: "It's more striking what hasn't changed—the hypernationalism, the leader cult, the idea that this is a leader who is going to save us, the fear of white population decline, anti-feminism, anti-left, things like that."[4] Among Christians today, the conversation about racism has been tied to similar ideas. Instead of listening, there is a general fear of leftist thinking and the decline of the white population. The overwhelming support for Donald Trump among conservative Christians also reflects the belief in a cultlike leader who will save us all from the imminent threats of liberalism to "our" way of life.

Trump and others who support this way of thinking often

point out and harp on the threat liberals pose to the religious liberties of Christians. For what it's worth, many American Christians today often speak out louder for their religious liberties than they do for biblical justice for the poor and marginalized. The principles of the gospel lead us to realize that what we do or don't do with the spiritual liberty we already have in Christ is much more important than fighting for our constitutional religious liberties. As American citizens, we should be thankful for these liberties and should reasonably address them in our civic interactions, but we must also recognize that legally guaranteed religious liberties are not found in Scripture. Tethering the idea that anything remotely contrary to conservative political thinking is an imminent threat to one's religious liberties oversimplifies and demonizes all dissenting viewpoints, even minor ones. It uses fear and conspiracy to manipulate and mobilize large numbers of people to action under a singular extremism.

As we can see, it is not a new tactic, but it's an effective one.

Understanding Nationalism and Patriotism

Fascism finds its strength in nationalism. After scouring scholarly sources, Georgetown University professor and research fellow with the Ethics and Religious Liberty Commission Paul D. Miller defined nationalism as "the belief that humanity is divisible into mutually distinct, internally coherent cultural groups defined by shared traits like language, religion, ethnicity, or culture. . . . Nationalists believe that these groups should each have their own governments; that governments should promote and protect a nation's cultural identity; and that sovereign national groups provide meaning and purpose for human beings."[5] Nationalists believe that a certain cultural group—in the case of American Christian nationalistic thinking, white Christians (or Anglo-Protestants)—characterizes the success of our past, and that "we will lose our identity and our freedom if we do not preserve our cultural inheritance."[6]

Though many Christian nationalists would deny that race is a component of their nationalism, it is embedded in this way of thinking, if nothing else, by the idea that there is always an adversary who is fundamentally an outsider (ethnically, ideologically, religiously, or otherwise) and whose existence in our nation is a threat to *real* Americans.

Nationalism tends to elevate individual freedom as the highest of ideals, even to the detriment of the collective good. It leads us to circle the wagons to an unhealthy degree, seeing only certain people as "real" Americans and most everyone outside of this circle, both foreign and domestic, as a collective enemy. The nationalistic mindset is devoted to protecting and conserving what we have because someone—the social justice warrior, the liberal, the communist, or the "other"—is intent on taking it away. As a result, nationalism creates a constant sense of scarcity, suspicion, and conspiracy thinking. Reason and logic that contradict this mindset are often disregarded, and at its worst, nationalistic thinking manifests as pathological narcissism, filtering every event and every other person in the world through a narrow, self-serving ideological lens.

Nationalists who claim to be Christians may think they believe that God is sovereign, but they behave as if they are the ones in control. American nationalistic thinking has promoted the idea that Christianity can falter if all Christians don't join in their ideological battle, even if it means using tactics that violate Christian principles. In an October 2, 2020, interview on the North Dakota radio show *What's on Your Mind?* Eric Trump stated that his father "literally saved Christianity" from the "full-out war on faith in this country by the *other* side."[7] This is the apex of nationalistic thinking, albeit mixed with Christianity—or, as some call it, Christian nationalism.

From a theological standpoint, there absolutely is an "other," an enemy who seeks to "steal and kill and destroy" all that we are and all that we love (John 10:10). However, he is not a liberal or a socialist, nor is he a physical enemy. The apostle Paul makes it clear that "we do not wrestle against flesh and blood, but against the rulers, against the authorities, against the cosmic powers over this present darkness, against the spiritual forces of evil in the heavenly places" (Eph. 6:12). These may be mysterious words for the enemies that are waging battle against us, but they clearly point away from flesh-and-blood enemies as our greatest concern. As Christians, we are at best misguided when we engage in endless battles against all manner of flesh and blood in our thoughts, words, and attitudes, as well as in our social media posts rather than fighting against our real spiritual enemy.

So what does this mean for Christians who want to be responsible citizens? Delineating the differences between patriotism and nationalism is key. In contrast to nationalism, patriotism is simply a love of or loyalty to one's country. Patriots love their country, but they don't worship it. They love it well by recognizing the need to hold it accountable to its own values. They do this through constitutional processes such as voting, amending the Constitution, and holding their leaders accountable (through elections, checks and balances, impeachment, and other means). As Christian hip-hop and spoken-word performance artist Propaganda says, "I don't hate America, [I] just demand she keeps her promises."[8] Such a statement reflects the ideals of our nation's founders, who, despite all the ways they faltered on matters of race, endeavored to create a system that could be held accountable to its stated ideals.

Nationalists, on the other hand, believe the nation is beyond reproach simply because they—the passionate nationalists—live within its borders, and regardless of who else lives within its borders. In this respect, the intrinsic value of a nation is established not by its belief systems, governmental structure, or diversity of citizenry but rather by the presence of a certain kind of citizen who is a truer citizen than others. As Paul Miller says, "Patriotism is the love of country. It is different from nationalism, which is an argument about *how to define* our country."[9]

Those with a nationalistic mindset treat anyone who questions government policies as an imminent and existential threat, and they devote significant energy (more than it takes to simply listen or focus on peacefully governing) to identifying and denouncing those they deem lesser Americans. We have witnessed this dynamic in social media posts in recent years, with a number of people, including some high-ranking elected officials, suggesting in a knee-jerk response that anyone who criticizes the government or seeks change should leave the country.

Are there viewpoints and policies worth challenging and opposing? Sure. But why are opposing viewpoints no longer the normative reality of a nation built on checks and balances? Why should those who disagree with nationalistic-minded Americans leave America, especially when most nationalists are calling for some kind of change themselves?

These are the dissonances in a nationalistic mindset and in the outcomes it seeks to achieve. Nationalism may raise a lot of American flags and amplify America-first rhetoric, but it is fundamentally un-American because it diverges from what the founders intended. More important, nationalism is contrary to the gospel.

Nationalism becomes even more problematic when it's mixed with religion. An example from early Christian history illustrates why. When Roman Emperor Constantine converted to Christianity in AD 312, Christianity went from being a persecuted faith to an established religion. Certainly, ending persecution was a good thing, but having a ruler who exercised command over both church and state ultimately became a contributing factor in the downfall of the Roman Empire. How could this be?

This downfall was a result of mixing two opposing ideologies—the nationalism of ancient Rome (distinct from modern American nationalism) and Christianity. The sovereign ideals of each could not coexist, and unfortunately, the lesser ideals of Roman nationalism significantly diminished the greater ideals of Christianity. Christians began looking less like followers of Christ and more like followers of the emperor, even though he claimed to follow Christ. Church historian Bruce Shelley writes that "Constantine ruled Christian bishops as he did his civil servants and demanded unconditional obedience to official pronouncements, even when they interfered with purely church matters."[10] Some church leaders hobbled into the new Christian emperor's presence with missing limbs or eyes—evidences of the harsh persecution they suffered under previous emperors.

But the official sanctioning and merging of the Christian faith with the Roman state shifted attitudes away from a once-selfless way of living. "Many [new Christians] came [to have influence in Constantine's regime] who were politically ambitious, religiously disinterested, and still half-rooted in paganism. This threatened to produce not only shallowness and permeation by pagan superstitions but also the secularization and misuse of religion for political purposes."[11] In addition to new Christians, many of the once-persecuted leaders also vied for political clout with the emperor, even asking him to intervene in infighting over doctrines.

Ultimately, Christianity was a factor in the downfall of the Roman Empire not because something was wrong with Christianity but because Christ's kingdom is incompatible with human kingdoms. Jesus does not share power with an emperor, a president, or a political party. His kingdom cannot be fully integrated into the ideologies of any other kingdom. Only one will be left standing: his. While it is good and necessary for Christians to live and even lead in human kingdoms, trying to create a Christian kingdom will always end in downfall. Christ's kingdom has already come. We can't use governmental structures to usher it in through our own efforts.

White Nationalism

If religion and nationalism are incompatible, you can imagine what happens when the racial component of nationalism is emphasized: tragedy and chaos, as we've seen in recent events. The term *white nationalism* is all too common in conversations these days. At its core, it refers to groups of militant white people who espouse white supremacy and advocate some form of racial segregation. Much of the nationalism we see today contains traces of white nationalism with less overt rhetoric, though some people freely espouse white supremacy.

Most Christian conservatives would never consider themselves adherents of white nationalism. And yet their political viewpoints often fall in line with this ideology. There is always a group of "others" out there who pose a threat to law and order—Black, Middle Eastern, South American, or another group of nonwhite persuasion. "These people," they insist, "are always bringing crime into our neighborhoods and lowering our property values. They are always marching toward our borders to take our property, hurt our families, and ruin our democracy." Donald Trump regularly stoked such fears among supporters who wouldn't necessarily consider themselves white nationalists. When the infamous migrant caravan marched toward the southern border of the United States in 2018, Trump tweeted, "Sadly, it looks like Mexico's Police and Military are unable to stop the Caravan heading to the Southern Border of the United States. Criminal and unknown Middle Easterners are mixed in."[12]

Nationalistic rhetoric like this is enough to scare and mobilize white citizens and Christians, though they may not realize this is what they're responding to. But in this case, the fear tactics were not based on fact. The *New York Times* reported that of "the more than 300,000 people apprehended at the southern border in the last fiscal year, 61, or 0.02 percent, were from countries the State Department deems the Middle East or Near East. Of those, 14 were citizens of the four Middle Eastern countries—Libya, Iran, Syria and Yemen—included in Mr. Trump's travel ban. The Department of Homeland Security had '2,554 encounters with individuals on the terrorist watch list' traveling to the United States, according to a January government report. The vast majority—2,170—were trying to enter by air. Just 335 were trying to enter by land, and the report does not note whether those encounters occurred at the southern border."[13] His tweet was more fearmongering than fact.

White nationalists fear the loss of whiteness in America, particularly from the influx or influence of immigrants and minorities. When religious differences between white Americans and these groups are added to the mix, it's obvious how religion and race become so easily married to white nationalism. Yet the idea that whiteness somehow represents the quintessential American is both a social construct and an unfortunate legacy of our founders' belief systems and the system of government they created—a constitutional democracy whose Declaration of Independence acknowledged the divinely granted rights of "Life, Liberty, and the pursuit of Happiness" for white, voting-age males only, most of whom also called themselves Christian.

The founders missed the target not only by failing to protect the rights of so many others—women, children, Blacks, Native Americans, and more—but also by failing to acknowledge that God had granted these rights to all people. They acknowledged that "all men are created equal [and] are *endowed by their Creator* with certain unalienable Rights."[14] They acknowledged God's ways and their desire to build systems reflective of them but then failed to ensure that these systems lived up to God's values for millions of people outside the prevailing power structure and privilege of their day.

For the founders, the issue was not so much whiteness or Blackness as land ownership and status. Yet race was undeniably the epicenter of the matter, and slavery produced the need to define racial identity on a much broader scale. Whiteness became a racial identity because it was the opposite of Blackness—a way to prove and maintain the superior status of white people as citizens and human beings rather than slaves and property.

This is not to say that the eighteenth-century founders did not acknowledge white and Black people—they certainly did. The first national census in 1790 had three categories related to race: "free whites, all other free persons and slaves."[15] There was a time in history when people of European descent would have identified themselves not as white but rather as Polish, French, German, or the like.

Throughout the nineteenth and twentieth centuries, the concept of whiteness continued to evolve in the United States. Early on, as wave upon wave of immigrants settled in predominantly urban areas, white nationalists directed racism toward certain ethnic groups that would be considered white today, including immigrants from Italy, Ireland, and Poland. Anti-Semitism was also prevalent, as white nationalists discriminated against Europeans of Jewish descent or violently mistreated them.

Over time, as more and more groups assimilated into an increasingly diverse America, whiteness began to eclipse European cultural heritage as a marker of privilege and status. Privileges accorded to whiteness included the right to vote, the right to own property in certain areas, due process in the justice system, access to various governmental positions, and membership in private clubs. These privileges developed as a consequence of slavery and Jim Crow policies, a way to distinguish whiteness from Blackness and other ethnicities, such as Latinx, Asian, or Native American.

Above all, whiteness carried with it the right not to be enslaved. Identifying as white became more important—as well as safer and more advantageous—than identifying as Scottish, Irish, Italian, Jewish, or German, though all of these were still preferable to being Black or Native American.

As the concept of whiteness evolved, immigrants began to lose more and more of their cultural heritage. Enculturation—setting aside ethnic cultures and assimilating into American culture—was promoted, especially in the early twentieth century.

President Theodore Roosevelt celebrated the "melting pot" concept of American society. The diversity of people who chose to become Americans remains a strong point of our history and national identity. However, the melting pot concept had devastating side effects as well.

Historian Jon Meacham notes that Roosevelt was "welcoming to certain groups *if* those groups put away their cultures of origin." Meacham elaborates, "TR's capacity on some occasions to stand for equality and for openness and in other contexts to argue that it was the destiny of the Anglo-Saxon peoples to rule the world was a particular example of a more universal American inconsistency. We believed in life and liberty for some; we simultaneously believed in imposing our will on the lives and liberties of others on the grounds that they were innately inferior."[16]

As we continued to define what it meant to be a citizen of this melting pot nation, all of the nations from which we came began to melt away in the pot. What was left was something much simpler to observe and delineate: the color of one's skin. As pastor and activist John Perkins attests, "Whiteness, it turns out, is a very recent idea in the grand scheme of history, but it's a powerful one that was used to create categories and systems that would place value, economically and otherwise, on skin color and the groups of people who were either blessed or burdened by it. If race could be used to indicate a group's level of intelligence, its work ethic, and its tendency to do wrong, then the majority culture could justify all types of bigotries and discriminations."[17]

Unlike being born Scottish, Irish, Nigerian, South African, or even American, technically no one has ever been born white or Black. Since white and Black are more recent cultural appropriations, they are less accurate descriptions of our ethnicity. This shouldn't be insulting to us. It is merely a fact of history and immigration. We don't believe it's necessary to stop using the terms *white* and

Black, since these have come to mean something in our American context, for better and for worse. We only encourage believers to choose the better over the worse, letting our heavenly ethnicity in Christ supersede and inform all of our earthly ethnicities so that we are defined by our lives together in Christ more than by our whiteness or Blackness.

Just as the apostle Paul not only considered his privileges as a prominent Jewish Pharisee and scholar of no value compared with knowing Christ (Phil. 3:7–8) but also maintained a sense of gratitude and honor for his Jewish heritage and his fellow Israelites (Rom. 9:1–5), we, too, can allow the gospel to help us strike a balance between honoring our history and traditions, while intentionally allowing our relationship with Christ to eclipse any cultural bias, prejudice, or privilege. Our primary identity as Christians is not in our skin color or nationality but in our status as citizens of Christ's eternal kingdom. That is our truest identity.

Our kingdom identity does not diminish our human identity as members of various cultures and ethnicities but rather enhances it in a biblical way. There is so much in our nation's history, culture, and diversity that we can celebrate as gifts granted by an infinitely loving Creator. It is time for churches in America to engage in conversations about our earthly differences as a means of worshipping the one who has adopted many ethnicities into one family.

Political Homelessness and Healing

When we begin to see that mixing race or religion with nationalism is harmful to our nation and seek to keep our faith separate from our patriotism, we may still claim a political party or tribe, but we won't be blind followers of a particular ideology or charismatic leader. Many people today are feeling the tension of choosing God's ways at a time when certain political parties claim to be defending God's ways, yet seem to be doing so by ungodly, nationalistic means. On the other hand, they see no viable alternative in other political parties whose beliefs and platforms more directly contradict key elements of their faith. Some of the people feeling this tension have told us they feel like men and women "with no country," a common expression indicative of a sense of belonging rather than actual citizenship. Any time we choose not to play the game of extremes, the extremists will banish us because there is no room for reasonable conversations in narrow-minded circles. As our friend Jonnie W. says about this kind of tribal thinking, "Rarely do people join tribes and then immediately say, 'Ooh, let's go have dinner with the other tribe!'"

Being politically homeless may be uncomfortable, but be encouraged. If you feel like you have no country because you're avoiding the extremes of nationalism, there's a good chance you are exactly where you should be. Pastor Thabiti Anyabwile says, "Political homelessness is not a curse but a blessing. We were never meant to repent for being homeless in this world; we are meant to repent for seeking a home here. Political or otherwise. We are 'looking forward to the city that has foundations, whose designer and builder is God.'"[18]

If we are courageous enough to leave behind those places—political or religious—that are filled with adversarial thinking and bombastic speech, we will enter instead into a quieter place where there is room for empathy and confession. Christ will most certainly meet us there and do the healing work we could never do on our own. As he does this work in our lives, our willingness to confess wrongs and pray for one another contributes to our healing (James 5:16). We can bring into the light what has been hidden in shadows, perhaps allowing a friend of a different color to express the pain of discrimination from people who look like us—maybe even from us.

Bringing past wounds into the light can be painful and messy, but like a surgeon's scalpel, a targeted moment of pain can heal a wound that has been festering for years under the surface. The apostle John alludes to this when he says, "If we walk in the light, as he is in the light, we have fellowship with one another, and the blood of Jesus his Son cleanses us from all sin" (1 John 1:7). Note the progression here. We have to be willing to walk in the light—to allow what is dark and painful to be exposed rather than hidden. If we do so, we have "fellowship" with each other, a biblical word denoting community and intimacy.

It all begins with walking into the light together.

Jesus does something in these moments that we could never do on our own: he "cleanses" us. The Greek word John uses for "cleanse" is the same word other biblical writers use to describe a leper being cleansed from leprosy. To be cleansed is to heal from a terminal, dismembering disease.

Racism is a disease that plagues our nation—not only in the hearts of individuals but also in governmental, business, institutional, and church systems. But cleansing is offered to us through the healing ways of Christ. That healing begins by coming into the light and admitting where we've slipped in our history and our thinking.

CHAPTER 11

DANGEROUS RADICALS AND FATAL EXTREMES

Everybody today loves to quote Martin Luther King Jr.," Reggie said, "but he was the most hated man in America in his time."

"How could people hate someone who talked so much about love?"

"That's what happens when you can't see what you're not seeing. One man who opened my eyes was Reverend G. H. Williams. He lived in Atlanta and used to work with Dr. King. We both spoke at a conference there, but he stole the show."

"I can't even imagine the stories he had to tell!" John replied.

"Oh, man, he was a legend. He told us that when they would get ready to go to a sit-in or a rally—and they knew it was going to be rough and they would be arrested—they would take only three things with them: a toothbrush, a washcloth, and a dime. He said that the police wouldn't give you a washcloth in jail, but if you brought your own, you could wash the blood off your face and brush your teeth. That way, you could always smile in your mug shot."

"Smile? With a bloody face? It sickens me that they knew what they were walking into. It wasn't right. What was the dime for?"

"For making your one phone call. At the event, they showed several pictures of his mug shots. He was smiling through black eyes and a busted nose from rioters and police. But he was the one accused of being a thug, even though he never fought back."

"That's so tragic and wrong," John said with deep sadness.

"I know. At the end of the weekend, I got to drive Dr. and Mrs. Williams home from the event. I peppered them with all kinds of questions. It was unbelievable. They were still so sharp and so full of life and energy. I asked Dr. Williams if it was hard to smile in those pictures. During the event, he had been smiling most of the time, cracking jokes. But his face became more somber and he said, 'Reggie, sometimes it was hard to just breathe. We got many more miles to go before we sleep.'"

● ● ●

The year was 1967, but much of it could have passed for 2020. The nation was divided on many fronts, including civil rights for minorities and women, as well as the Vietnam War. From 1965 forward, riots and violence built up pressure that eventually erupted in major cities across the country, prompting the nickname of the "long, hot summer of 1967."

Most riots were sparked by violent incidents between white police and Black residents, originating in the Watts neighborhood of Los Angeles in 1965. The violence resulted in thirty-four deaths, one thousand injuries, and more than $40 million in property damage.

As tensions rose from the Watts riots, eleven other riots broke out in 1966, and then twenty-five more in 1967. The worst violence occurred in Detroit, Michigan, leaving forty-three people dead.[1]

In 1967, President Lyndon B. Johnson appointed a commission to study the causes of civil disorders in urban areas in the United States. Originally named the National Advisory Commission on Civil Disorders, it ultimately became known as the Kerner Commission, named after its chairman, former Illinois governor Otto Kerner.

The eleven-person commission comprised two Blacks and nine whites, including two US senators (one Republican and one Democrat), two US representatives (one Republican and one Democrat), the mayor of New York, and one woman. Johnson hoped the commission and its report would reflect kindly on all of the social advances of his Great Society domestic policies, including civil rights progress for Black Americans. However, after months of research, investigative study, and personal interviews conducted across the nation, the commission arrived at conclusions that sent even more shock waves reverberating across an already shaken nation.

The Kerner Commission concluded what many are debating now: that the true cause of the social unrest was white racism embedded in various systems. One of the most damning statements from the report was this: "Segregation and poverty have created in the ghetto [inner cities] a destructive environment totally unknown to most white Americans. What white Americans have never fully understood—but what the Negro can never forget—is that white society is deeply implicated in the ghetto. White institutions created it, white institutions maintain it, and white society condones it."[2]

This was not the glowing endorsement of his progressive policies that Johnson had hoped for. Nevertheless, it was a definitive statement that systemic racism was embedded in many aspects of life for Black Americans, especially those living in impoverished inner-city environments. Martin Luther King Jr. called the commission's findings a "physician's warning of approaching death, with a prescription for life."[3]

One cannot overstate the importance of the fact that the commission was nonpartisan and thus not a reflection of a radically liberal viewpoint. It should also be noted that while having only two Black members on the commission may seem regrettable, the racial disparity of its members strengthened the impact of their findings. The report could not be dismissed as a product of disgruntled Black liberals advancing their reverse-racism agenda.

In the end, a politically diverse group of mostly white men was the first government-sanctioned body in modern American history to point a finger at systemic racism. This was obviously not news to Black Americans. As the *Chicago Daily Defender* reported, "The Negro press and civil rights organizations have been pointing this out to the nation for more than a decade. While there is nothing new in the report, the commission . . . did emphasize in stern language the severity of the sickness with which the American society is inflicted and prescribe the needed remedy."[4]

The commission's recommendations were strikingly similar to ideas being debated today, many of them revolving around the need for diversity and inclusion training, as well as increased education and training for police officers. The commission also called for increased funding of alternate social services to deal with issues better suited for social workers than law enforcement officers.

Today, the rallying cry for law enforcement reform has coalesced around the phrase "defund the police." In our polarized political environment, there seems to be room only for extreme measures, with little tolerance for the messy middle or for nuance. For what it's worth, we support law enforcement and stand against calls for a radical singular swoop that slashes the budgets of these departments.

Rather than denouncing every American police officer as racist, we should be able to acknowledge that while most police officers are doing their jobs with honor, there is room for evaluating and adjusting our nation's law enforcement systems. Both can be true. Both *are* true. As pastor and scholar Esau McCaulley attests, "We can create a society where those who are suspected of breaking the law are treated as image bearers worthy of respect. A Christian theology of policing, then, must grow out of a Christian theology of persons. This Christian theology of policing must remember that the state is *only* a steward or caretaker of persons. It did not create them and it does not own or define them. God is our creator, and he will have a word for those who attempt to mar the image of God in any person. We are being the Christians God called us to be when we remind the state of the limits of its power."[5]

Truth spoke to power in 1968, and thousands of Americans resonated with *The Kerner Report*, purchasing more than 750,000 copies of the published version in less than three weeks. Even so, the collective cultural response was divided, just as it is today. Many people, mainly conservatives, were not ready for this conversation about race, including, ironically, the one who commissioned the report—President Johnson.

The president was not a fan of the report's findings, largely because it concluded that his progressive social agenda had not been effective in reversing the tide of poverty and violence in America. His agenda included the Civil Rights Act of 1964, groundbreaking legislation that President John F. Kennedy pressed Congress for in 1963 and Johnson championed to passage following Kennedy's assassination. The law federalized enforcement of racial desegregation in schools and public institutions and prohibited workplace discrimination based on "race, color, religion, sex, or national origin."[6] Johnson also championed the Voting Rights Act of 1965, which targeted state and local barriers designed to keep minorities from voting.

The Conservative "Christian" Reaction

President Johnson believed his efforts had struck a powerful blow against racism—indeed, he made more strides than any American president in the twentieth century. However, as we have learned, while legislation is a critical step in combating racism, it is also a limited one. The battle to eliminate systemic racism from American life continues to this day.

The legacy of the Kerner Commission is a sad but familiar one. Instead of leading to national repentance and confession, values Christians embrace, the report was weaponized for political gain as rising conservative politicians began to coalesce their power with the influence of evangelical leaders and organizations. Sadly, conservatives and Christians allowed themselves to become pawns to advance a new agenda.

Rather than listening to the report's findings and responding with humility, this new political tribe demonized the Kerner Commission's efforts to address the underlying causes and complexities of social unrest in the Black community, portraying the upheaval as nothing more than an assault on law and order. The convergence of evangelicals and conservative politicians had already begun in the late sixties, and findings like those in *The Kerner Report* contributed to their ideological fusion. This convergence sparked a movement in the 1970s that had a significant impact on American politics and elections for years to come. That movement, led by Baptist minister Jerry Falwell and composed primarily of white Christians, became known as the Moral Majority. In the seventies, the terms *conservative* and *Christian* were not yet synonymous with the Republican Party as they are today. Had that been the case, evangelical Christians likely would not have voted a Southern Baptist Sunday school teacher and Democrat named Jimmy Carter into the White House in 1976.

On the heels of the 1968 presidential election, Richard Nixon seized on the fears and biases of this evolving Republican base, amplifying conservative critiques that the Kerner Commission had "condoned and even commended a breakdown in law and order that . . . was the chief source of the nation's ills."[7] Nixon, eager to win the Oval Office and recognizing the potency of law-and-order rhetoric, stated that the report "blames everybody for the riots except the perpetrators of the riots."[8]

Conservative commentator William Buckley Jr. voiced what many began to believe: "[What caused the riots] isn't segregation or poverty or frustration. What caused them is a psychological disorder that is tearing at the ethos of our society as a result of boredom, self-hatred, and the arrogant contention that all our shortcomings are the result of other people's aggressions upon us."[9] We can see elements of white nationalism at play in his assertion that something is fundamentally, even psychologically, disordered in the minds of one's political and ideological opponents.

Georgia governor Lester Maddox offered another telling and perhaps prophetic summation of the report, foreshadowing a perspective held by many conservative Christians today: "I say it isn't racism. . . . It's communism. I know it is."[10] It didn't matter that the commission was made up of eleven people, including bipartisan elected officials at various levels of leadership, and that the context of their findings reflected a concerted effort fostered by elected leaders of the strongest democracy the world has ever known. Just saying the word *communism* (and repeating it as many times as possible) was enough to end the conversation for many conservative Americans. It still is.

The backlash against the report and the subsequent election of Richard Nixon ushered in an era in which many conservative leaders used law-and-order rhetoric to denounce virtually anything they considered liberal, socialist, or communist. The result was that even research-based systemic examinations of racism, such as *The Kerner Report*, were exiled to the political badlands of liberalism and socialism, regardless of their narrative or scholarly accuracy, at least in the eyes of the voting conservative base.

In spite of this, advances were made in the years that followed, including the emergence of a Black middle class and the general agreement that openly racist remarks were socially unacceptable. Racist language became politically incorrect, and many people no doubt experienced legitimate shifts in their belief systems on racism. However, over the years, white Americans had heard so much about the evils of racism that many assumed it had mostly disappeared, except in the hearts of a few extremists.

What we failed to realize was that many systems continued to evolve based on overtly racist policies, which meant their legacies were still affecting people of color. We didn't know this because the public narrative on racism had been effectively redirected from a focus on systems to the invisible space of an individual's heart. Hence, in the minds of many white people, and especially conservative Christians, racism had disappeared.

By the early 1980s, white conservatives had become a formidable political base comprised largely of single-issue (abortion) Republican voters who identified almost exclusively as evangelical Christians. Most conservatives today assume that modern Republicanism has always been tied to evangelical Christianity. We personally know plenty of people today who believe you can't be both a Democrat and a Christian.

Yet as the election of Jimmy Carter proved, sharing the same pew was not always an impossibility for Democrats and Republicans. Political and religious affiliations were not always fused, but they eventually became so, and not by accident. Contrary to popular belief, the Christian-conservative fusion started not over the issue of abortion but over desegregation. Some Christian institutions didn't want to lose their tax-exempt status over racist policies, which included the prohibition of interracial relationships at certain evangelical colleges. As Christian conservatives shifted their focus to fighting for what they considered their religious liberties—in this case, the freedom to racially discriminate—the national inventory of the Kerner Commission was forgotten.

Today, we must refuse to repeat this injustice. We cannot continue allowing our conservative traditions to become traditions of unbiblical discrimination. We would do well to consider why we, as conservatives, seem to have a blind faith in our systems of government and justice. Do we really believe we have come so far as a society that these systems couldn't possibly retain any racial bias? How can evangelicals decry the ways of the world, yet simultaneously put great trust in our worldly systems?

History reveals that we've been here before, but we don't have to stay here. We don't have to be afraid of taking honest inventories or responding to the findings with humility, grace, and a willingness to change. This is not only the way our governmental systems are intended to work, but it is also the way of the gospel.

Exiled to the Extremes of Either-Or

In our polarized climate, we have to remember that not only are there more than two sides to every issue, but there is also a lot of room between the extremes. People who try to convince you otherwise are, at best, questionable sources or questionable leaders. At worst, they are manipulating you for their own gain.

Jesus often found himself caught between two extreme, opposing viewpoints. For example, the Pharisees expected meticulous adherence to the Sabbath, which included doing no work. And yet ordinary people who suffered from various diseases sometimes came to Jesus for help on this day. According to the Pharisees, healing was work and was therefore prohibited on the Sabbath. Should Jesus strictly adhere to the Sabbath rules and turn people away, or should he heal those who were sick? Instead of declaring an either-or winner, Jesus chose a both-and approach. He not only healed people on the Sabbath, but he also explained why his actions honored God's intentions for this holy day. In one instance Jesus healed a woman with a disability that kept her bent over for eighteen years. Afterward, he said to those who objected to the healing, "You hypocrites! Doesn't each of you on the Sabbath untie your ox or donkey from the stall and lead it out to give it water? Then should not this woman, a daughter of Abraham, whom Satan has kept bound for eighteen long years, be set free on the Sabbath day from what bound her?" (Luke 13:15–16 NIV).

In another effort to entrap Jesus in an either-or scenario, Jewish religious leaders asked him, "Is it lawful to pay taxes to Caesar, or not? Should we pay them, or should we not?" (Mark 12:14). It was a loaded question in more ways than one. "Caesar" referred to the corrupt Roman authorities who occupied the Jewish nation by force. Was it better to be compliant or defiant?

Instead of flipping a coin and choosing a side on either political extreme, Jesus took a coin and let it speak for itself: "'Bring me a denarius and let me look at it.' And they brought one. And he said to them, 'Whose likeness and inscription is this?' They said to him, 'Caesar's.' Jesus said to them, 'Render to Caesar the things that are Caesar's, and to God the things that are God's'" (12:15–17). Talk about a both-and statement! Jesus kept his eye on the will of his Father and the ways of his Father's kingdom, refusing to be exiled to the extreme perspectives of any lesser earthly kingdoms.

As believers, we must learn to refuse the same exile to extreme perspectives, especially in our politics. Author and pastor Scott Sauls says, "Partisan politics might be the greatest threat to unity in the American church. Truth: Neither Right nor Left has a corner on truth, justice, or neighbor love. Both (a) have some blood on their hands, and (b) imperfectly align with *some* aspect/s of Christ's own agenda. Follow the whole Christ and you will find it impossible to align wholesale with any party."[11]

Perhaps no other issue in the current conversation about racism pushes us (especially as conservatives) to extremes and insults us more than the rioting, looting, and violence surrounding the protests that erupted following the deaths of Ahmaud Arbery, Breonna Taylor, and George Floyd. Democrats and Republicans alike have stoked the ideological fires surrounding such violence for their own objectives. It's no longer possible for a person to support peaceful protests without also being accused by conservatives of supporting violence. It's difficult even to acknowledge the legitimacy of the injustices that sparked some of the violence without being labeled an anarchist.

The truth—and the way of Christ—lies not in a false choice between extremes but somewhere in the middle.

We do not condone violence against police officers or citizens or destroying public and private property. However, we do believe that, as the Kerner Commission pointed out some fifty years ago, those who protest racial injustices are not randomly taking to the streets to overthrow a peaceful, democratic society. They have legitimate reasons to be outraged by injustice—as when Ahmaud Arbery is shot while jogging, when Breonna Taylor is shot in her own apartment, when George Floyd suffocates under the knee of a police officer. While legitimate outrage does not justify violence and rioting, we can at least understand what Martin Luther King Jr. meant when he said of the Watts Riots, "A riot is the language of the unheard. And what is it that America has failed to hear?"[12] Even today, would there be such violence if we listened, engaged in honest dialogue, and committed to changing the injustices embedded in our systems?

Yes, extremists on both sides are opportunists. Yes, both have manipulated the narrative to benefit their own dubious causes. Yes, both need to stop. Yes. Yes. Yes. However, none of these yeses justifies a blanket no to listening and responding to the legitimate injustices that sparked these issues in the first place. The pundits or politicians who keep telling us we have to choose between law and order and fighting against systemic injustice are lying. We can live in the freedom of the middle ground, gracefully exercising wisdom and discretion in our responses.

We don't have to decry everything to decry something.

Not everyone marching in a protest against racism is a godless liberal, an authoritarian socialist, or a bloody anarchist. Dr. Martin Luther King Jr. was none of these. We don't have to be either. We don't have to drive into the left ditch or the right ditch; we can stay on the road and do the driving (listening, healing, leading, changing) that is possible only when we remain there.

If you believe that any person with a viewpoint that remotely disagrees with your own is a dangerous radical, then by definition, *you* are a dangerous radical.

When we move to middle-ground thinking, we can expect a backlash, which should reinforce the conviction that we are where we need to be. When we stop thinking of protest events as riots, we can open our ears to the complexities of the issues people are protesting. We can condemn undue violence without condemning the need for systemic change, especially in areas where policing and judicial policies have a history of corruption and unnecessary violence.

The Kerner Report echoed these middle-ground perspectives: "Some experts and analysts conceived of the violent outbreaks not as signs of oppressive poverty and social breakdown but as righteous political protests against racist institutions, in particular the police. The events in Watts, Detroit, and elsewhere were not riots, these analysts claimed, they were rebellions; instead of seeking to quell the outrage in the nation's inner cities, responsible government officials needed to awaken to the racism so deeply and systematically entrenched in American life, and then attack it head-on."[13]

The church can adopt a similar attitude by not writing off every violent event that follows peaceful protests over racial injustice and attributing it to only one thing—a liberal conspiracy, a socialist agenda, an attack on our religious liberties, or whatever else renders us too angry to listen. Instead, we can allow for complexity and view such events as the convergence of many factors, some of which are bad and some of which arise from valid issues that need to be heard.

We would also do well to note that most valid and noble movements have extreme elements that do not reflect the best intentions or actions of honorable people in the center. During the American Revolution, possibly the most revered event in our nation's history, there were among the patriots extremist elements who took things too far.

In 1775, as anti-British sentiment was growing to a fever pitch in New York, an angry mob of politically zealous, intoxicated patriots formed on the campus of King's College (known today as Columbia University). They were incensed by an article accusing the college president, Dr. Myles Cooper, of being responsible for the deaths of colonists at Lexington and Concord at the hands of British soldiers. Cooper had remained loyal to the British crown and was an outspoken opponent of revolutionary sentiment in the colonies.

Alexander Hamilton happened to be a student at King's College at the time and had been personally instructed by Dr. Cooper. Hamilton was a patriot in every sense of the word—a high-ranking officer who fought for the Continental Army and became the chief aide to General George Washington. Upon seeing the angry mob coming for his professor, Hamilton stopped them from carrying out their violent intentions by giving a long speech. This bought Dr. Cooper enough time to escape out a window, in his nightshirt no less.

Hamilton never decried the patriotic cause of the revolution because such extremists attempted such actions. From a political and ideological standpoint, he disagreed with Dr. Cooper and agreed with the mob, but in this instance, a higher ethic prevailed. Hamilton did not have to accept one cause and cancel the other.

Oh that we would adopt such a disposition today! We need not decry the fight to end racism because of angry mobs. Yes, anyone who breaks the law should be held accountable under due process of law, but extremists shouldn't cause us to dismiss millions of others (like the two of us) who march peacefully for the cause of racial justice. As Hamilton noted, "In times of such commotion as the present, while the passions of men are worked up to an uncommon pitch there is great danger of fatal extremes."[14]

The danger of fatal extremes still exists today, but the gospel leads us to seek middle ground, which won't be particularly pleasing to either extreme. Ironically, when we choose the gospel center, both sides will accuse us of being extremists, just as they accused Christ. But living in the center, we'll be wiser in faith and politics and, like Dr. Martin Luther King Jr. and Alexander Hamilton, perhaps in a better position to effect lasting change.

CHAPTER 12

Systemic Racism in the Modern Age

"Even if they keep from getting caught up in the hot-button terms being used today," John observed, "it seems like a lot of conservative Christians get tripped up over the idea that systemic racism still exists."

"Yeah," replied Reggie, "I guess seeing it in our past is one thing, but seeing it today is another."

"That's especially true since things have changed for the better in so many ways. I mean, a Black man was elected president, you know?"

"That's right," Reggie replied. "When I was growing up in a Black neighborhood of Knoxville, and even when I went to college, I never would have thought that was possible in my lifetime."

"Doesn't that prove that racism is still embedded in our systems in some way?" John said. "If the law didn't stop a Black man from becoming president, why did you think it was impossible?"

"That's a great question," answered Reggie. "I guess that goes right along with a lot of the other things we've been talking about, like Black men training their children to avoid bad interactions with police or the fact that I knew my neighborhood was a Black neighborhood in the first place."

● ● ●

Now that we've explored the history of racism in America and have taken an honest inventory of our ways of thinking and responding to racial issues, we have the foundation we need to consider where systemic racism exists today. Legacies of racism from our past continue to affect Black communities, which is why it's important never to detach past history from present systems.

In this chapter, we'll focus on three systemic issues: redlining, policing, and mass incarceration.

Redlining

Redlining is the systematic discriminatory practice of denying loans for houses in certain areas based on race. For decades after the Constitution guaranteed equal rights for Blacks, federal agencies prohibited Black families from buying houses in the "good" parts of town. These agencies used overtly racist strategies, including New Deal policies enacted through the Federal Housing Administration (FHA), to segregate Black families from white neighborhoods to avoid lower property values. This is where the phrase "the other side of the tracks" comes from. Consequently, Blacks were also denied higher paying jobs and better policing on the other side of town.

After the assassination of Martin Luther King Jr. on April 4, 1968, and the riots that followed, redlining was outlawed when President Lyndon B. Johnson signed the Civil Rights Act of 1968, which included the Fair Housing Act. It was a beacon rising out of a dark chapter in American history, and a momentous step forward from a legal perspective.

The objective of the Fair Housing Act was to prevent housing discrimination based on race, religion, sex, or national origin. However, the law could not, and did not, reverse the consequences of many decades of segregation and discrimination, nor did it prevent the practice of redlining from continuing in different forms.

In 2017, the Center for Investigative Reporting determined, after examining 31 million mortgage records, that redlining persists in sixty-one metropolitan areas, including Detroit, Philadelphia, Saint Louis, and San Antonio, with African Americans experiencing the most discrimination in Southern cities such as Mobile, Alabama; Greenville, North Carolina; and Gainesville, Florida.[1] One study in 2020 found that between 2012 and 2018, "for every dollar banks [lent] in majority-white neighborhoods in Chicago, they [lent] just 12 cents in majority-Black and majority-Latino areas."[2] Problems persist today, especially since changes in housing markets occur over longer periods of time, and a rise or fall in neighborhood property values do not generally occur overnight. The trends in an area, as well as economic changes in surrounding areas, often span generations of families. Author Richard Rothstein said in an interview on NPR, "The segregation of our metropolitan areas today leads . . . to stagnant inequality, because families are much less able to be upwardly mobile when they're living in segregated neighborhoods where opportunity is absent. . . . If we want greater equality in this society, if we want a lowering of the hostility between police and young African-American men, we need to take steps to desegregate."[3]

Redlining is a both-and issue. America's legacy of discriminatory housing practices is still affecting Black people. And as Rothstein pointed out, housing and policing—the most volatile racial issues today—are not mutually exclusive.

Policing

Policing in America has evolved into a modern institution that parties on all sides of the political and social spectrums vehemently criticize or defend. Modern definitions of policing center on the administration of law and order to detect, prevent, and prosecute crime when it arises. The history of policing is too broad to fully explore here, so we will limit our focus to issues that relate to systemic racism in our nation today.

One study on policing found that between 2013 and 2018, Black men were about two and a half times more likely to be killed by police than white men. Black men have a one in one thousand (0.001 percent) chance of dying at the hands of police, while the odds for white men are about thirty-nine in one hundred thousand (0.00039 percent).[4] Some counter these statistics with their own, pointing out that Black men commit a much higher percentage of crimes. While this is true in some areas, a disproportionate number of police-related deaths also occur with other ethnicities,[5] such as Latinx and Native American men, who don't commit a higher percentage of crimes but are significantly more likely to be killed by police than white men. This indicates that crime rates do not proportionately affect the death rate at the hands of police. If they did, other ethnicities would not also be more likely to be killed by police than whites.

Another report examined data from more than eleven thousand police stops in the District of Columbia over the course of about four weeks and found that while Black people make up 46 percent of the city's population, they were involved in 70 percent of police stops.[6] A report out of Los Angeles revealed similar findings in more alarming contexts. When stopped by police, "24 percent of Black drivers and passengers were searched, compared with 16 percent of Latinos and 5 percent of whites." The same study revealed that whites, who were searched four times less than Blacks, were more likely to be in possession of illegal drugs, weapons, or other contraband.[7] This refutes the idea that Black people are stopped by police solely because a higher rate of criminal activity occurs among Blacks.

Similar findings were noted in studies conducted in other cities, such as Portland, Oregon; Indianapolis, Indiana; Springfield, Missouri; and Burlington, Vermont. And all were congruent with findings from a Department of Justice study, which concluded that Black drivers were 31 percent more likely to be pulled over than a white driver.[8] Another study analyzed approximately ninety-five million traffic stops conducted by fifty-six police agencies around the nation and found that not only were Blacks much more likely to be pulled over and searched, but alarmingly, they were also "less likely to be stopped after sunset" because it was harder for police to detect the race of a driver at night.[9]

Do all of these studies mean that law enforcement agencies across the country are made up of mostly bad apples? We think not. It would be a mistake to attribute racism on this scale primarily to individuals rather than systemic issues.

It is more likely that the majority of these officers are decent cops doing their jobs in a system of policing that carries the legacy of our racist past. When we see racism solely in the acts of some bad apples, we overlook the fact that the apple tree itself—the system producing the apples—might be the issue. The way officers are trained may have a subconscious built-in bias that affects how police officers perceive Black people and enforce the law. If we are unwilling to admit that there may be systemic problems, the only conclusion we can draw from the facts is that we have a staggering number of racist individuals who work within our law enforcement systems. And we will fail to address the lingering systemic bias embedded in these agencies that continues to produce bad-apple policing, even by good apples.

As we have shown throughout this book, our systemic problems are at least in part a result of our historical legacy of racism. Most historians believe that policing in the US developed not just parallel to racism but as a means of enforcing it. Criminal justice journalist Radley Balko writes, "When you consider that much of the criminal justice system was built, honed and firmly established during the Jim Crow era—an era almost everyone, conservatives included, will concede [was] rife with racism—this is pretty intuitive. The modern criminal justice system helped preserve racial order—it kept Black people in their place. For much of the early twentieth century, in some parts of the country, that was its primary function. That it might retain some of those proclivities today shouldn't be all that surprising."[10]

Pastor and scholar Esau McCaulley concurs: "By my count, I have been stopped somewhere between seven and ten times on the road or for existing in public spaces for no crime other than being Black. These words may make it seem as if I dislike police officers. I do not. I have known many good police officers. I recognize the dangers that they face and the difficulties inherent in the vocation they choose. But a difficult job does not absolve one of criticism; it puts the criticism in a wider framework. That wider framework must also include, if we are going to be complete, the history of the police's interaction with people of color in this country."[11]

The convergence of the historical roots of policing with many present-day experiences of Black citizens like Dr. McCaulley reveals a compelling truth about an ongoing systemic problem. In some cities, this problem has seemingly gone on unchecked, becoming deeply embedded and more overtly racist than other issues. A 2016 US Department of Justice report concluded that the Baltimore Police Department (BPD) was rife with systemic racism. The report stated the BPD had "routinely violated the constitutional rights of citizens, used excessive force, and discriminated against African Americans."[12] It also found the following:

> Officers seemed to view themselves as controlling the city rather than as a part of the city. Many others, including high ranking officers in the Department, view themselves as enforcing the will of the "silent majority." . . .
>
> Almost everyone who spoke to us—from current and former City leaders, BPD officers and command staff during ride-alongs and interviews, community members throughout the many neighborhoods of Baltimore, union representatives of all levels of officers in BPD, advocacy groups, and civic and religious leaders—agrees that BPD has significant problems that have undermined its efforts to police constitutionally and effectively.[13]

Based on the sources the DOJ cited within the Baltimore community, including the police department itself, it is evident that this report is not a witch hunt or political grandstanding, as some believe.

Statistics and politics aside, it is important to note that the consequences of systemic racism extend far beyond the horrors we read about in the news or the victims of brutal encounters with police. They are a legacy passed down to future generations.

In her book *Mother to Son: Letters to a Black Boy on Identity and Hope*, history teacher and blogger Jasmine Holmes shares a sobering human reality of how these statistics about systemic racism affect real people. In a letter to her young son, she writes, "My fear for you, my son, is not so much that you will be lynched like Emmett Till. Make no mistake, I will train you—as I was trained—to respond to authority in a way that will make you appear as nonthreatening and compliant as humanly possible. And I will hope and pray that this compliance will serve as some kind of barrier against the brutality that your young black form may incur. I will watch every news story of a black man gunned down by police with a twinge of fear, wanting so badly to trust that those charged with protecting our communities would not harm you without just cause, but fearing every scenario where they might."[14]

As we have learned from the personal stories others have shared, including the experiences of one of this book's authors, biases in our systems of policing affect not just our families but generations down the line if those biases are not corrected. This is the nature of systemic things—they are generational. And perhaps nothing has a greater generational impact on Black families than mass incarceration.

Mass Incarceration

The term *mass incarceration* refers to the stark racial dividing line in American prisons: Black people are imprisoned and given longer sentences at an exponentially higher rate than whites. According to a recent study by the Pew Research Center, the Black imprisonment rate "is nearly twice the rate among Hispanics and more than five times the rate among whites."[15]

Former Harvard Law School professor William J. Stuntz provides some context for understanding this disparity: "A substantial portion of that disparity will and should remain: crime rates among blacks are much higher than among the rest of the population, so, at least in part, the prison population should reflect that truth. But there is no explaining the massive racial tilt in the drug prisoner population in terms of different crime rates: what evidence we have on the subject suggests that blacks, whites, and Latinos violate the drug laws at similar rates."[16]

What Stuntz is referring to is a systemic issue. The judicial system dispenses harsher prison sentences for Black offenders, which has created a larger Black prison population. This is the legacy of historically racist policies in which Blacks were given longer prison sentences than whites for identical crimes.

Now consider some of the trickle-down consequences of this systemic issue. For one thing, imprisonment removes earning power for inmates, which creates economic hardship and stress for families and often results in divorce. It also removes fathers from their children, traumatizes the young men who experience violence in prison, and reinforces distrust of the justice system in Black communities. The consequences themselves have now also become systemic.

We aren't opposed to people of any color going to jail for the crimes they commit. That is justice. However, mass incarceration is not about justice; it's about harsher treatment under the law for millions of Black men *because* of the color of their skin. That is injustice.

The federal government took steps to address this injustice

when Congress passed the Fair Sentencing Act of 2010. Attorney Deborah England points out that prior to the act, "someone convicted of possessing one gram of crack would receive a sentence 100 times longer than someone possessing one gram of powder cocaine. What is the chemical difference between crack cocaine and powder cocaine that justified this disparity? Answer: There is no significant chemical difference—crack and powder cocaine are both forms of cocaine."[17] The only real difference was that the majority of those arrested for crack were Black, while those arrested for cocaine were white. This legislation reduced the disparity in sentencing from a hundred-to-one ratio to eighteen to one,[18] but again, a disparity remains that affects Black men more than white men. The ratio should be one to one.

It would be hard to lay the cause of such disparities at the feet of individuals. It is most certainly the consequence of legacy racism in our judicial system, and it disproportionately affects family structures, economic potential, educational opportunities, and more in Black communities. We can't just say, "Blacks commit more crimes," and yet fail to acknowledge that whites get shorter sentences for many of the same crimes, which in turn has less of an impact on white communities. Both facts are true, but many white people in politics and the church tend to acknowledge only one.

To be clear, the racial disparities in sentencing have been narrowing in recent years. According to the Council on Criminal Justice, "Black-white disparities in state imprisonment rates fell across all major crime categories. The largest drop was for drug offenses. In 2000, Black people were imprisoned for drug crimes at fifteen times the rate of whites; by 2016, that ratio was just under five to one."[19] The conviction rate of Blacks for violent crimes, including rape, robbery, and aggravated assault, "declined by an average of 3 percent per year between 2000 and 2016."[20] That is the equivalent of a 45 percent drop over that period. Yet even as crime rates go down, the percentage of Blacks being incarcerated remains staggeringly high. Until sentencing for identical crimes is statistically the same across all ethnicities, undeniable evidence of racial bias continues to exist in our criminal justice system.

Obviously, justice is not perverted in every instance of incarceration among Black people. However, under all administrations since the late 1970s, the government has convicted and incarcerated Black men at exponentially higher rates than any other race, and for the same crimes. Many white moderates don't seem to question these conclusions or convictions, but many Black communities do, and that is not unreasonable.

It is helpful to note that even following the violence of the civil rights movement of the 1960s, incarceration rates among Blacks were not nearly at the level they are today. This has at least partially been the result of a systemic shift in policing and sentencing policy from the war on drugs in the 1980s and 1990s. Law professor William Stuntz acknowledges this change: "Before the 1990s, conventional wisdom on policing emphasized police officers' role as the first step in the process that leads to criminal punishment."[21] The police were the first step, but a tough-on-crime approach by multiple Democratic and Republican administrations led to the goal of catching and punishing more criminals. According to Stuntz,

> In order to catch more offenders and hence make more arrests, doctrine stressed speed and surprise. Urban police forces invested in reducing their response time to 911 calls, and in high-speed, violent SWAT teams—the policing equivalent of "shock and

awe"—that could roll into crime scenes with overwhelming force, make arrests, and roll out. The goal was more efficient punishment, and that goal was reached: the number of arrests per officer rose steadily through the 1970s and 1980s. But greater efficiency didn't produce desired outcomes. On city streets, "shock and awe" generates shock and anger, plus sympathy for the young men the police are targeting. Violent, in-and-out raids and quick street stop-and-frisks are bound to have a high error rate, meaning that innocent residents of high-crime neighborhoods pay a large price for efforts to catch guilty ones.[22]

This systemic change in policing is one of the reasons the United States leads the world in incarcerations—and there's not even a close second.[23] Are our citizens really so much worse than those of other countries? The gospel would say no, since we're all equally in need of grace because of our sin.

A study in the late 1990s found that only one-ninth of stop-and-frisks led to arrests,[24] which means that eight out of nine people were stopped and frisked for no criminal reason at all, a high proportion of them Black. In one instance, the Black mayor of a town in Prince George's County, Maryland, was mistakenly targeted in a drug raid, and his family was grossly mistreated and robbed of their dignity.

As we have seen, changes are occurring in drug laws and search policies because obvious inequities are contributing to the mass incarceration of Black men to a disproportionate degree. This problem is all too easy for white Christians to ignore because it generally doesn't affect them directly. The gospel, however, leaves no room for an out-of-sight, out-of-mind mentality. We are called to pay attention to injustices that affect those around us.

Purposeful Inventions and Purposeful Change

The data we've presented offers compelling evidence of the systemic racism embedded in redlining, policing, and the mass incarceration of Black people. We must not act as if these are just random occurrences, especially in light of their historical origins. Austin Channing Brown states, "Racial injustices, like slavery and our system of mass incarceration, were purposeful inventions, but instead of seeking to understand how we got here, the national narrative remains filled with myths, patchwork timelines, and colonial ideals."[25] Recognizing the purposeful steps that got us here can help us avoid an ambivalent attitude toward injustice that seemingly has always existed and is therefore all too easy to consider normal.

Progress has been made in the fight against systemic racism, but the battle is far from over. Equipped with an understanding of our past and the courage the gospel provides, we can forge ahead as we seek to listen with empathy, respond rightly, and work together toward change.

CHAPTER 13

A Time to Lament and
Lean Forward Together

"When I first started out as a public speaker," said Reggie, "I traveled with Dave Roever."

"Oh, I remember Dave. He was the guy in Vietnam who had a grenade explode in his hand, right?"

"Yeah, that's him. Well, one time he couldn't make it to a church event, and he asked me to speak for him. When I got there, the pastor brought me into his office to talk. I could hear the music starting in the sanctuary, so it was almost time to take the stage. The pastor handed me an envelope from his desk and told me to give it to Dave. Then he said, 'Thank you for coming, but I feel God leading me to preach today.'"

"What?"

"Yeah, man. He went on to tell me that I needed to go speak to my own people in the Church of God in Christ because they were my type."

"He did not!" John said in a loud voice.

"He did. So I wished him well and went on my way. I wasn't mad, but I did think, *Someday I'll be back here, and it won't be because of Dave Roever.* Eight years later, that's exactly what happened. I wasn't traveling with Dave anymore, and I received an invitation to speak. Honestly, I was traveling so much that I didn't put two and two together until I pulled into the parking lot. I thought, *You've got to be kidding me. There's no way the same pastor is still here.*"

"Was he?"

"Yep. We didn't talk much before service, but when I got the microphone and began to speak, I made a few funny but pointed comments about race in my message. At the end, I couldn't believe it when the pastor was the first to come down for prayer. In my heart, I knew God wanted me to pray for him, so I did."

"Did you talk afterward?" John was on the edge of his seat.

"Oh yeah, I went out to eat with him and his wife. He told me that he deserved what I had said in my message. I told him that I didn't think he would remember what he had done. He remembered all right. He was so apologetic."

"Wow, bro."

"It was amazing. Now he texts me every few months just to check on me. When COVID hit and I wasn't traveling, he sent me money for groceries."

"That's unbelievable! You guys should not be friends."

"That's what we tend to think," Reggie agreed. "But anyone can change. In this case, it only took eight years. It was definitely worth the wait."

● ● ●

When we started this journey together, we described what it feels like to stand at the edge of an airplane ramp twelve thousand feet in the air, just waiting to jump. That's what we did in this book. We jumped into a host of conversations about the gospel, history, politics, policy, and a lot more. If you've made it this far, hopefully you've not succumbed to insults or the depths of despair, and we are grateful for your courage to grow with us in these conversations.

So what happens now? There is no way to tie up the topic of racism in a neat little bow. Chances are, you may still be at an impasse with family members, your political party, or your church. It has been our hope that the questions and insights in this book will equip you to build stronger bridges of thought that will lead to building bridges of conversation and action.

As we close, we'd like to share a couple of stories, along with a few thoughts on hope, lament, and keeping the conversation on race going. We believe Scripture shows that these are God's ways, along with others we have explored in this book. We believe that when God's ways are fully practiced by God's people, he will allow us to be a part of his work to end racism.

Lowering the Temperature

It was August 2020, and the coronavirus craziness was still raging. I (Reggie) was beginning to travel again and speak at a few weekend events and churches (with masks and social distancing, of course). That day I was flying to Minneapolis on Delta, my airline of choice.

I had taken my seat in first class and was excited to watch the NBA playoffs from the "bubble" in Orlando, Florida—the quarantined area of Disney World where players lived for a few months, isolated from the outside world. Anyone who came or went had to undergo COVID testing and quarantining. A few weeks earlier, I had been to the bubble to speak, so I was extra pumped to see the teams play on the plane's video feed.

Before the game, they played the national anthem, and as is common these days, players on both teams took a knee. I was wearing headphones, but nothing was coming through them yet, so I could still hear everyone around me. Just then a voice said, "Those niggers should be standing!"

Before I could react, I heard a young boy say, "Mama! That man just said the N-word!"

We weren't the only ones who heard it. The whole plane suddenly felt as if it had been pressurized, and not in the normal way. It felt like it could explode at any second.

I took off my headphones and turned to the little boy. "Hey, son, listen. Sometimes adults say things they don't mean to say out loud. So don't hate him. I saw a tattoo on his arm, and I'm pretty sure that he is a military man who fought for our country, so this stuff really hits home to him. He's a hero, and I'm sure he didn't mean it like that, so please forgive him for it."

Before I could finish speaking, the man himself stood up and turned to us. I braced myself for the worst.

"He's right, son," the man humbly said. "I didn't mean to say that, and I'm sorry."

I was floored, but then he turned to me and continued. "And I would like to apologize to you too, sir."

"No problem, bro," I said. "And thank you for your service."

I thought that was that and returned my attention to the game, but then the boy's mom tapped me on the shoulder. "Thank you so much for what you said."

Then another man across the aisle said, "Who are you?"

"What do you mean?" I asked.

"I mean that it was a cool seventy-two degrees on this plane until he said that, and then it got up to over a hundred. But whatever you just did, it brought the temperature right back down."

It's a sad thing that it is so rare to see the temperature come down in all the heated debates over race today. I hadn't done anything that shouldn't be normal for those who follow Jesus. Did the man's use of the N-word make me mad? Yes. Was there any justifiable excuse for him to use it? No, there wasn't.

But regardless of other people, we always have a choice, even when others make bad choices that affect us. I'm certainly not justifying the man's choices, nor am I saying that we always need to overlook overt expressions of racism like this one. Yes, we have talked about standing up for what's right; we just need to learn to fight the right way.

As an old adage says, when all you have is a hammer, everything looks like a nail. If everything looks like a fight, we can dismiss the value of the humans we are fighting against—human beings who may be dead wrong in the way they are thinking or acting but are nonetheless image bearers of God.

It is all too easy to feel that the choices of others leave us with no choices, especially when black-and-white issues abound. It's hard to consider the humanity of people who treat others as subhuman, but we can learn not to treat every situation regarding race as if it were a nail that needs to be banged with a hammer.

There is always right and wrong. There is always good and bad. There is always up and down. But just because someone else goes wrong, bad, or down does not mean we can't still choose right, good, and up. Nelson Mandela said, "We must strive [to] be moved by a generosity of spirit that will enable us to outgrow the hatred and conflicts of the past."[1] It is this generosity of spirit that can change our conversations and hearts so that we can change the systems.

I had the honor of meeting Nelson Mandela in South Africa before he passed away in 2013. After I finished speaking at a rally, he sent someone to request a sit-down with me. It was a life-changing experience. He lived everything he is quoted as saying, even enduring prison for it. You can tell when people are willing to keep their hearts and minds open to change. For him, this meant being open to others, even those who mistreated him.

Yes, other measures besides kindness and tolerance are required to address systemic racism. In our nation's past, we fought a bloody but just civil war over these issues. Many times, slaves rightly rebelled against their violent masters or ran away to save their families from brutal conditions. There were riots throughout America during the civil rights movement. There are riots today. My point is that we do not have to choose either a humble, nonadversarial response that allows systemic racism to continue or a bold, head-on response of rising up, speaking out, and marching to bring about change. There is a time for both—a time when both are called for.

In terms of our individual lives, we need to be open to both responses. And in terms of the gospel, we have to first be open to Christlike responses to very non-Christlike actions. Part of what made Christ's reactions so radical and effective was how strikingly opposite they were to the actions taken against him. He could have not forgiven his enemies if he had never had any enemies. He could have not returned gentleness for derision if he had never faced derision. British writer G. K. Chesterton says, "Charity [love] means pardoning what is unpardonable, or it is no virtue at all."[2] Modernized renditions of this quote attributed to Chesterton say,

"Love means to love that which is unlovable, or it is no virtue at all; forgiving means to pardon that which is unpardonable, or it is no virtue at all." The presence of the negative—the unlovable and unpardonable—was Christ's cue to respond with the positive—with love and forgiveness—not a justification for going negative himself.

I am no Jesus. I am no Nelson Mandela. I am just Reggie, and I, like you, face a million little choices in my life every day. I often get it wrong, but even when I do, the gospel offers me the chance to use that wrongness as the reason to change direction and pursue what is right instead. The life of following Jesus is a life of constantly seeing where he is walking and where I am walking and then correcting the distance, pace, and gait between the two.

Do I sometimes want to scream? Yes. Do I sometimes want to take a swing? Sure. Is there a time for more action? Yes. But in that moment on the plane, there was more going on than the racist actions of one individual. The man and I began to talk more. I found out that he served in Iraq and suffered from PTSD (post-traumatic stress disorder). I was able to tell him that he was going to make it, and then I was able to pray for him. I missed the basketball game, but I found out that he was a broken human being like me, just for different reasons. He asked for my email address when we parted.

Like so many, he had been exposed to and influenced by countless nuances of the race conversation in this nation, including how it intersects with politics and nationalism. It was doubtful he was putting on white sheets and marching in Klan rallies, yet surely most of us would agree that there was a degree of racism in his life.

Scripture is clear that there is a time for different actions depending on circumstances and seasons.

For everything there is a season, and a time for every matter
under heaven:

> a time to be born, and a time to die;
> a time to plant, and a time to pluck up what is
>   planted;
> a time to kill, and a time to heal;
> a time to break down, and a time to build up;
> a time to weep, and a time to laugh;
> a time to mourn, and a time to dance;
> a time to cast away stones, and a time to gather
>   stones together;
> a time to embrace, and a time to refrain from
>   embracing;
> a time to seek, and a time to lose;
> a time to keep, and a time to cast away;
> a time to tear, and a time to sew;
> a time to keep silence, and a time to speak;
> a time to love, and a time to hate;
> a time for war, and a time for peace.
>
> —Ecclesiastes 3:1–8

Life entails a variety of seasons and circumstances and thus
requires a variety of nuanced responses, including "a time to kill,
and a time to heal" (v. 3). The point is that we must learn to address
the situation at hand and not treat every season or circumstance as
a time to break down rather than a time to build up.

If we want to lower the temperature of our conversations about
race, it must begin with one or two people at a time being willing to
break the cycle of pride and anger within themselves—to take the

foundational truths of the gospel and apply confession and repentance to real conversations. It doesn't end there, so resist the urge to quote this part of the book in a social media post. We won't end the problem of racism by telling everyone else they shouldn't be angry. That's not what I'm saying. What I am saying is that we need to do something about racism, not just be the anger police.

So how can you help? Start by believing that you are already a part of the story of racism in America in some way. This is a fact, not an opinion. Humanity is made up of humans, so each human has a role. God knew this and has equipped us to play our parts, first by continually learning what it really means to follow Christ. This is why changing the way we think should be normal for us as Christians.

Philip Yancey, a well-known influential Christian author and speaker who has written many bestselling books about the wonderfully radical nature of the grace of God, is a prime example of someone who allowed the gospel to change the way he thought about race. In his watershed book, *What's So Amazing about Grace?* he shares, "I grew up a racist. . . . We used to call Martin Luther King Jr. 'Martin Lucifer Coon.' We said that King was a card-carrying Communist, a Marxist agent who merely posed as a minister. Not until much later was I able to appreciate the moral strength of the man who, perhaps more than any other person, kept the South from outright racial war."[3] It is this kind of vulnerable, honest inventory that reminds us that Christ joyfully changes anyone who is willing to allow him to do so—in Yancey's case, from a willful racist to a humble yet effective voice espousing the love of God to all races of the world. It wasn't until he was willing for his heart to be changed that God used him to help change others as well.

The kind of heart change we need is not the kind we keep

clamoring for others to make. Instead, we must first commit to a continuous process of listening, learning, and changing our ways of thinking. Such a commitment goes far beyond religious rhetoric; it requires that we acknowledge and embrace our brokenness, especially as Christians.

If we want to lower the temperature in conversations about race, we must begin by being willing to let our minds be changed and to see the humanity in those with whom we disagree, always remembering that anyone can change.

Don't All Lives Matter?

I (John) previously acknowledged that when I heard the phrase "Black lives matter," my first response was, "Don't all lives matter?"

On August 10, 2014, my wife and I were watching the news as the horrifying events in Ferguson, Missouri, played out before us. The day before, an eighteen-year-old Black man named Michael Brown had been fatally shot by police. I was living less than ten hours from Ferguson at the time, but I might as well have been a million miles away from the realities in which Black people in that community— and in communities across the nation—were living. It wasn't a sin to be white, and there was no need to feel guilty about my race, yet all of the unrest and heated rhetoric felt like an accusation. I felt accused of all the things I had not done, things I thought I stood against.

As I was trying to verbally process all the pain I was seeing on the news, as well as my own conflicted thoughts and emotions, my wife said, "You know, John, you are making a lot of really logical points, but there is one thing that people who don't look like us are asking us to do, and you're not doing it."

"And what is that, exactly?" I asked.

"You're not listening to them," she said.

It felt like an insult, but it was the one I most needed to hear from someone I trusted. Though I wasn't yet an ally in the fight against racism, it was in that moment and in the slight shift of my mindset that so many other things began to change.

In the months and years that followed, I began to listen differently—not just to filter the experiences or perspectives of Black people through my lenses but rather to hear what they were saying. I lamented along with them, even joining thousands of mourners at a rally in downtown Nashville. I faced resistance from some white Christians for getting too involved in what they considered radical activity, but I was only there to mourn with those who mourned. Pastor Mark Vroegop says that such mourning "expresses spiritual outrage against the effects of the fall. Laments appropriately declare, 'This isn't right.'"[4]

It was a small beginning, but it was time for me to express that the mistreatment of Blacks I was finally seeing more clearly isn't right, and not just socially but also spiritually. I stopped trying to defend myself against any indictment of racism, mainly because I didn't want to be one of the well-meaning people who end up defending racism in the process.

I began to speak differently to my community and our church. Hopefully, none of us had ever intended to support racism, and both claiming and desiring not to be racist were most certainly good things. However, it was time to admit that the gospel calls us to much more than simply not being racist. We can and should be doing so much more to help eradicate racism. If that seems impossible to us, perhaps our expectations of God are set far too low. After all, Christ came "to destroy the works of the devil"

(1 John 3:8), so as his body, should it not be our work to do the same?

I began to take seriously these words of Martin Luther King Jr.: "Injustice anywhere is a threat to justice everywhere. We are caught in an inescapable network of mutuality, tied in a single garment of destiny. Whatever affects one directly, affects all indirectly."[5] As a white pastor, I chose to become a stronger thread in this garment of destiny, to become part of God's work to heal the wounds of hundreds of years of racism.

Perhaps you can relate to my experience. Like me, maybe you are a white person who hates racism but isn't sure what you can do to make a difference. You might have been offended by others' insinuating that you are a racist or felt pressure from others who fear you will suddenly burst into flames of socialism or liberalism if you admit that Black lives really do matter.

Maybe, like me, you're looking for what's next.

What Now?

Our goal on this journey has been to explore what the gospel really calls for: a willingness to listen and repent, to keep changing the way we think as we learn, and to keep learning more about the historical and theological issues behind racism so that we can take steps toward ending it. These gospel actions reflect the disposition of fully devoted disciples.

It takes three components to live out the ways of Christ: God's Word, God's Spirit, and God's people. If we lean into only one of these, we are leaning into none of them. We can't interpret God's Word with accuracy without the help of God's Spirit (John 14:26) and God's people, which is why we are supposed to "let the word of Christ dwell in [us] richly, teaching and admonishing one another in all wisdom" (Col. 3:16).

We can't grow without real community. Proverbs tells us that "whoever isolates himself seeks his own desire; he breaks out against all sound judgment" (18:1). When we go it alone, which includes listening only to viewpoints that support what we think, we swim against the current of good judgment.

Similarly, we can't live in community without the God-breathed guidelines of his Word. It is the Word of God that teaches us about selfless love, mutual humility, preferring one another, and how to lovingly admonish and correct each other so we "spur one another on toward love and good deeds" (Heb. 10:24 NIV).

We also can't seek the feel-good manifestations and gifts of the Spirit while ignoring the clear directives of living according to the gospel, which includes seeking justice for the poor and marginalized and doing so with others in authentic Christlike community—the kind of community we've seen God's people live out in the early church (Acts 2:42–47).

All three of these—God's Word, God's Spirit, and God's people—must be active in the lives of Christ's disciples.

Remember the dispute in the early church over the feeding program for Greek and Hebrew widows? Remember how they handled such an ugly moment? God's Spirit led them to the principles of God's Word lived out in the community of God's people. Could you imagine what might happen if this were our reality today? It seems like a dream. We're so busy fighting each other over words that it has compromised our ability to collectively "fight the good fight of the faith" (1 Tim. 6:12).

Listening with empathy and responding with humility and

gentleness are the dispositions of Christ's disciples, no matter what topic they're discussing. As in the early church, these gospel actions will help us see the next steps we need to take.

Next Steps for Individuals

Moving forward in this fight can feel intimidating—there is so much to do! Jemar Tisby advocates an ARC approach: awareness, relationships, commitment.[6] We have spent most our time on awareness because without a gospel-based change in this area of our lives, it's impossible to build new relationships or commit authentically to antiracist actions as a new normal—as a lifestyle to be lived, not just a project to be completed.

There are a thousand practical things white people could and should be doing. As individuals, we may not be able to do them all, but we can do something. Here are a few ideas to consider:

- Study more history about slavery and racism in the United States, including the role of the church.
- Read fiction and nonfiction books by Black authors, watch documentaries and movies by Black filmmakers, and listen to podcasts with Black hosts.
- Follow Black authors, theologians, historians, and activists on social media.
- Normalize conversations about race by sharing what you're learning from books, movies, and podcasts with your friends and family.
- Attend Black churches and seek to develop authentic relationships there.

- Sponsor Black students in scholastic or missions endeavors.
- Start or join a mixed-race small group that reads and discusses issues of race together. Be the Bridge groups[7] are a great place to start.
- Visit civil rights museums, memorials, and landmarks around the nation, including the National Museum of African American History and Culture and the Martin Luther King Jr. Memorial in Washington, DC; the National Memorial for Peace and Justice in Montgomery, Alabama; and the National Civil Rights Museum in Memphis, Tennessee.
- When you take your children to visit museums and memorials, have conversations with them about the gospel and its call to end racism. Someone who read an early version of this book pointed out that conversations with our fathers laid the foundation for what we are writing and saying today. You never know what your words and actions today might do for your kids—and the world—in the future.
- Eat in Black-owned restaurants and shop at Black-owned businesses.

Above all, we can humble ourselves and listen to Black people we've never attempted to engage before—if they want to share. If they are reluctant to share, we could show them we are genuinely seeking to grow in our understanding of racial issues and their experiences as Black people. After all, it is not the job of our Black friends to educate every white person. We can learn to educate ourselves.

If we want to change, we must be brave enough to set aside the false belief that one party or one leader (apart from Jesus) fully represents Christianity. We must also be willing to make amends to family members or anyone we have belittled or trolled online. We must stop allowing the social media feed of those who perpetuate a nongospel approach (even if they're ministers of the gospel) to feed our minds and souls. Before we can change our tone, we must first change the tone of what we listen to.

Next Steps for Pastors and Ministry Leaders

Pastors and other Christian leaders can also take steps to better equip those they shepherd. If you are a Christian leader, we hope that what you've read has motivated you to engage the topic of racism in your church or organization. Yes, you may alienate some people who think you're a little too "social justicy" for their tastes. Both of us have lost people from our churches over this, and it hurts, but it also clarifies our mission: to be and make disciples of Jesus. If we have disciples who won't discuss racism out of fear, bias, or anger, what kind of disciples are we shepherding?

Help those you shepherd to understand that the gospel calls them to see their complete need for a Savior—not just their sin-by-sin need. Then point out why this is great news. Encourage them to become willing to change the way they think, to listen to others, and to follow the gospel boldly in community with others who will do the same. Along the way, remember that the goal is not to stop seeing color or deny our ethnic differences but to listen to and prefer one another. This is how we demonstrate the attitude of Christ that supersedes our whiteness or Blackness, rightly ordering our differences under our higher citizenship.

The gospel rightly lived out with others can create exactly what it did in the early church: a sense of awe. Much of this awe was felt as a result of what God's Spirit did in people of different ethnic backgrounds. They didn't stop having differences. Rather, they were no longer insulted or threatened by these differences, and certainly, any who experienced discrimination were heard and heeded so that the church systems could be adjusted without offense.

This is part of the good news of the gospel for white Christians—that we are free to acknowledge our differences as well as the complex history of our nation that has left many people in legitimate need of healing. We need to listen and learn about our own patterns of thought, speech, and action so we can stop allowing these to be the centerpieces of the way we think, speak, and act toward others and instead allow the experiences and perceptions of our Black brothers and sisters to take center stage.

Whatever your role—pastor, community-group leader, Sunday school teacher, Christian school educator, or ministry leader—move forward with humility and boldness. Speak truth and break down barriers of foolishness, beginning with the foolishness in you. Separate nationalism from faith with confidence. Lean into difficult conversations instead of running from them. Do so prayerfully, with gentleness, and with honesty, realizing that your ultimate approval comes from God alone. This same realization is why Paul combined boldness with humility in his words to Timothy: "Reprove, rebuke, and exhort, with complete patience and teaching" (2 Tim. 4:2). Have conversations that help those you lead grow in their understanding of where systemic change is needed, addressing the systems (in civic and religious institutions) that have no heart, even as you let the gospel address your heart at all times.

We can joyfully imagine churches so willing to constantly walk in repentance, constantly listen and prefer one another, and constantly go out of their way to honor one another (including their ethnic and cultural differences) that it makes more sense for them to merge into one local church in which all of the cultures are not only represented but also heard, loved, and celebrated. If you wax eloquently on the one-race vision of Revelation, why wait for heaven when you could pursue relational oneness with other races now?

If nothing else, right now we can listen and share in the grief of this huge story of racism that characterizes our nation and the church.

A Time to Mourn

Libraries are filled with books addressing racism, which is why we encourage you to continue reading on the topic and engaging others in conversation. But in doing so, we can easily get caught up in the minutiae over what's right and wrong in matters of racial terminology, political alliances, and the like. Christians need to address and engage these issues, but we encourage you not to drown in conversations about them. Take a breath and, above all, lean into Christ through times of silence, solitude, prayer, and rest.

When you do, we are confident that he will lead you back to what matters most to him: loving him and loving others. If you love others, you will be fulfilling God's plan for your life. You will also be unable to sit idly by while someone you love suffers. You will be compelled to mourn with those who mourn.

We pray that your life will model what it means to listen to and lament with others without becoming defensive and immediately jumping into fix-it mode. Four hundred years of racial injustice can't be healed with a bandaid of good intentions, good deeds, or good gospel rhetoric. Say less and listen more.

Lament is what many conservative white Christians lack when

engaging racism. They often express no emotion or empathy for the staggering losses in Black communities, past and present. Instead, there is dismissal, rationalization, and a lot of what-abouts. Again, these words from the apostle Paul show us how we are to think and react: "Let your gentle spirit [your graciousness, unselfishness, mercy, tolerance, and patience] be known to all people. The Lord is near" (Phil. 4:5 AMP).

To be anything less than gentle and compassionate about the enslavement, rape, lynching, or murder of anyone, regardless of circumstance, is antithetical to the gospel. There is no wiggle room here. We must refuse to cancel the violence we don't want to acknowledge (slavery, discrimination, race-based violence) with another form of violence that we do want to acknowledge (deaths of police officers, rioting, looting). We can stand against both without using one to negate any meaningful conversation about the other. We must truly lament both if we want things to change.

After the murder of Ahmaud Arbery, pastor and author Osheta Moore shed light on the necessity of living with these tensions:

> Okay, White Peacemaker, what are you going to do? You see, I can't do anything more with this today—it's almost too much to process. Again. I'm going to have to pull away and grieve, so it's time for y'all to step up. . . . Let the Spirit empower you to make peace and demand justice for Ahmaud. I'll promise you this though, I'm a Black peacemaker, so I'm going to try to hold in tension my desire for justice for Ahmaud, a beloved Black man who experienced unspeakable trauma, who experienced a modern-day lynching, and a kind of compassion for the McMichaels, who were so consumed by their sickness of racism they took his life. Holding this tension is going to be difficult,

but it's necessary because I will not let my anger consume me. I have no more words, just a short prayer:

> Lord, have mercy.
>
> Lord, bring justice.
>
> Lord, weep with us.[8]

Mercy. Justice. Weeping. There will be no lasting change if these do not first permeate our hearts. We *can* be healed. We must believe this. We must remember that healing is God's work, and he will be faithful to complete it. May we be faithful to think differently so the work God is doing can also be entrusted to us as we engage in it with him and lean forward into his strength.

In his Nobel Peace Prize acceptance speech in 1964, Martin Luther King Jr. says, "I believe that unarmed truth and unconditional love will have the final word in reality. This is why right temporarily defeated is stronger than evil triumphant."[9] At present, right has most definitely been "temporarily defeated" with respect to racism, but truth that disarms lies and love that disarms division are stronger. Take heart. Stay the course.

The system doesn't have a heart, but you do, and God wants to change them both.

ACKNOWLEDGMENTS

Reggie's acknowledgments: To Michele, my wife of almost forty years: you are my best friend and a voice of truth in my life. To my son, Dominic: we are proud of the man you are. You are my main reason for writing this difficult book.

To my partner, friend, and brother from another mother, John Driver: thank you for dreaming with me. You are the smartest brother I know.

To everyone at First Assembly of God, Fort Myers: if everyone had a church family like you, world peace would already be achieved.

Thank you, Kim Shelton, for being my English teacher during the course of writing this book. I greatly appreciate your skills and your encouragement.

To Sister Janice Shaffer-Blythe: you were the first to believe in me and look past the color of my skin.

To Bill and Lelia Dabbs: you raised me right to believe in people no matter their color or their past.

To the church: let's love the way Jesus loves and change the world as he is changing it.

To all my friends: you know who you are, and I love you.

J ohn's acknowledgments: To my friend of so many years, Reggie: thank you for your courage to share your stories and take this dive with me into the gospel, history, and new (sometimes scary) arenas of cultural engagement in our tribes.

Thanks to Austin Wilson and Robert Wolgemuth, my wonderful friends and incomparable literary agents, who continue to take chances on me as a writer.

Thanks also to Webb Younce, Carolyn McCready, and the entire team at Zondervan—what an incredible honor to work with you all. Carolyn, your thoughtful insight and careful attention to detail in every aspect of this book were such gifts to the writing and to us personally.

Thanks also to Andrew Wharton, my pastor, dear friend, and gospel coconspirator, as well as everyone from the Church at Pleasant Grove who continues to bravely step into changing the way we think about the gospel and race.

Thanks to Jonnie W., my best friend of more than two decades and podcast cohost: working a lot of this out with you over lunch and on the air was so critical to growing in my understanding and empathy, something I'm still trying to do.

To the people we do life with every day, Matt and Linnea Stewart and the rest of our community group: thank you for enduring me, supporting me, sharpening me, and always loving me.

Dad, I miss you more every day. Thanks for showing me an example of gospel-based diversity when it wasn't common to do so.

To my dearest Sadie: you are my favorite! I pray that someday a book like this one will spur you on to your own gospel endeavors.

And finally, to Laura, my wife of more than twenty years: thank you for loving me well enough to challenge the way I was thinking about race. You probably didn't think that would lead to my spending hundreds of hours on the deck writing this book in the middle of snowstorms and a pandemic while you kept our world afloat. God holds me together with the beautiful binding of you.

I can't believe God let me, the least of these, help to write this book. The greatest of thanks goes to him. These pages emerged out of painful and difficult stories in others' lives, so to everyone who was willing to share their experiences as Black people and white people in America—and to those of all ethnicities who courageously stand for the gospel call to end racism—we are humbled, uplifted, and moved to action by your faithfulness to Christ.

NOTES

An Invitation to Honest Conversations about Race and Faith

1. Ahmaud Arbery, age twenty-five, was jogging in Glynn County, Georgia, when he was pursued and fatally shot by a white man on February 23, 2020. Breonna Taylor, age twenty-six, was fatally shot by police in Louisville, Kentucky, on March 13, 2020, while asleep in her apartment. George Floyd, age forty-six, was killed by a white police officer in Minneapolis, Minnesota, on May 25, 2020, while being arrested for allegedly using a counterfeit twenty-dollar bill.
2. Latasha Morrison, *Be the Bridge: Pursuing God's Heart for Racial Reconciliation* (Colorado Springs: WaterBrook, 2019), 2–3.
3. Larry Buchanan, Quoctrung Bui, and Jugal K. Patel, "Black Lives Matter May Be the Largest Movement in U.S. History," *New York Times*, July 3, 2020, *www.nytimes.com/interactive/2020/07/03/us/george-floyd-protests-crowd-size.html*.
4. Jemar Tisby, *The Color of Compromise: The Truth about the American Church's Complicity in Racism* (Grand Rapids: Zondervan, 2019), 197.

Chapter 1: Looking Where We've Slipped

1. Bill Haslam, *Faithful Presence: The Promise and Peril of Faith in the Public Square* (Nashville: Thomas Nelson, 2021), 19.
2. Thabiti Anyabwile (@ThabitiAnyabwil), "May God, the omniscient and just Judge," Twitter, September 23, 2020, *https://twitter.com/ThabitiAnyabwil/status/1308895738026434560*.
3. Adelle M. Banks, "SBC President J. D. Greear Says 'Black Lives Matter,'" *Baptist Standard*, June 10, 2020, *www.baptiststandard.com/news/baptists/sbc-president-j-d-greear-says-black-lives-matter/*.
4. "Why We Say: Presbyterians Affirm Black Lives Matter," Presbyterian Week of Action: Black Lives Matter, Presbyterian Church (USA), August 24–30, 2020, *www.pcusa.org/weekofaction/#2*.

5. Nicola Menzie, "Nation's Largest Pentecostal Denominations Affirm That 'Black Lives Matter'; Call for Christian Solidarity despite Personal Opinions," *Christian Post*, December 12, 2014, *www.christianpost.com /news/nations-largest-pentecostal-denominations-affirm-that-black-lives -matter-call-for-christian-solidarity-despite-personal-opinions.html*.

6. Rev. D. Anthony Everett, "Why Black Lives Matter: A Spiritual View," United Methodist Church, January 29, 2016, *www.umc.org/en/content /why-black-lives-matter-a-spiritual-view*.

7. Esau McCaulley (@esaumccaulley), "People keep warning us," Twitter, August 29, 2020, *https://twitter.com/esaumccaulley/status /1299776687819849730?s=21* (tweet unavailable as of April 23, 2021).

8. Justin Giboney (@JustinEGiboney), "Do you know what's more effective . . .?" Instagram, December 2, 2020, *www.instagram.com/p /CITG82yn5Jg/*.

9. Dr. Martin Luther King Jr., "Social Justice" (address), Western Michigan University, December 18, 1963, *https://libguides.wmich.edu /mlkatwmu/speech*.

10. Osheta Moore (@oshetamoore), "I've learned that systems of oppression," Instagram, May 12, 2020, *www.instagram.com/p/CAFz3uwHtK3/*.

11. Justin Giboney (@JustinEGiboney), "Unwillingness to change systems that have," Twitter, December 22, 2020, *www.twitter.com /JustinEGiboney/status/1341385573198606338* (emphasis added).

12. Charles H. Spurgeon, *The Treasury of David*, vol. 7, *Psalm CXXV to CL* (London: Passmore and Alabaster, 1886), 404.

13. Timothy Keller, "How Do Christians Fit into the Two-Party System? They Don't," *New York Times*, September 29, 2018, *www.nytimes.com /2018/09/29/opinion/sunday/christians-politics-belief.html?smid=tw-share*.

14. George Carlin, "Stuff on Driving" stand-up routine, quoted in "Cars and Driving: Part One," *Long Live Carlin* (blog), accessed April 23, 2021, *http://georgedpcarlin.blogspot.com/2014/01/cars-and-driving-part -one-george-carlin.html*.

15. John Onwuchekwa (@JawnO), "When it comes to repairing past injustices," Twitter, October 13, 2020, *https://twitter.com/JawnO/status /1316047464106004482/*.

Chapter 2: A Twenty-Dollar Life

1. If you're too young to know who Fat Albert is, he was a character in the cartoon series *Fat Albert and the Cosby Kids* from the 1970s and 1980s

(with a movie reboot in the early 2000s). Just google "Fat Albert" and compare our physical characteristics.

2. Attributed to Dr. Martin Luther King Jr., "The Trumpet of Conscience" (speech), Steeler Lecture, November 1967, in Wikiquote, "Silence," accessed April 24, 2021, *https://en.wikiquote.org/wiki/Silence#K.*

3. Martin Luther King Jr., "Beyond Vietnam: A Time to Break Silence" (speech), Riverside Church, New York, April 4, 1967, *https://kinginstitute.stanford.edu/king-papers/documents/beyond-vietnam.*

4. John M. Perkins, *One Blood: Parting Words to the Church on Race and Love* (Chicago: Moody, 2018), 17.

5. Latasha Morrison, *Be the Bridge: Pursuing God's Heart for Racial Reconciliation* (Colorado Springs, WaterBrook, 2019), 23–24.

6. Morrison, *Be the Bridge*, 22.

7. Morrison, *Be the Bridge*, 22.

8. Lecrae, quoted in Jemar Tisby, *The Color of Compromise: The Truth about the American Church's Complicity in Racism* (Grand Rapids: Zondervan, 2019), 10.

Chapter 3: A White Christian Moderate

1. *Hamilton*, music and lyrics by Lin-Manuel Miranda, dir. Thomas Kail, original performance at the Public Theater, New York City, January 20–May 3, 2015.

2. Reggie Dabbs, *Reggie: You Can't Change Your Past, but You Can Change Your Future* (Nashville: Thomas Nelson, 2011). The book tells the full story of Reggie's life.

3. Martin Luther King Jr., letter to fellow clergymen (Birmingham, Alabama, April 16, 1963), *http://okra.stanford.edu/transcription /document_images/undecided/630416-019.pdf.* This letter was later published as *Letter from the Birmingham Jail* (multiple editions).

4. Matt Chandler (@mattchandler74), "We really like Martin Luther King Jr. right now," Instagram, June 8, 2020, *www.instagram.com/tv /CBMt__TlNQ-/?igshid=mckyp7452x4h.*

5. Martin Luther, *Luther's Works*, vol. 43, *Devotional Writings II*, ed. Jaroslav Jan Pelikan, Hilton C. Oswald, and Helmut T. Lehmann (Philadelphia: Fortress Press, 1999), 131–32.

6. Baby Yoda would be proud. (See the YouTube performance of "This Is the Way" at *www.youtube.com/watch?v=tf7y6EJLF_0.*)

7. Bruce Shelley, *Church History in Plain Language,* 4th ed. (Nashville: Thomas Nelson, 2013), 38.

8. John Piper, "Policies, Persons, and Paths to Ruin: Pondering the Implications of the 2020 Election," Desiring God, October 22, 2020, *www.desiringgod.org/articles/policies-persons-and-paths-to-ruin.*

Chapter 4: When Was the Last Time You Changed Your Mind?

1. C. S. Lewis, *Mere Christianity,* in *The C. S. Lewis Signature Classics* (New York: HarperOne, 2017), 112.

2. "Calvinist Dog Corrects Owner: 'No One Is a Good Boy,'" Babylon Bee, March 1, 2018, *https://babylonbee.com/news/calvinist-dog-corrects -owner-no-one-good-boy.*

3. Tertullian, "Of Repentance," in *Tertullian,* vol. 1, *Apologetic and Practical Treatises,* trans. C. Dodgson (London: John Henry Parker, 1842), 366.

4. This might not be an *exact* comparison, but I'm sure you see the point.

5. Martin Luther King Jr., "Beyond Vietnam: A Time to Break Silence" (speech), Riverside Church, New York City, April 4, 1967, *https://kinginstitute.stanford.edu/king-papers/documents/beyond-vietnam.*

6. Sanya Mansoor, "93% of Black Lives Matter Protests Have Been Peaceful, New Report Finds," *Time,* September 5, 2020, *https://time .com/5886348/report-peaceful-protests/.*

7. KB (@KB_HGA), "I've watched a surge of people," Twitter, November 1, 2020, *https://twitter.com/kb_hga/status/1322929460673470465?s=21.*

8. Beth Moore (@BethMoreLPM), "Nobody's never wrong," Twitter, January 11, 2021, *https://twitter.com/BethMooreLPM/status/1348653033010425861.*

9. Justin Giboney, "An Opposition-Centered Public Witness," December 9, 2020, on *Church Politics* podcast.

Chapter 5: Getting Past the Idea of Getting Over the Past

1. Bryan Stevenson, commencement address at College of the Holy Cross, Worcester, Massachusetts, May 22, 2015, *www.holycross.edu /commencement-2015/2015-commencement-address-bryan-stevenson.*

2. Candacy Taylor, "The Roots of Route 66," *Atlantic,* November 3, 2016, *www.theatlantic.com/politics/archive/2016/11/the-roots-of-route-66/506255/.*

3. James W. Loewen, *Sundown Towns: A Hidden Dimension of American Racism* (New York: Touchstone, 2005), 16.

4. John MacArthur, quoted in Michael Gryboski, "John MacArthur Says 'True Believers' Will Vote for Trump, Can't Affirm Abortion and Trans Activism," *Christian Post*, September 2, 2020, *www.christianpost.com /news/john-macarthur-says-true-believers-will-vote-for-trump-cant-affirm -abortion-and-trans-activism.html.*

5. Timothy Keller, quoted in Michael Gryboski, "Tim Keller Rejects Claims that Christians Must Vote a Certain Way, Says Stop Demonizing Opponents," *Christian Post*, September 21, 2020, *www .christianpost.com/politics/tim-keller-rejects-claims-that-christians-must -vote-a-certain-way-says-stop-demonizing-opponents.html.*

6. Jon Foreman, afterword to *One Blood: Parting Words to the Church on Race and Love,* by John M. Perkins (Chicago: Moody, 2018), 179.

Chapter 6: Language, Laws, and Legacy

1. George Washington, "Washington's Farewell Address 1796" (transcript), Avalon Project, Yale Law School, *https://avalon.law.yale.edu/18th _century/washing.asp,* emphasis added.

2. US Constitution, Thirteenth Amendment, sec. 1.

3. *Encyclopedia Britannica,* s.v. "Black code," accessed May 4, 2021, *www .britannica.com/topic/black-code,* emphasis added.

4. Josh Dawsey, "Trump Derides Protections for Immigrants from 'Shithole' Countries," *Washington Post,* January 12, 2018, *www .washingtonpost.com/politics/trump-attacks-protections-for-immigrants -from-shithole-countries-in-oval-office-meeting/2018/01/11/bfc0725c-f711 -11e7-91af-31ac729add94_story.html.*

5. "1921 Tulsa Race Massacre," Tulsa Historical Society and Museum, accessed May 2, 2021, *www.tulsahistory.org/exhibit/1921-tulsa-race -massacre/#flexible-content.*

Chapter 7: The Historical Legacy of Slavery in the Church and the Nation

1. "What Is Slavery?" Abolition Project, accessed May 3, 2021, *http://abolition.e2bn.org/slavery_40.html.*

2. Henry Louis Gates Jr., "How Many Slaves Landed in the US?" TheRoot.com, January 6, 2014, *www.theroot.com/how-many-slaves -landed-in-the-us-1790873989.*

3. Modern translation of Virginia General Assembly statute, act 3, September 23, 1667, in William Waller Hening, ed., *The Statutes at*

Large: Being a Collection of All the Laws of Virginia (New York: R. W. G. Bartow, 1823), 260.

4. Austin Channing Brown, *I'm Still Here: Black Dignity in a World Made for Whiteness* (New York: Crown, 2018), 113.

5. Frederick Douglass, *Narrative of the Life of Frederick Douglass: An American Slave* (Boston: Anti-Slavery Office, 1845), 118.

6. Jemar Tisby, *The Color of Compromise: The Truth about the American Church's Complicity in Racism* (Grand Rapids: Zondervan, 2019), 24.

7. Brown, *I'm Still Here*, 113–14.

8. Tisby, *Color of Compromise*, 29.

9. John C. Calhoun actually coined the phrase "the peculiar institution" in the 1830s, three decades before the Civil War. *Encyclopedia Britannica*, s.v. "John C. Calhoun," accessed May 4, 2021, *www.britannica.com /biography/John-C-Calhoun.*

10. Ron Chernow, *Alexander Hamilton* (New York: Penguin, 2004), 210.

11. Chernow, *Alexander Hamilton*, 212.

12. Brown, *I'm Still Here*, 114.

13. Andrew Johnson, State of the Union address, December 3, 1867, quoted in Jon Meacham, *The Soul of America: The Battle for Our Better Angels* (New York: Random House, 2018), 63.

14. Eric Foner, quoted in Meacham, *Soul of America,* 63.

15. Meacham, *Soul of America*, 65.

Chapter 8: Rewriting History

1. Jon Meacham, *The Soul of America: The Battle for Our Better Angels* (New York: Random House, 2018), 59.

2. Jemar Tisby, *The Color of Compromise: The Truth about the American Church's Complicity in Racism* (Grand Rapids: Zondervan, 2019), 94.

3. Charles Reagan Wilson, *Baptized in Blood: The Religion of the Lost Cause* (Athens, GA: University of Georgia Press, 1980), 49.

4. Frederick Douglass, quoted in Meacham, *Soul of America*, 60.

5. "Oaths of Enlistment and Oaths of Office," U.S. Army Center of Military History, accessed May 4, 2021, *https://history.army.mil/html/faq/oaths.html.*

6. Sean Kane, "Myths and Misunderstandings: Lee as a Slaveholder," American Civil War Museum, October 4, 2017, *https://acwm.org/blog /myths-misunderstandings-lee-slaveholder/.*

7. Wesley Norris, quoted in Kane, "Myths and Misunderstandings."

8. Kane, "Myths and Misunderstandings."

9. "The Declaration of Causes of Seceding States," American Battlefield Trust, accessed May 4, 2021, *www.battlefields.org/learn/primary-sources /declaration-causes-seceding-states.*

10. "Declaration of Causes of Seceding States."

11. James Bryce, *The American Commonwealth*, cited in Sean Wilentz, "The Return of Ulysses," *New Republic*, January 25, 2010, *https://newrepublic .com/article/72699/the-return-ulyses-s-grant.*

12. Frederick Douglass, *U. S. Grant and the Colored People* (Washington, DC: Union Republican National Committee, 1872), 4, 7, *https://tile.loc .gov/storage-services/service/rbc/lcrbmrp/t2407/t2407.pdf.*

13. Ron Chernow, *Grant* (New York: Penguin Books, 2017), 101.

14. Chernow, *Grant*, 101.

15. Chernow, *Grant*, 106.

16. Chernow, *Grant*, 516.

17. Ulysses S. Grant, quoted in Chernow, *Grant*, 516.

18. "How Statues Are Falling around the World," *New York Times*, June 24, 2020, *www.nytimes.com/2020/06/24/us/confederate-statues-photos.html.*

19. Laura Vozzella, "Northam Can Remove Lee Statue in Richmond, Judge Rules," *Washington Post*, October 27, 2020, *www.washingtonpost.com/local /virginia-politics/richmond-judge-lee-statue-removal/2020/10/27/6fe87166 -1893-11eb-82db-60b15c874105_story.html.*

20. Bryan Stevenson, interview on *CBS This Morning*, quoted in "Bryan Stevenson: 'The North Won the Civil War, but the South Won the Narrative War' on History of Racism," CBS News, June 24, 2019, *www .cbsnews.com/news/bryan-stevenson-we-are-all-complicit-in-our-countrys -history-of-racism/.*

21. David H. Bennett, *The Party of Fear: From Nativist Movements to the New Right in American History* (Chapel Hill, NC: University of North Carolina Press, 1988), 211.

22. Meacham, *Soul of America*, 111.

23. W. E. B. Du Bois, *Black Reconstruction in America* (New York: Free Press, 1962), 708.

24. Tisby, *Color of Compromise*, 102.

25. Jennifer Rae Taylor, "A History of Tolerance for Violence Has Laid the Groundwork for Injustice Today," American Bar Association, May 16, 2019, *www.americanbar.org/groups/crsj/publications/human _rights_magazine_home/black-to-the-future/tolerance-for-violence/.*

26. Tisby, *Color of Compromise*, 109.

Chapter 9: White Privilege and the Liberal Bogeyman

1. Peggy McIntosh, "White Privilege: Unpacking the Invisible Knapsack," *Peace and Freedom Magazine*, July/August 1989, 9–10, *https://nationalseedproject.org/Key-SEED-Texts/white-privilege-unpacking-the-invisible-knapsack*.
2. Dr. Martin Luther King Jr., "Remaining Awake through a Great Revolution" (speech), National Cathedral, Washington, DC, March 31, 1968, *https://kinginstitute.stanford.edu/king-papers/publications/knock-midnight-inspiration-great-sermons-reverend-martin-luther-king-jr-10*.
3. Jordan B. Peterson, "White Privilege and Safe Spaces," YouTube, November 11, 2017, accessed May 5, 2021, *www.youtube.com/watch?v=kRz0i0gh2iE&feature=youtu.be*.
4. *Encyclopedia Britannica*, s.v. "kulak," accessed May 5, 2021, *www.britannica.com/topic/kulak*.
5. Image of 1930s poster, courtesy of the Alabama Department of Archives and History, *https://digital.archives.alabama.gov/digital/collection/voices/id/2020*.
6. Martin Luther King Jr., "Beyond Vietnam: A Time to Break Silence" (speech), Riverside Church, New York City, April 4, 1967, *https://kinginstitute.stanford.edu/king-papers/documents/beyond-vietnam*.

Chapter 10: When God and Country Don't Go Together

1. Martin Niemöller, quoted in "Martin Niemöller: 'First They Came for the Socialists . . .,'" Holocaust Encyclopedia, United States Holocaust Memorial Museum, accessed May 6, 2021, *https://encyclopedia.ushmm.org/content/en/article/martin-niemoeller-first-they-came-for-the-socialists*.
2. James Whitman, "Why the Nazis Loved America," *Time*, March 21, 2017, *https://time.com/4703586/nazis-america-race-law/*.
3. Adam Serwer, "White Nationalism," interview by Sam Sanders, *Throughline* (podcast), NPR, May 9, 2019, *www.npr.org/transcripts/721165704*.
4. Ruth Ben-Ghiat, "What to Know about the Origins of Fascism's Brutal Ideology," *Time*, March 22, 2019, *https://time.com/5556242/what-is-fascism/*.
5. Paul D. Miller, "What Is Christian Nationalism?" Christianity Today, February 3, 2021, *www.christianitytoday.com/ct/2021/february-web-only/what-is-christian-nationalism.html?utm_source=CT+Weekly+Newsletter&utm_medium=Newsletter&utm_term=365095&utm_content=2199&utm_campaign=email*.

6. Miller, "What Is Christian Nationalism?"
7. Eric Trump, interview by Todd Mitchell, *What's on Your Mind?* October 2, 2020, quoted in Josephine Harvey, "Eric Trump Claims His Dad 'Literally Saved Christianity,'" HuffPost, October 6, 2020, *www .huffpost.com/entry/eric-trump-literally-saved-christianity_n_5f7d2355c5b 6e5aba0d1d927*, emphasis added.
8. Propaganda, "Crooked Way," *Crooked*, lyrics by Terence F. Clark (Humble Beast, 2017).
9. Miller, "What Is Christian Nationalism?"
10. Bruce Shelley, *Church History in Plain Language*, 4th ed. (Nashville: Thomas Nelson, 2013), 102.
11. Shelley, *Church History*.
12. Linda Qiu, "Trump's Evidence-Free Claims about the Migrant Caravan," *New York Times*, October 22, 2018, *www.nytimes .com/2018/10/22/us/politics/migrant-caravan-fact-check.html*.
13. Qiu, "Trump's Evidence-Free Claims."
14. Preamble to the US Declaration of Independence, July 4, 1776, emphasis added.
15. Kim Parker et al., "Chapter 1: Race and Multiracial Americans in the U.S. Census," in *Multiracial in America: Proud, Diverse, and Growing in Numbers* (Washington, DC: Pew Research Center, 2015), *www.pewsocialtrends.org/2015/06/11/chapter-1-race-and-multiracial -americans-in-the-u-s-census/#:~:text=The%20first%20census%20in%20 1790,were%20included%20in%20subsequent%20counts*.
16. Jon Meacham, *The Soul of America: The Battle for Our Better Angels* (New York: Random House, 2018), 75–76, emphasis added.
17. John M. Perkins, *One Blood: Parting Words to the Church on Race and Love* (Chicago: Moody, 2018), 46.
18. Thabiti Anyabwile (@ThabitiAnyabwil), "Political homelessness is not a curse," Twitter, October 29, 2020, *https://twitter.com/ThabitiAnyabwil /status/1321827198425305088*.

Chapter 11: Dangerous Radicals and Fatal Extremes

1. Sean Wilentz, general editor's introduction to *The Kerner Report: The National Advisory Commission on Civil Disorders*, edited by Sean Wilentz (Princeton: Princeton University Press, 2016), ix.
2. Julian E. Zelizer, introduction to the 2016 edition of *Kerner Report*, edited by Wilentz, xiii.

3. Martin Luther King Jr., quoted on the back cover of Wilentz, *Kerner Report*.

4. "Riots Panel Tells Truth," *Chicago Daily Defender*, March 5, 1968, quoted in Wilentz, *Kerner Report*, xxxi.

5. Esau McCaulley, *Reading While Black: African American Biblical Interpretation as an Exercise in Hope* (Downers Grove, IL: InterVarsity, 2020), 40, emphasis added.

6. "Transcript of Civil Rights Act of 1964," title VII, sec. 703, in OurDocuments.gov, accessed May 7, 2021, *www.ourdocuments.gov/doc .php?flash=false&doc=97&page=transcript*.

7. Wilentz, *Kerner Report*, xi.

8. Richard Nixon, quoted in Wilentz, *Kerner Report*, xxxii.

9. William Buckley Jr., "Mistakes of the President's Riot Commission," *Newsday*, March 21, 1968, quoted in Wilentz, *Kerner Report*, xxxi.

10. Richard L. Lyons, "Riot Report Sends Out Shock Waves," *Los Angeles Times*, March 2, 1968.

11. Scott Sauls (@scottsauls), "Partisan politics might be the greatest threat," Instagram, September 5, 2020, *www.instagram.com/p/CEwfN3Mhh1T/*.

12. Martin Luther King Jr., "The Other America" (speech), Stanford University, April 14, 1967, Civil Rights Movement Archive, accessed May 7, 2021, *www.crmvet.org/docs/otheram.htm*.

13. Wilentz, *Kerner Report*, x.

14. Letter to John Jay, November 26, 1775, quoted in Harold C. Syrett, ed., *The Papers of Alexander Hamilton*, vol. 1, *1768–1778* (New York: Columbia University Press, 1961), 176.

Chapter 12: Systemic Racism in the Modern Age

1. Aaron Glantz and Emmanuel Martinez, "Modern-Day Redlining: How Banks Block People of Color from Homeownership," *Chicago Tribune*, February 17, 2018, *www.chicagotribune.com/business/ct-biz-modern-day -redlining-20180215-story.html*.

2. Jared Brey, "Housing in Brief: 'Modern-Day Redlining,'" June 5, 2020, *https://nextcity.org/daily/entry/housing-in-brief-modern-day-redlining*.

3. Richard Rothstein, interview by Terry Gross, *Fresh Air*, quoted in "A 'Forgotten History' of How the U.S. Government Segregated America," NPR, May 3, 2017, *www.npr.org/2017/05/03/526655831/a-forgotten -history-of-how-the-u-s-government-segregated-america*.

4. Frank Edwards, Hedwig Lee, and Michael Esposito, "Risk of Being

Killed by Police Use of Force in the United States by Age, Race-Ethnicity, and Sex," *Proceedings of the National Academy of Sciences* 116, no. 34 (August 2019), *www.pnas.org/content/116/34/16793*.

5. Edwards, Lee, Esposito, "Risk of Being Killed."

6. Paul Duggan, "A Disproportionate Number of D.C. Police Stops Involved African Americans," *Washington Post*, September 9, 2019, *www.washingtonpost.com/local/public-safety/a-disproportionate-number -of-dc-police-stops-involved-african-americans/2019/09/09/6f11beb0-d347 -11e9-9343-40db57cf6abd_story.html*.

7. Ben Poston and Cindy Chang, "LAPD Searches Blacks and Latinos More. But They're Less Likely to Have Contraband than Whites," *Los Angeles Times*, October 8, 2019, *www.latimes.com/local/lanow/la-me -lapd-searches-20190605-story.html*.

8. Christopher Ingraham, "You Really Can Get Pulled Over for Driving While Black, Federal Statistics Show," *Washington Post*, September 9, 2014, *www.washingtonpost.com/news/wonk/wp/2014/09/09/you-really -can-get-pulled-over-for-driving-while-black-federal-statistics-show/*.

9. Emma Pierson et al., "A Large-Scale Analysis of Racial Disparities in Police Stops across the United States," *Nature Human Behaviour* 4 (July 2020), *www.nature.com/articles/s41562-020-0858-1.pdf*.

10. Radley Balko, "There's Overwhelming Evidence That the Criminal Justice System Is Racist: Here's the Proof," *Washington Post*, June 10, 2020, *www.washingtonpost.com/graphics/2020/opinions/systemic-racism -police-evidence-criminal-justice-system/?itid=ap_radleybalko&itid=lk _inline_manual_6#Policing*.

11. Esau McCaulley, *Reading While Black: African American Biblical Interpreta- tion as an Exercise in Hope* (Downers Grove, IL: InterVarsity, 2020), 28.

12. US Department of Justice, Civil Rights Division, *Investigation of the Baltimore City Police Department*, August 10, 2016, cited in David A. Graham, "The Horror of the Baltimore Police Department," *Atlantic*, August 10, 2016, *www.theatlantic.com/news/archive/2016/08 /the-horror-of-the-baltimore-police-department/495329/*.

13. Department of Justice, *Investigation of the Baltimore City Police Department*, 157, 4, *www.documentcloud.org/documents/3010223-BPD -Findings-Report.html*.

14. Jasmine L. Holmes, *Mother to Son: Letters to a Black Boy on Identity and Hope* (Downers Grove, IL: InterVarsity, 2020), 32.

15. John Gramlich, "Black Imprisonment Rate in the U.S. Has

Fallen by a Third Since 2006," Fact Tank, Pew Research Center, May 6, 2020, *www.pewresearch.org/fact-tank/2020/05/06/share-of-black-white-hispanic-americans-in-prison-2018-vs-2006/*.

16. William J. Stuntz, *The Collapse of American Criminal Justice* (Cambridge, MA: Belknap, 2011), 296.

17. Deborah C. England, "Crack vs. Powder Cocaine: One Drug, Two Penalties," Criminal Defense Lawyer, accessed May 8, 2021, *www.criminaldefenselawyer.com/resources/crack-vrs-powder-cocaine-one-drug-two-penalties.htm*.

18. England, "Crack vs. Powder Cocaine."

19. William J. Sabol, Thaddeus L. Johnson, and Alexander Caccavale, *Trends in Correctional Control by Race and Sex* (Washington, DC: Council on Criminal Justice, 2019), 1, *https://cdn.ymaws.com/counciloncj.org/resource/collection/4683B90A-08CF-493F-89ED-A0D7C4BF7551/Trends_in_Correctional_Control_-_FINAL.pdf*.

20. Sabol, Johnson, and Caccavale, *Trends in Correctional Control*.

21. Stuntz, *Collapse of American Criminal Justice*, 291.

22. Stuntz, *Collapse of American Criminal Justice*, 291–92.

23. Paola Scommegna, "U.S. Has World's Highest Incarceration Rate," Population Reference Bureau (PRB), August 10, 2012, *www.prb.org/us-incarceration/*.

24. Stuntz, *Collapse of American Criminal Justice*, 388, citing State of New York, Office of the Attorney General, Civil Rights Bureau, "The New York City Police Department's 'Stop & Frisk' Practices: A Report to the People of the State of New York from the Office of the Attorney General," 111 (1999).

25. Austin Channing Brown, *I'm Still Here: Black Dignity in a World Made for Whiteness* (New York: Crown, 2018), 113.

Chapter 13: A Time to Lament and Lean Forward Together

1. Nelson Mandela (@NelsonMandela), "We must strive to be moved," posthumously posted to Twitter, December 25, 2014, *https://twitter.com/NelsonMandela/status/548335266428379138*.

2. G. K. Chesterton, *Heretics* (New York: John Lane, 1905), 158.

3. Philip Yancey, *What's So Amazing about Grace?* Apple Books, *https://books.apple.com/us/book/whats-so-amazing-about-grace/id387707180*.

4. Mark Vroegop, *Weep with Me: How Lament Opens a Door for Racial Reconciliation* (Wheaton, IL: Crossway, 2020), 137.

5. Dr. Martin Luther King Jr., letter to fellow clergymen (Birmingham, Alabama, April 16, 1963), *http://okra.stanford.edu/transcription /document_images/undecided/630416-019.pdf.* This letter was later published as *Letter from the Birmingham Jail* (multiple editions).

6. Jemar Tisby, *The Color of Compromise: The Truth about the American Church's Complicity in Racism* (Grand Rapids: Zondervan, 2019), 194.

7. "Join the #IAmABridgeBuilder Movement," BTB Groups, Be the Bridge, accessed May 9, 2021, *https://bethebridge.com/groups/.*

8. Osheta Moore (@oshetamoore), "Okay, White Peacemaker," Instagram, May 6, 2020, *www.instagram.com/p/B_19rwcJTRW/.*

9. Dr. Martin Luther King Jr., "Acceptance Speech," (Nobel Peace Prize, Oslo, Norway, December 10, 1964), transcript from Nobel Prize, accessed May 9, 2021, *www.nobelprize.org/prizes/peace/1964/king /26142-martin-luther-king-jr-acceptance-speech-1964/.*